Praise for

TELL NO ONE

'This powerful debut by Brendan Watkins
takes the reader on a confronting and gripping
journey from the very first pages. Brendan's
voice is compelling throughout, and he peppers
his own story with excellent research on the
children of priests.'

SUZANNE SMITH,
author of *The Altar Boys* and
multi-Walkley Award–winning journalist

'I read *Tell No One* in one sitting. I could not
put it down. Everyone needs to know where
they come from. It is such a core need. Brendan's
persistence against secrecy and lies was a powerful
reminder that many end their lives without
knowing. I so wanted a fairytale ending and then
I remembered how cruel institutionalised religious
power is to children and women. Read it and
weep and then get strategic—it has to end.'

WENDY McCARTHY,
author of *Don't Be Too Polite, Girls*

THE SON OF A PRIEST AND A NUN
UNCOVERS LONG-BURIED SECRETS

TELL NO ONE

BRENDAN WATKINS

ALLEN&UNWIN
SYDNEY•MELBOURNE•AUCKLAND•LONDON

First published in 2023

Allen & Unwin
Cammeraygal Country
83 Alexander Street
Crows Nest NSW 2065
Australia
Phone: (61 2) 8425 0100
Email: info@allenandunwin.com
Web: www.allenandunwin.com

Allen & Unwin acknowledges the Traditional Owners of the Country on which we live and work. We pay our respects to all Aboriginal and Torres Strait Islander Elders, past and present.

A catalogue record for this book is available from the National Library of Australia

ISBN 978 1 76106 999 4

Index by Puddingburn Publishing Services
Set in 12.5/17.25 pt Bembo Std by Bookhouse, Sydney
Printed and bound in Australia by Pegasus Media & Logistics

10 9 8 7 6 5 4 3 2

'If you hush up a ghost, it grows bigger.'

—GREENLANDIC PROVERB

CONTENTS

CONTENTS

AUTHOR'S NOTE

I have kept a journal for much of my life—hundreds of thousands of words recorded over decades. That discipline got me match fit for what's written here, the book I've craved to read all of my life.

This is a memoir, my personal recollection of a fifty-year quest. As my story has been deliberately shrouded in secrets and lies—by others—it has not been possible to verify some details from alternate sources. I've tried to tell the story with absolute integrity but acknowledge I may have unintentionally misrepresented, or misunderstood, some people or their actions. Some of the conversations reported are as I recall them, others from recordings, some paraphrased from letters, articles or phone conversations. My motivation, in the first instance, was to understand myself, and much later, fearing the weight of the secrets that I uncovered would crush the life from me, I pursued publication.

In order to protect the living, in some instances I have changed the names of individuals, their places of residence and minor descriptive details, while remaining true to the profound and fundamental truth of their stories. The chapters evoking the experiences of a priest have been imagined using news articles, extensive archival records and oral histories.

Over the past four years I have engaged with sons and daughters of priests, mothers of the children of priests, nuns, several male priests, a female priest, failed priests, priests who've married and had families, individuals who have found their parents via DNA databases, and several adoptees. I've also interviewed lawyers, psychologists, barristers, professors, a social anthropologist, doctors, sex-abuse counsellors, social workers and journalists. Add to this my contemporaneous journals, family archives and audio recordings of interviews relating to my ancestry, and this is what I found.

It is the story of me. This is who I am.

INTRODUCTION

A few years ago, on a brilliant sun-bathed September afternoon in a run-down Melbourne pub, I delivered a presentation to a group of around twenty ex-seminarians, all now elderly men, some never ordained, some priests, but most not. They wanted my life story. That afternoon unexpectedly jolted me to a revelation.

Sharing my story with people for the first time underscored just how painful it is. To protect myself, I'd become adept at throwing the facts down, detached, as though they belonged to some random anecdote. To rein in any emotion, and to accurately recall the complexities of my familial story, I had to go deep into myself, and as a result I became detached from the audience.

After around thirty minutes I finished talking, and really saw the men I faced, frozen as though posing to have their portrait painted. The stunned expressions staring back sharply amplified my trauma, a complex story of being the hidden son of a priest and an ex-nun. As I scanned the room, aside from a clattering afternoon tram labouring up the hill outside, it was pin-drop silent.

At that moment, a nameless weight of dark sorrow came pushing down on my shoulders and chest. I steadied myself to avoid stumbling.

Afterwards, sitting down with the men, I was to hear much about the inner workings of the church and their thoughts about my parents. One ex-seminarian, a respected professor, felt certain my parents would have had an ongoing sexual and emotional life together, and disclosed that he had been sexually harassed by several female parishioners when he was a young priest: 'I was entirely ill-equipped to contend with women and the intensity of sexual politics—there are two sides to every coin, Brendan.' It was a presumptuous response; how would he have any idea of who initiated the liaison, or what took place when I was conceived? Was he saying my mother initiated whatever happened with my father? I suspected many others in this group shared his thoughts about women. Regardless, I didn't buy what he was selling.

Still shaken as I drove home, it occurred to me that for thirty years I'd maintained I wasn't a victim out of sheer bloody-minded loyalty to my cherished adoptive parents. But on that day, it dawned on me that I'd been treated appallingly by my birth parents and the institution that owed the core duty of care to me, the Catholic Church. I am a child of the era of closed and often forced adoptions, and also a member of an ignored clan of rejected souls: priests' hidden children. We are Christ's orphans.

Part One

SECRETS

Chapter 1

MELBOURNE, 1969

We lived behind a sandwich shop that Mum ran in Bridge Road, Richmond. My older brother, Damien, and I enjoyed unfettered access to the shop out front. I was strictly a Fanta, Golden Gaytime and Cherry Ripe kid. He was Coke, Eskimo Pie and Flake.

Damien was the sort of kid who'd happily talk to customers who came into the shop, while I hid behind Mum's apron. He was compact, strong, dark-haired, with rounded features. I was gangly-long, all elbows and knees, with mousy hair. Though we happily spent hours together, the two of us were opposites in every conceivable way.

I entertained a suspicion that I wasn't cut from the same cloth as the rest of my family, though I never said it out loud. Not only did we look different, but my brother and I also thought and acted differently. Maybe one of us was adopted? But who was the odd one out?

It was 1969. Damien was ten and I was eight.

We were given the news by our parents, Roy and Bet. It was just another grey winter's Sunday morning (or so I thought), until we got home from mass and Bet asked Damien and me to go and lie on our beds in our shared bedroom. Our parents wanted to have a talk. 'It won't take long.'

It was before *World of Sport* kicked off at 11 am—we adored sport—so I'd make it around 10.30 am. Roy and Bet followed us into the room and perched together on the end of Damien's bed. We could smell Bet's roast pork, the mouth-watering aromas wafting in from the kitchen. While they'd all be gnawing on the greasy crackling, Bet would give me a head start on the apple pie.

Bet did the talking. 'Boys, we need to tell you something. Firstly, please understand that what I'm going to tell you will never change the fact that Roy and I will always love and care for you. You will continue to live with us and you'll always be our sons.'

My mother had her hands in her lap. I saw them tightly gripping the sleeve cuffs on the heavy winter coat she'd worn to mass.

She began, 'Your father and I aren't your real parents.' Roy stared silently at the ground. 'Your real parents, even though they loved you, weren't able to bring you up. So they asked the church to find a nice married couple to adopt you.'

Bet looked first to Damien and then to me. 'Do you know what adopted means?' Somehow I knew she'd rehearsed these words many times. She sounded so stilted, not her usual cheery self. Without waiting for an answer, she rushed on. 'Sometimes, if people are poor, or they die . . . if they're sick or are too young, they just can't bring up their children. So they ask the church to have somebody else do it. Your dad and I agreed to help out and raise you both as our sons.'

'Adopted children are just so very lucky that the church is able to find a home for the babies that can't stay with their parents.

'Your father and I won't be having other children,' she added. 'It's just us.'

I stared at her. Our eyes locked. I must have looked frightened, because she gave me one of her intensely reassuring smiles. It radiated pure kindness, and I knew then that everything was going to be okay.

Roy was still peering at the floor. Was he sad? Did he feel sorry for Damien and me? Or was he sorry for himself? He wasn't saying anything. Bet had always allowed my father to think he ran the show. We knew he didn't.

She continued. 'Damien, Brendan, you both have different parents—but we will take care of you both forever . . . and ever.' Her voice caught, and she inhaled quickly. I looked up and saw my mother's eyes were glassy. She wasn't able to talk. For a moment we all bowed our heads, as though we were back in church.

Composed again, Bet asked, 'Do you have any questions?' I looked across at Damien. He said, 'No,' and so I did, too. The news had hit me like a hammer. Nothing made sense, and yet somehow everything made perfect sense.

Psychologists use the term 'flashbulb memories' to describe strikingly vivid recall of a significant life event, including many seemingly unimportant details: what you were wearing, the temperature, maybe even the smell of the air, all coalescing into one single moment. Though it was more than fifty years ago, I can recall the moment my mother uttered those words. I can still see Damien's posters on the wall: *Doctor Who*, *Lost in Space* and that robot stuff I had zero patience for. He adored the escape of sci-fi, but it left me cold.

I lay still on the bed as the enormity of Bet's disclosure pushed me into the mattress, immobilised. I waited for gravity to release me so I could get up and walk around, shake myself off and work out what had happened.

Roy was the timekeeper with the Richmond Football Club and the Tigers were flying in the 1960s. Sport, and in particular a love of the Tigers, was an unfailing common denominator that we would all rely on in the years to come. The neddies, footy or cricket were usually blaring from the wireless on Saturdays. But there was no live sport on the radio on a Sunday. It was the day of rest. A good day to make an announcement. The house seemed unnervingly quiet after the big news was delivered.

Bet and Roy had just severed the lines that moored us boys safely in our sheltered harbour. What a message for Bet to have to deliver. Adrift, we could float out to sea or become beached on the shore. I was only a little boy, but I knew my life would be profoundly different after hearing those few sentences.

After an unusually quiet lunch, Damien and I lay on our beds against opposite walls of our little bedroom and talked. My brother wasn't overly perturbed by the adoption news. I found his lack of angsty contemplation reassuring. We've been the closest of allies since that day.

In the days that followed, we all walked on eggshells. There wasn't any further explanation about our adoptions. Just go about your business, boys. I'm sure Bet hugged us, but we weren't a touchy-feely family—who was, in the 1960s? After that day, an invisible force field silently descended on that momentous subject. Adoption was a ridiculously complex concept for an eight-year-old to wrestle with alone, and not talking about it meant I retreated into my head, withdrawing even further into my books, music and daydreams. I found control within myself.

Roy and Bet were terrific parents. They were reliable, present and hard-working; Damien and I loved them for all they did for us. And what a profound gesture, to accept two relinquished babies into their home, newborns with no ancestral footsteps to follow. To adopt or to foster a child is simply the greatest gift anyone can ever give. My parents' unconditional love was never in question, though my mind sometimes raced with thoughts of who my real parents were and why they gave me up.

Living behind a shop in Richmond suggests we were poor, but it didn't feel like it. We struggled, but we didn't go without. When Damien and I were supposed to be out of earshot, I remember listening to my parents discussing the family budget. In serious, muted voices, they deliberated on how to afford expenses such as school uniforms. The knees and elbows in our clothes were well-darned. Clothing was handed down from Damien to me, repurposed or worn paper thin.

I'd later dwell on why Roy and Bet didn't discuss the adoption with us again in greater detail. It wasn't as though the subject was forbidden. It came up superficially on occasion, but there was no nitty-gritty talk—certainly not about how we felt, how Roy and Bet felt, or what had transpired when we were born.

I never once asked who my birth parents were, or where they were, because I thought it would be perceived as being ungrateful. I didn't *really* think that I'd be sent back to where I came from if I started asking questions or misbehaving—but I wasn't about to push my luck. Though not conscious of it until adulthood, one of my first responses was to become super-independent—just in case. I kept my powder dry. I became the ever-watchful child.

It would take more than half a century before I had the answers to the questions that began to circle in my head on that day in 1969.

Chapter 2

MELBOURNE, 2019

Not so long ago, I described my 'flashbulb memory' of the day we were told of our adoption to Damien, and he said with a shrug, 'I thought we'd always known.'

While I've spent countless hours researching my past, Damien simply wasn't that interested in pursuing blood kin. I respect his decision not to plunge blindly down the rabbit hole, but for me there simply wasn't a choice.

Interestingly, one of my brother's clear childhood recollections was of me being annoyed at him for telling kids at school that we were adopted. I certainly wasn't proud of the fact; to me it was corroboration that I'd been declined, overlooked. NQR— or 'not quite right'.

Growing up, I'd often despair that no effort had been made to try to allocate Damien and me, the little orphans, to families where there was at least some vague physical resemblance. Could it really be that hard? We were four people: Roy, Bet, Damien and I. But we were seemingly made up of spare parts. We couldn't have been more different.

It didn't help that I had a 'turned eye' before starting school. I had numerous visits to the ophthalmologist, who gave me Buddy Holly–style glasses with one lens blurry and the other clear. The glasses failed to fix the problem. I was then administered endless courses of drops that also failed. I had to sit in the front row of class with the teacher's pets and the No-Friends-Nigels.

In the playground, there was some teasing about my wonky eye. 'Footy eyes,' they said—one at home, one away. I was what some teachers referred to as an FLK: a Funny Lookin' Kid.

An NQR FLK.

In Grade 2, I had an operation to fix my eye. The left one straightened, but as it'd always been a different shape, the operation still didn't work—it was never going to. I had a handful of formative early years of school looking different, and I hated the attention.

Many adopted people, regardless of when they're told (or find out), have some nagging inkling that they're mismatched, don't quite fit, or are outsiders, a recurring sense that they've lost something. Like aliens dropped onto earth in one of Damien's crazy sci-fi books, quietly biding their time, waiting for the mothership to return and take them home. That was me. I wasn't unhappy; there was no shortage of love. But I'd see someone on a bus with my hair, or nose, or gait, and ever-hopefully think . . . could they be my mother, my father, my brother or sister? As Jeanette Winterson says in *Why Be Happy When You Could Be Normal?*, 'Adoption drops you into the story after it has started. It's like reading a book with the first few pages missing . . . The feeling that something is missing never, ever leaves you—and it can't, and it shouldn't, because something *is* missing.'

The upside of adoption was that it allowed me to feel limitless. There was no compulsion to be something—a doctor, a bus driver, or an accountant like Roy. I could be anything. As I grew older, I never hesitated to pursue opportunities that I was entirely unqualified for. I succeeded in talking myself into several sought-after jobs I simply had no right to. I bluffed my way in with the thought that I'd work out what was required after I'd started. Why not? Maybe this was where I was meant to fit?

A common response for adoptees is to invent for themselves a place of belonging. I was free to create a persona out of thin air. It was more than mere teenage fantasising; I inhabited alternative lives, physically present but mentally living other, more complete existences. These identities provided an unredacted history and offered much-needed certainty. I was obsessed with the pursuit of identity. Books provided vital templates, because I had no familial starting point, no point of reference. Biographies, memoirs and autobiographies all helped crystallise the ways people articulate self-motivation and inclinations. I devoured hundreds that dealt with one's purpose in life.

For a long time I was George Johnston living the tempestuous bohemian life with Charmian Clift in Hydra, Greece. I've visited the island numerous times to re-trace the scenes from my imagination, fact and fiction blurring into one. I've also inhabited W. Somerset Maugham's Larry Darrell from *The Razor's Edge*. The story follows a soldier who, after a traumatic World War I experience, wanders the globe looking for purpose and identity. Larry studies religion and philosophy in Paris, tramps across Europe and lives with Benedictine monks. Those long-ago scenes of misplaced protagonists searching for connection will forever be a part of me.

During school years I spent much of the time living in my head, detached from the outside world. Though I knew I was loved by my family, a foggy sense of purposelessness, of being misplaced, arose often. I felt that finding out where I came from might provide direction, or clues about how I should live my adult life. I could easily have floated out to sea, never to return, but Roy and Bet's unconditional love not only anchored me, but also provided a profound foundation for the rest of my life. However, there remained an overwhelming need for an explanation of my ancestry.

It has proven insatiable.

Chapter 3

MELBOURNE, 1975

When Damien and I were teenagers, Roy told us a story about the parish priest from St Ignatius Church in Richmond, my parents' local church. The venerated priest had long been friendly with them.

My parents were hoping to raise the deposit for their first house by breeding dachshunds. One evening when walking the dogs out the front of St Ignatius, my father was approached by the priest, who told him: 'A good Catholic couple like you and Bet deserve children.' He encouraged Roy to adopt a baby boy; that baby was Damien.

Although my parents knew that there was often a surplus of surrendered babies available for adoption, they felt blessed to have been chosen and quickly agreed to proceed.

The church had long played an active role in finding homes for surrendered Catholic children among parishioners. Sometimes it resorted to advertisements, like the following, which appeared in *The Southern Cross*, a Catholic newspaper published in Adelaide, in 1954:

BABY BOYS FOR ADOPTION

THERE is an urgent need for homes for baby boys who are awaiting adoption into Catholic homes. At the moment there are three of these children for whom no home can be found, and there is a danger that they may be sent to *non-Catholic families.** There are several families waiting to take baby girls, but the need is for someone to take baby boys.

(* their italics)

A telegram arrived at the end of August 1959 advising Roy and Bet of my brother's birth and imminent arrival. The over-joyed parents-to-be received instructions about where and when to collect him. They were given a few days' notice to prepare and make arrangements. Damien was a handsome, contented baby and settled into his new home with ease.

By 1961, Bet was thirty-eight and Roy thirty-six, and considered far too old to adopt a second child. However, on 9 February they received not a telegram but an urgent call from the Catholic Family Welfare Bureau saying there was a 'special child' the church would like them to raise. The call sent Bet into a tizz. She was without the essentials for a newborn: 'All I had was two balls of baby wool.' Nevertheless, the following day, having never expected another baby, my new parents collected me from the Mother Superior of the Sisters of St Joseph Receiving Home in Carlton, and an unanticipated family of four was created. Roy and Bet struggled financially, were without higher education, and were devout and compliant—not the sort to ask questions. They were ideal candidates for a 'special child'.

From day one I was a restless, colicky baby, my stomach often in knots. Bet was frequently kept up well into the night soothing this unsettled new arrival. She battled through, as mums of newborns do, and eventually I adjusted to the unfamiliar sounds, smells and routine of my new environment.

Like all surrendered Catholic babies, Damien and I were both baptised before being adopted. Roy and Bet dutifully took us to mass every Sunday, come rain, hail or shine. Mass was never something I looked forward to; it was more an hour to be endured. Even the priests looked as though mass was the last place they wanted to be. It was an endless cycle of sitting, kneeling, standing and mouthing the words to monotonous hymns. Often the sermon spoke of Christ and how he'd been nailed to a cross. Somehow we were, at least in part, responsible, which was why we were stuck here on earth.

When I was about twelve, it began to occur to me that church was all smoke and mirrors. We're going to burn in hell? A devil with pointy horns? Really? It was made abundantly clear in my early Catholic schooling that priests had superpowers and a hotline to God. Each one had taken a vow of celibacy and was the embodiment of Our Lord on earth. Given that the priests knew all the important stuff, there was no need for us dolts in the pews to think for ourselves. The pew-dwellers around us didn't appear to mind sitting for an hour each Sunday looking forward to the Sunday roast lunch. But I had questions, though I kept them to myself.

As I grew older, I was particularly taken with the claim that priests had the ability to annul sin. All sins, from the minuscule to the mammoth, could be erased, no questions asked. This meant there was no need to involve the police (or the headmaster— depending on the location of the evildoing). Nobody I knew had ever thought to ask the difference between a sin and a crime. Priests were untouchable, above the law—we were instructed to be forever grateful that they were in our lives.

One day, my friend, Vas, and I stole a couple of packs of playing cards from Target; it was the most evil thing I had ever done in my life. I knew it was a crime—but only if the police were called. And anyway, I knew if I went to confession afterwards (and I did) the law-breaking would be downgraded to a sin. Three Hail Marys and two Our Fathers made for an inexpensive pack of cards. And better still, I could blame Satan for making me do it.

We Catholics were (supposedly) able to sleep well at night, because we'd been blessed with exclusive access to whiter, brighter, soul-cleansing confession. No matter the gravity of the offence, parishioners' secrets were always safe under the 'seal of confession', whatever that was.

But being Catholic didn't protect us from punishment. My schooling, particularly when delivered by those who had taken vows, was at times a trial by ordeal. It was confounding that even though they had divine superpowers, they often resorted to ruling their classrooms with an earthly iron fist. As Jonathan Swift wrote, 'We have just enough religion to make us hate, but not enough to make us love one another.' At our school, St John's School, Hawthorn, which went from Prep to Form 4, some of the teaching Marist Brothers would intimidate, cane and bastardise at will. It came as no surprise that the school was closed at the end of 1976, the year I left.

Singing classes with Brother Raymond were notorious for his control-by-fear methodology. Known to all as Fudd (as in Bugs Bunny's easily exasperated Elmer), because he was both short and bald, he was also short of temper. Each week Fudd would march through the rows of us boys poking a ruler deep into our mouths as we sang. He was only satisfied when our mouths were as wide open as they could stretch. Sometimes we gagged when he penetrated too deeply.

On one occasion, after probing rounds with his ruler, Fudd stood in front of my friend, Tony, who'd just stifled a laugh (another boy, Kev, had farted). Making any sound other than contributing to our tuneless dirge was unforgivable. Punishment from Fudd could include detention, public belittling, caning or all three. This time, he elected to keep time with the song by fiercely thumping the top of Tony's head with an open hand. The timekeeping quickly progressed to a pounding with clenched fist, then uppercuts and full swings to my friend's stunned face. Fudd grew bright red and wild with rage. After absorbing more than half-a-dozen blows, a semiconscious Tony collapsed to the floor and pissed his pants.

The police weren't called. Maybe Fudd went to confession, maybe not. He was later shunted off to a boarding school in New South Wales. These occurrences were only ever spoken about in whispers. Secrecy was hardwired into the church, our school and community.

Some days at school made *Lord of the Flies* look like a pleasant Sunday outing. Left unsupervised by teachers, one boy was dangled by a leg from a second-storey balcony by classmates. Another was held down while students spat into his forced-open mouth. One boy was savagely beaten by a lay teacher in front of a stunned class.

It wasn't all bad, though: a few of the brothers acted with generosity and sincere compassion, and I made several life-long cherished friends. The threat of violence was always there, niggling at the back of my mind, but for the most part school was just monotonous. In the end, I left with far more good memories than bad—but with no thanks to the religious brothers who taught us.

I was moderately bright, sensitive and disengaged. Anyone different from the herd was vulnerable: the overly expressive, the uncoordinated, loners, mouth-breathers, kids without a dad, wogs, the poor kids, freckle-heads, the smelly ones—their lives could be made unbearable. All of this was a good reason to keep my adoptive status quiet. The church, and therefore society in general, looked unfavourably on 'illegitimate children'.

I didn't want to be associated with adopted kids. Of all the kids I knew, the ones with the most pronounced emotional disturbances were always adopted. For example, one deeply troubled classmate was expelled from school for continual poor behaviour and, during his absence, in a dispute with his mother, poured mower fuel over himself, demanded 'Don't take a step closer,' and then lit a match. It didn't take long for that story to make its way to the schoolyard. The shrugged-shoulder explanation among our classmates: 'Well, he *is* adopted.' Months later I happened upon him, in his typical wild-eyed state, in the street. With what I remember as perverse pride, he rolled up his sleeves and urged me to inspect the haunting wax-like scars.

Being called a bastard was a sharp, shame-laden slur; we bastards had few comebacks other than attempting to belt the accuser (which only confirmed the deeper truth). I don't recall ever being called a bastard by friends in a way intended to hurt deeply, but then I'd avoided the spiteful slurs by being selective in sharing my adoption secret. I restricted knowledge of my vulnerability to a handful of allies. To my knowledge, none of my close friends had been adopted—I kept a distance from those weirdos. On the few occasions when close friends ribbed me with the 'bastard' term, they would have seen from my tight smile that the subject was out of bounds.

Though I refused to publicly acknowledge my adoption, questions about the identity of my birth parents percolated at the back of my mind. Who were they? Where were they? Why did they give me away?

Perhaps knowing I was adopted increased my doubts about the Catholic faith. I started going to 7 pm Saturday night mass in my early teens. Night mass was a funky new invention for groovers who wanted a sleep-in on Sunday morning while still securing the all-important tick from the beardy man upstairs. It also allowed wayward young soon-to-be-heathens like me to piously proclaim 'I'm off to church' and then zip off to a friend's place to kick the footy or listen to cassettes for an hour. I considered myself way too cool to be singing along to the acoustic guitar of a desert boot–wearing hippie in a corduroy jacket at the front of the church. Night mass was not my scene.

In my early teens I was questioning everything and reading widely. I was fascinated by how the world worked, and began absorbing *National Geographic*, *The Bulletin*, *Life* and *Time* magazines, as well as any international papers I could lay my hands on at the library. There were plenty of logical atheists to follow—Peter Singer, Richard Dawkins and Phillip Adams (not forgetting the hedonists: Jagger and Richards). Much of the reading I did scrutinised both religion and politics.

When I turned sixteen, I decided it was time to tell Roy and Bet that Catholicism was no longer for me. We sat down one Sunday evening and I explained my enlightened thoughts on spirituality and all things celestial, concluding with 'and there-fore . . . (gulp) I'm not going to go to church anymore'.

What followed was one of the longest pregnant pauses in the history of pregnant pauses. The clock stopped. Even the dog held its breath. Finally, Roy and Bet looked at each other before Roy spoke: 'Okay. You're able to make your own decisions.'

Yes! He didn't explode; Bet didn't get all teary (my greatest fear). Finally, no more pretending to go to those inane services. Hallelujah! And then, from the far corner of the lounge room, my big, strong elder brother's voice squeaked, 'And me!' I had made a crazy-brave leap into the darkness, and Damien saw his chance and jumped on for a free ride. He thought church was all mumbo jumbo, just as I did. And in that moment, we were out, together. Brothers.

Several months later, still on a high, I dared an even greater assertion of independence. This time the very fabric of our family bond would be tested like never before. My father had issues with blood pressure and anxiety. He was a terrific dad but was trying to keep a lid on his own wounding experience of rejection and emotional trauma (one we kids knew nothing about). Like most kids, we were expert at reading our parents' body language, so I watched, and plotted, and chose my moment judiciously. When the right moment finally arrived, I blurted out across the dinner table, 'Roy, Bet . . . I've decided to barrack for Hawthorn!'

This time the stakes were too high. Damien held his tongue.

He always was smarter than me.

Chapter 4

IRON KNOB, SOUTH AUSTRALIA, 1953

He'd set out from a station in Iron Knob well before dawn. He was driving north for the weekend work in Pimba and Woomera. A couple too many drinks the night before explained the sore head and dry mouth, but at least he'd enjoyed a rare full night's rest. It was a respite from the dreams about the ten-day-old baby boy he'd sent to Sydney to be adopted by his elder brother. To push those thoughts from his mind, if only for a night, was a blessing.

Out on the open track, the red dirt silently fell away under the big sky. The track rolled forward as far as the eye could see; there'd be little evidence of people for several hours now. Out here, shortly after the sun rose, the distant view became distorted by heat haze. It could make a driver question what he'd seen. The sun robbed all moisture from the plain, and the odd mulga, eucalypt or desert quandong fluttered and winked in the sunlight.

Woomera this week, Coober Pedy the next. The opal miners in Pedy lived underground like rabbits. They spent their days throwing gelignite down mine shafts and their nights—or most of them—drinking and fighting. But he knew a few of the locals near Pimba would be pleased to see the dusty man in the VW Kombi as it dack-dacked up the track later that evening. The Kombi had two side doors immediately behind the passenger's seat. Using his carpentry skills, he'd decked out the rear cabin for both work and rest. The foolish smile of the VW badge on the front belied the disposition of the man behind the steering wheel. He felt as empty as the landscape.

Setting out for Pimba in the gathering heat of December was not what he'd have chosen if he had any say in things. He'd been tending to his outback flocks in the Nullarbor, Quorn, Hawker, Leigh Creek, Andamooka and Oodnadatta for eleven years now. It was not for the faint-hearted or the easily offended. This was a parched and unwelcoming terrain, interrupted only by salt pans and the mighty Flinders Ranges. It's where men came to hide from prying eyes, often with torment and guilt.

Midmorning he stopped to brew a billy of tea; he would let the vehicle cool and gather his thoughts. In a past life, he'd been a house builder in Balmain, in Sydney. He was surrounded by water, even as a kid. His family lived close to one of the world's most picturesque harbours. At night in bed he'd smell the salty sea air. In his late teens, he'd been a lifesaver at Bondi Beach. It was a cruel twist to be banished to this godforsaken arid outpost.

As he thudded over corrugated gibber tracks, the sun blasted him from the east through the driver-side window. It shone on him fully by noon. He could never decide if it was more comfortable with the windows open or closed. In long sleeves or short. Fair-skinned Irishmen weren't cut out for this caper. The passenger-side window was half open, allowing a fine desert dust to cover everything and leave a red patina on his spectacles.

He took it as a daily blessing when the sun was overhead, as then it was just his hands and knees that copped the baking. His shoulder and hip ached from the years he'd spent earning a living through hard manual labour. He braced for every jolt along the weather-beaten track. Late last year, an X-ray taken by a doctor in Adelaide had revealed a small tubercular lesion on his lung. He'd be seeing a Sydney specialist soon to learn more.

Bumping up north, he had too much time to think. Worrying about his brother in Sydney and the burden of the baby boy he'd sent from Iron Knob knotted his stomach—it was a big ask of his brother. He'd made several people swear to keep some big secrets and was having trouble recalling who, exactly, knew which part of what story. There were also the two young women, no longer girls, he'd sent from Port Augusta to stay with his Sydney family. He felt they both needed direction; pleasingly, one of them was now committed to becoming a nun. He wondered if people back home in Sydney were curious about his relationship with these women.

Out on the open track, his mind wandered. Most of the dangers here were unseen. The fine red aeolian dust they called bulldust concealed treacherous potholes. Bulldust was one of the many pitfalls for the unfamiliar on the outback tracks. Front wheels sometimes slid into a rutted holes, causing drivers to lose all ability to steer. Abandoned vehicles on the side of the road punctuated the trek, their bonnets up and windscreens sometimes shot out.

Tinned produce was the only food that could survive the heat of the journey—all else spoiled. But even so, the occasional mid-afternoon pop of a tin of fruit exploding in the back of the Kombi sometimes jerked him upright. It took him back to air raids, bombs and the horrors he'd seen in Europe. He was a changed person after the war. Many of those who'd returned suffered severe shell shock. In truth, he had little to complain about—though he'd suffered through several bombings as a younger man, he had been exempt from taking up arms as he was studying in England. He'd made it back to Australia in one piece. Nobody had even taken a single shot at him: somehow that made it worse.

The smell of hot, fruity syrup filled the van, and he was sweating through his shirt and pants; he'd be stuck to the seat until he arrived.

After pushing further up the rocky gibber track for another hour or two, he spotted a dingo next to a large salt pan. He was pressed for time—they expected him up at the homestead before dark, and the shadows had already grown long—but he also knew the station manager had been bedevilled by a rogue male dingo for a good six months.

In the desert, dingos are nocturnal. They hunt mainly at dusk and dawn. They're highly efficient, opportunistic predators—now it was time for the hunter to become the hunted. Slowly poking his rifle out of the driver's window, he steered the vehicle onto the high side of the track and then cut the engine. He'd only get one shot; he had to make it count.

The sky was cobalt blue above, but it was beginning to show blood red on the horizon—there was no time to waste. The breeze had died. For some reason his side ached more in this eerie quiet. On the edge of the lake was a smattering of low-growing native grasses. He released the brake, inching toward his prey, slowly manoeuvring the van downward whenever the dingo turned the other way.

It's not a sin to kill a predator; nor is there shame in taking the life of one of God's creatures. The dingo has a certain nobility—the best are more intelligent than a domestic dog. In the desert they only survive a few years, as the terrain is so brutal. The young males, like this one, are nomadic and solitary in nature. All they desire is food, a mate and, while raising their pups, a pack. This dingo hunter was also nomadic, solitary and had been cut from his pack. He regularly contemplated the need to procreate that was evidently in the soul of all men and beasts. It was impossible to deny the truth of his own desires and urges. Not that he told anyone about them.

Careful to stay downwind, he trailed the dingo for close to two hours. Just before complete darkness fell, he delivered his shot.

Though it was night, he was guided forward by the stars and the heavens above. The cooler air brought out all manner of wildlife that had been hiding who knows where. He drove with caution.

The people in the homestead had heard the Kombi dack-dack up the miles-long drive to the station and were all outside to bid him welcome. He came to rest at the steps of the enormous verandah surrounding the homestead and wordlessly opened the van's tailgate to reveal the dead dingo. The station manager and rouseabouts rejoiced. Some threw their hats in the air. He then opened the side doors of the Kombi, revealing the altar and tabernacle, robes hung above. Caked in red dust, he began preparations for the mass to be held at dawn the next day.

Later, at the evening meal, the station manager toasted: 'To Father Vin Shiel, our protector!' The priest raised his glass with a crooked grin. He didn't know who he was, but he knew he wasn't one of them.

Chapter 5

MELBOURNE, 1990

I was twenty-nine years old when I decided to find my birth parents. While my twenties had been relatively carefree, my adoption was regularly brought to front of mind: introducing friends to family (the older I got, the less I looked like any of them); doctors posing the 'is there a family history of?' question; many innocuous run-of-the-mill conversations about family traits, intelligence, things that 'run in the family'. These moments underscored the profound, unresolved issue that I'd put off dealing with.

I was working at Australia's largest audio studio. We'd recorded a who's who of the entertainment world, including U2, Mick Jagger and Madonna. The charts were full of our artists' hits, while TV and radio were filled with our clients' voice-overs and jingles. I loved the place; I was with my tribe. My girlfriend, Kate, and I revelled in our frenetic social life, but we also knew it was the right time for kids. We decided to do a backpacking trip through America and Europe in 1992 and then start a family.

Though there are many words to describe relationships, I've not found the right one to categorise ours. We're not

'spouses'—we didn't get married, because it seemed too predict-
able when everyone we knew seemed to be getting hitched. (Half
of them have since divorced.) 'Best mates' is blokey and shallow;
'life partners' could mean anything, and 'soul mates' is warmer
but still too New Age-y for us. All I know is we've been pretty
much inseparable since 1984.

Once Kate and I resolved to have a child, thoughts of genetics,
ancestry and identity swirled in my head—I knew it was time to
educate myself about adoption. Before birth control became freely
available in Australia in the 1960s, adoption was one of the great
unquestioned practices in our society. Abortion was illegal and
treacherous for those who risked 'backyard' procedures. There
was no financial support for unwed mothers. Single women who
found themselves pregnant had few options.

It's estimated that more than 200,000 Australian children have
been adopted since 1940. The peak decades were the 1950s and
1960s. Due to family dysfunction, displacement, neglect or abuse
of adoptees and unintended outcomes, various Australian state
governments were compelled to periodically revisit adoption legislation. I furtively read every report and news item on the subject.

When a new adoption Act passed through Victorian parliament in 1984, it attracted widespread media attention. The Act
gave adult adoptees access to their original birth records for the
first time. In short, the new laws 'opened' what had always been
intended to be permanently 'closed' adoptions. Adoptees were free
to apply for their unabridged birth certificates, which revealed
the names of their birth mother and, for the fortunate minority,
birth father.

Though well aware in my mid-twenties that I was legally
allowed to learn the identity of at least one of my birth parents,
I'd never tried. I'd been wrestling with a number of issues, one of
the most obvious being the stigma surrounding adoption. Birth

parents who surrendered children were seen as promiscuous, irresponsible or ignorant—bad people—while adoptive parents were seen as unquestionably noble. Most people thought that adoptees should consider themselves fortunate and that searching for your birth parents was ungrateful. Though always unspoken, it was expected we would express thanks for our predicament.

Without ill-intent, this thinking was accepted as fact by my friends and peers. At a party in my early twenties, I became enraged at a friend who offhandedly blurted, 'Adoption, what does it matter? You're so lucky to have your family!'

But it did matter. 'I've never met another person on the planet who looks and thinks like me! You people take for granted that you've always known who you are and where you're from,' I fumed, and I stomped out the back gate. The inherent anguish of closed adoptions is unique—adoptees who know nothing of their past are expected to wordlessly bury their pain.

Once Kate and I had committed to starting a family, I became increasingly concerned about a rare medical disorder she'd inherited called malignant hyperthermia. In short, it meant she could have a severe reaction to certain drugs used in anaesthesia. Without prompt treatment, sufferers dramatically overheat, and it can be fatal. Some of Kate's relatives had died on the operating table when undergoing seemingly benign procedures—we now knew why. Kate would need specialised attention while giving birth, and our children were likely to inherit the disorder.

I had zero knowledge of what was swimming around in my gene pool. Maybe I had malignant hyperthermia, too, or was harbouring other obscure genetic time bombs. If I'd known my family history of cancers, strokes and heart problems, I could have put preventive strategies in place and acted quickly if symptoms emerged—but I didn't have even the most basic details. As a borderline control freak, I'd always been troubled by not knowing my medical predispositions, and this malignant-hyperthermia twist provided an unarguable justification to investigate my ancestry.

During my research, I read accounts of both joyful and permanently scarring experiences when adoptees made first contact with birth parents. I was filled with equal measures of blind hope and fear; it was obvious 1 could be devastated by this venture. I naively reasoned that I'd first ask my birth parents specific medical questions, and if I liked the sound of them, I'd become more emotionally engaged. I thought I could steer the process. I have never been more wrong about anything in my life.

Once I'd made the decision to obtain my birth records, I acted quickly. After a formal application to Community Services Victoria, I waited for the bureaucratic process to unfold. The first step was to go through a psych assessment, presumably to ensure I'd handle the news appropriately. At this session, the counsellor tempered my assumption of a successful outcome. I dismissed him as a pessimist. I'd always been lucky. Why wouldn't my birth parents want to meet me?

The Watkins family of four was extremely close, and Damien and I had always been reasonably popular, sporty, happy kids. Every family occasion—Christmas, New Year, Easter, birthdays, anniversaries, new jobs, whatever—called for celebration. We cherished long Sunday afternoons together at barbecues in the backyard celebrating our deeply supportive family. We were more forgiving than the majority of my friends' families who shared DNA—maybe we unconsciously tried harder. But there was no denying we were four independent streams with no shared genetic source, four distinct tributaries forming our family river.

I resolved to put my loyalty to Roy and Bet to one side. I had an obligation to Kate and our future children. The laws had been changed to assist people like me. It was my birthright to know, or so I thought.

I didn't tell Roy and Bet what I was up to. Not only did I fear they'd interpret my desire to contact my birth parents as rejecting them, but Bet would doubtless worry that I'd be hurt. All she ever wanted was for her boys to be happy. There could be no questioning of the depths of our emotional bond; they would always be my true parents. But this was a leap into the unknown, and I was anxious enough—I didn't need them to stress about a response they couldn't influence.

And, of course, it could all go horribly pear-shaped. Painful secrets could be unearthed, information I'd wish I'd never discovered. Roy and Bet had done everything imaginable for Damien and me. There was no gain for them in a wretched outcome. Though I put on a brave face, I suffered tormenting anxiety about the possibility of finding out something sinister about my birth parents. What if I was the result of rape? What if they were criminals? What if they were in gaol? What if they'd both died young of a genetic disorder?

Or worse, what if my parents wanted nothing to do with me?

I told myself I'd learn all I could, and if the outcome was positive, I'd share it with Roy and Bet. But as it turned out, they both went to their graves without me sharing a single thing about my astounding discoveries.

Chapter 6

MELBOURNE, 1990

I learned my birth mother's name close to thirty years after the severing of our umbilical cord.

I was sitting in the office of a counsellor from the Catholic Family Welfare Bureau. It was cold in the room. A box of tissues had been placed on the table next to where I sat. After brief introductions, the counsellor unceremoniously handed me my original birth certificate. As my hands shook with adrenaline, I could only focus on two unfamiliar words printed on the certificate. I slowly scanned each letter: M a g g i e B e c k e r. It was a puzzling, foreign-sounding name. I tried to conjure a kind-hearted face to match the name, but all I could see was Boris Becker, the spring-heeled German tennis prodigy.

Maybe because I'd often felt like a square peg in a round hole among the working-class vanilla Micks in Richmond, I was elated to learn of my non-Anglo ancestry. Give me a salty Germanic heritage any day. The certificate showed that Maggie had been born in South Australia and was twenty-seven years old when she gave birth. That made her much older than most mothers who'd put their children up for adoption.

And my birth father? There was an empty box on the form that should have contained his name. The counsellor, an abrupt woman named Jenny Abbott, told me it was common for the father's name to be missing from birth records. And there was more: Maggie had actually named me. *Paul Becker.* A solitary bon voyage gift. Learning this name, Paul Becker, was the beginning of a second identity that I would pursue for the next thirty years.

Jenny handed me more papers, which revealed that Roy and Bet had immediately claimed me for their own by changing my name to Brendan Watkins. This was common practice, but so much for Maggie's parting gift. The thinking at the time was that a 'clean break' from the abiding shame of illegitimacy was for the best. There was concern that the birth parents might one day change their mind and want their child back; a new identity would make it that little bit harder for the surrendering parents to trace the child. Adoptions were also kept quiet to protect the adopting parents from the stigma of infertility. Closed adoptions were always shrouded in layers of secrets. With this new name, for better or worse, I was a different person to the child I'd been the week before.

I wasn't told if my mother held me after I was born. I wasn't told how much I weighed or what time I was born. I didn't learn how long Maggie's labour was or if mine was an arduous birth—nothing connected me to Maggie but this piece of paper. I gripped it tightly. I knew many adoptees received at least some of these answers in such meetings. I had no inkling of it at the time, but I later discovered I was being treated very differently from everyone else.

Jenny described the typical scenarios that led to 'unwanted' babies being made available for adoption: teenage couples incapable of bringing up a child, couples of limited means unable to afford an extra mouth to feed, 'inappropriate' relationships . . . A lot of 'ins' and 'uns'. She was subtly discouraging me from making contact with my birth mother. I was astounded that she appeared to not fully comprehend why I was so keen to meet my very own birth mother. We discussed my desire for contact for some time; reluctantly, she concluded, 'Well, all right—if that's your wish— the best way forward is to have me make contact on your behalf.' I felt I had no choice, that this was my only option.

In those days, the influence of the Catholic Church was everywhere to be seen, at least in the world I lived in: crusty clerics were forever pontificating about how we should live our lives, sour-faced old men defending the status quo. And Jenny, of course, was a senior agent of the church, a position that gave her a tangible moral authority. Her tone of repression would be a potent, if subconscious, influence. For decades, Jenny would be the invisible presence behind me, looking over my shoulder, the disapproving voice in my head urging me to stay silent whenever I wanted to lash out at the church for my all-pervading sense of powerlessness. As a wide-eyed Catholic schoolboy, I was encouraged to be curious. We were told that the most inquisitive students would make profound discoveries and travel to far-off places; there'd be rewards for seeking answers. But the unmistakable message from Jenny was to let sleeping dogs lie. The unsaid instruction was to bury my emotions.

But I didn't need time to 'go home and think about it'. Despite Jenny's urging, I told her I wanted her to call this Maggie Becker straight away and tell her that her son wanted to talk. Kate and I were planning a family—I needed information, and the help of the only person in the world capable of providing it. I had a fabulous life and wanted to tell my birth mother about it. I had so many questions, too: Do I have brothers and sisters? Who is my father? What were the circumstances of my birth? Why couldn't she keep me? She'd named me Paul—was that my father's name? Or was Paul Maggie's father's name?

And when do we meet?

Jenny slowed me down . . . First, she needed to locate Maggie Becker and then, 'assuming she is alive', find her phone number.

Alive? My jaw clenched. I'd never seriously considered she could be dead. I'd come this far. I was her son. Surely not, she couldn't be dead?

Thousands like me, and a small number of parents who'd relinquished children, were clamouring for their original birth records around this time. If I wanted more information, I had to take a number and join the queue. I left Jenny's office and returned home to brood. At night, before drifting off to sleep, I would fabricate fabulous fantasies of family reunions with my wonky-eyed forebears. And sometimes, well before the dawn, I woke with stomach-churning nightmares of rejection.

Chapter 7

WOOMERA, 1954

A small mob of roos was idling in the late-morning sun by the track up ahead. It'd be easy for Father Vin to pull the Kombi over, grab the rifle from under the altar in the back and get a feed for the local peoples up the way.

Vin was an hour from the Woomera Prohibited Area. The local peoples were being pushed off their land by the government. Some of the waterholes appeared to have been poisoned by the atomic bomb tests, and the animals they'd once hunted had scattered. Though Prime Minister Menzies had guaranteed that 'no conceivable injury to life, limb or property could emerge' from the tests, some were saying that the Black Mist from the blasts made the local peoples ill—horrid sores and cancers were beginning to be reported. 'What a sorry state of affairs,' Father Vin mumbled to himself. He consoled himself that what he offered was heavenly salvation through the word of Our Lord. It was not too late for the souls of the local peoples to be saved. His mission was to advance the Catholic faith; it was for their own good.

His gun was buried under an assortment of holy robes and sweat-stained builder's overalls. By the time the priest had messed about trying to uncover it, the roos had scattered. 'Not to worry . . . short on time anyway,' he shrugged. He resolved to drop a couple on the return trip and deliver them to those who could sometimes be found near the railway sidings at Pimba. He was astonished at how the local peoples had developed a means to withstand these godforsaken lands. Some of them spoke about their 'Dreaming'. It was a spiritual connection to the land itself. What a mysterious concept, and a profoundly different spirituality to what Father Vin preached up in these parts.

Quite a number of the white trappers, fettlers, well-sinkers, miners and station hands had had children with the women of the local tribes. Much murderous violence and sinful activity had taken place. During the Depression, men would come out and try their hand at shooting or trapping dingos—the government paid handsomely for a pelt. Many of these white men had stayed away for too long. The desert changed them; there'd be no going back. Father Vin was far from perfect, he knew he risked the same fate, and that things must change.

Now that he was out of the vehicle, standing in the full sun next to the Kombi, he decided it must be time for a cuppa. He eased the van off the corrugated track and parked under a lone quandong tree. He was dry as a chip. All he could taste was dust. Aside from the occasional undulation, the only sight for 360 degrees was red dirt and rugged gibber outcrops. The engine needed to cool, and so did the sweating priest, who was still wearing his full-length black robe and dog-collar. As there was nobody around for miles, he decided to strip down to his white underpants and singlet. He lit a flame, put the billy on and lay on the stretcher in the back of the van. He'd doze until the billy boiled. But after only a few moments he began to snore loudly.

A thorny devil lizard emerged from under a rock beside the quandong and listened to the vibration of the snoring cleric. The devil tilted its head.

In his dreams, Father Vin relived the many adventures he'd packed into his life before entering the seminary. He'd lived by the motto 'Don't die wondering'. As a teenager, he couldn't wait to get out of school, and as soon as he did, he found himself a job in the building trade, where he'd shown great enterprise. Young Vin had energy in abundance and was quickly promoted to be trained in architectural design. He never tired of the gratification that only a builder can experience as a house rises from the dirt solely by the sweat of their brow.

Soon enough, the daring young man started a construction business of his own and employed several relatives. He went on to own a number of houses, a few of which he rented to friends and family. Surplus funds allowed him to venture into new commercial opportunities. In 1930, at twenty-seven years of age, he opened a wholesale household-supply store on Darling Street, in Sydney's Rozelle. He was also known for his sweet tooth, and so it only made sense to open a specialist chocolatier on Victoria Road, Rozelle. He was on his way.

The booming economy halted when the American stock market crashed in 1929 and the Great Depression spread to Australian shores. Vincent weathered the early years of the Great Depression but eventually had to wind back his businesses as the challenging times took hold.

The young Vincent was forever restless. As construction work slowed, he contemplated what else he could do with his life. There had to be more to it than simply amassing assets. A vocation with a deeper meaning, perhaps? He mulled over the possibility of a religious life, which would certainly please his adored mother, Margaret.

Born in 1859 in Ireland, Margaret Shiel had had fourteen children. Vin was the youngest. He was the apple of her eye, and he adored her. Margaret frequently said that to be blessed by just one of her brood offering themselves to Our Lord would make her time on earth of value. There was no doubting her hopes for her last child when she gave him 'Bede' as his middle name. It means to pray; also, to offer, to proffer. Sharing a name with Saint Bede the Venerable, Vincent was the last hope, and she let him know it. The young man would do anything to win her praise.

Fitfully snoring in the desert, the troubled priest dreamed of Margaret; a mother's love for her child is the purest of all devotions.

Crash! The billy had fallen from over the small fire, and boiling water sizzled into what was now bright red mud. The startled priest sat bolt upright in his cot, belting his head on the edge of the altar in the rear of the van. The wind had turned north and blew smoke from his fire through the side windows of the van. Thinking the cabin was on fire, he panicked and jolted to attention. He moaned and cradled a throbbing welt in the middle of his forehead.

As Father Vin struggled out of the back of the van, clutching his aching head, a trickle of blood snaked down his forearm. Still in his sweaty underwear, he caught sight of the thorny devil peering back at the extraordinary sight from the safety of his nearby rock.

The priest shook his head at the lizard and said, 'Well, Mr Beelzebub, I would like to formally advise you that I have made a profound decision. It brings me enormous pleasure to advise that you will never again enjoy the pleasure of my company. I'm leaving—for good!'

Chapter 8

MELBOURNE, 1990

After several weeks, Jenny called and asked me to meet her again at her office. The following week, I rushed to the appointment, certain she'd located my mother, and that Maggie was alive and keen to reunite. Like Bet, I was an optimist: think positive and positive things will happen.

But the moment I entered Jenny's office and noted her demeanour—unnervingly grim—I knew the news wasn't going to be good. Jenny told me to take a seat. As she began to talk, I realised that she had an accent. Why hadn't that registered in our previous meeting? Was she American? I didn't feel entitled to ask.

Without fanfare, Jenny announced that she'd spoken with my mother. My heart skipped—*she's alive!* I was told my request for contact was stressful for Maggie. She'd spent her entire life believing communication with me would never occur. Intentionally or not, Jenny's disapproving tone and expression made me feel like what I wanted—contact with my mother—was selfish. My mind accelerated into overdrive. I knew she might have been left high and dry by my father, and that a black hole of guilt was likely to have accompanied the decision to relinquish me. Assuming she was a believer, the church would have added its own layer of existential angst to the storm—hell and damnation awaited the mothers of the illegitimate.

'Maggie Becker is in Sydney,' Jenny said, 'where she's lived all of her adult life.'

'Terrific,' I replied. 'What'd she say? Are we going to meet?'

'Brendan, she has told me she can't ever meet you. There will be no contact.'

The words pinged in my head. *She can't ever. No contact.*

'Maggie is a very intelligent, determined and devout woman,' Jenny continued. 'It's not that she doesn't love you—in fact, she prays for you every day . . .'

If this addendum was intended to soften the blow, it failed.

'. . . but there will be no communication with Maggie.'

I couldn't gather my thoughts. How could I be rejected a second time? Jenny's next instruction scythed into my core: 'You need to go home and forget about Maggie Becker forever.'

After a pause, she said, 'In my experience, determined mothers who don't want contact never change their minds.'

My hard-as-nails mother had made up her mind and that was that. She wanted nothing to do with me. I decided that Maggie must be a heartless woman, just like Jenny. The certainty of my mother's refusal fused Jenny's foreboding persona with Maggie's. I would never see Maggie's face, so my subconscious made it Jenny's.

It felt as though I'd entered earth's atmosphere at speed and splashed down in a deep, dark ocean. Where the fuck was I now? All I wanted was information, stories—acknowledgement from my own flesh and blood. I didn't want money. I posed no threat. 'Why? Why did Maggie say we'll never meet?'

Jenny wouldn't say.

My brain became white noise. Discarded, I trudged home to Kate, unaware that a match had been struck, igniting an anxiety that would smoulder within me for decades.

Over the coming days, Kate and I pondered possible explanations. Maybe Maggie was married, and her husband didn't know about me? Or was there a traumatic secret she was protecting me from? But if that was the case, what was it? Maybe I really was the result of rape or incest. Is there anything worse?

Whatever the truth, it now seemed that I was shame personified. My appetite vanished; I slept poorly. Like a dog hit by a car, I lay low. I retreated into my head and reduced the size of the already small group of friends who shared the progress of my adoption story. I didn't cry (though I should have). Crying would mean letting my guard down.

My birth mother had given me not only an unused name but the oblivion of *damnatio memoriae*, a Latin phrase meaning 'condemnation of memory'. To condemn a person's memory is to remove them from official accounts of the past—to obliterate them from history. The second rejection hardened me.

A scream had lodged in the back of my throat. On occasion it filled me, overwhelmed me. I stifled it, ignored it. The only solace was that I hadn't told Roy and Bet what was going on. I thought of the words of novelist Alice Munro: 'You cannot let your parents anywhere near your real humiliations.' I felt lacerated, but at least I had spared my parents that hurt. Searching for a way to turn the loss into a draw, I immersed myself in self-help books. I already knew that many adoptees struggle with identity and self-esteem, but now I learned that this could lead to long-term psychological issues, dysfunctional relationships, antisocial behaviour and substance abuse. One of the more sobering statistics I read came from the American Academy of Pediatrics: adoptees were nearly four times more likely to attempt suicide than non-adopted offspring. I also read that the main reason adoptees don't make contact with birth parents is fear of a second rejection—a double-whammy of overwhelming grief that massively magnifies the potential for harm.

Paradoxically, after reading all of the (so-called) self-help books, I became even more anxious, fearful that I'd suddenly spin out of control. I'd learned about an array of previously unknown psychological maladies, which made me even more determined to control everything in my life. Most days I could persuade myself that Maggie didn't know me—that she'd shunned what I represented, not the person I was. I had a terrific life, I was loved, I had family, friends and financial security.

But on bad days, I was scared of being scared.

Chapter 9

MELBOURNE, 1991

It took weeks for the shock of my birth mother's rejection to subside. On occasion I was like one of those action movie characters who staggers from the burning car wreck—there was no sound, I felt as if I were wading through quicksand while the world moved past me at its regular speed. I didn't share my grief. I couldn't.

I'd been driven by a certainty that knowing my ancestry would make me whole, and I just couldn't let go of the idea of meeting my birth mother. What made matters worse was that the opening of the adoption laws attracted considerable media attention. Radio, TV and newspapers ran frequent stories of jubilant families welcoming long-lost children into their arms; answers provided to every adoptee question. Racing minds finally at rest. Seamless, heartwarming, happy endings. Every one of them filled me with envy.

After my fraught dealings with Jenny at the Catholic Family Welfare Bureau, I decided to look elsewhere for help. I made contact with a secular not-for-profit agency called Jigsaw, later subsumed by the less encouragingly named Vanish. Though run off their feet, the Jigsaw staff were knowledgeable, compassionate and keen to assist. At no stage did they attempt to steer my actions. Jigsaw produced a range of research guides and even a list of 'outreach phrases' for tongue-tied adoptees making first contact with birth parents. The materials promoted a positive 'rights of adoptees' view. In fact, Jigsaw encouraged adoptees to do all that was necessary to satisfy their mental health needs while being appropriately respectful of other parties, a position at odds with that of the Catholic Family Welfare Bureau, where I'd been made to feel self-centred.

Though I was still reeling, I hadn't given up, and I carefully contemplated my next step. I'd already been turned away by Maggie, yet she was almost certainly within reach—a Sydney phone book would likely contain her address and phone number. It was as if a Pandora's box had been placed on the table in front of me, if I were game enough to peek inside.

I decided to make contact. I knew it could go horribly wrong, but she hadn't shared a single thing, not even basic health information. It was unjust; we knew everything about our cocker spaniel's pedigree, but nothing about mine.

In 1991, there was no internet and no Google. Feeling like a fugitive, I caught the tram to the GPO (a disapproving Jenny Abbott breathing over my shoulder) to look for my birth mother in the Sydney phone book. I located the A–L directory and opened it at 'Bec' . . . and saw that there was less than half a page of Beckers in Sydney. As my finger glided down the alphabet, I found just one 'M. Becker'—it had to be her! My mother was hiding in plain sight. I scrawled the address and number onto a scrap of paper and rushed away from the city.

I wrestled with my conscience. What right did I have to stick my nose in when the almighty Catholic Family Welfare Bureau had warned me to stay away? But I told myself that if only Maggie got to know me, she'd see things differently. In the days that followed, I drafted and redrafted my letter. I started off too formal, then got too casual—it took a week to get it right. I decided to start by showing her that I posed no threat, to build a bridge. I'd leave the difficult questions for another day. I popped it in the postbox.

> This will probably come as a shock to you as I am Paul Becker born in Melbourne on the 10th February 1961 . . .
>
> I am happy and healthy as I hope you are, I'd like to say from the outset that I harbour no ill feeling and consider myself to have had a perfectly normal upbringing . . . I've been in a steady relationship for seven years and live in the suburbs—a very normal guy indeed! It's hard to verbalise why I'm writing. I would like to know about my history . . . the last pieces to the jigsaw. I'm most keen to ascertain medical information relating to my ancestors . . .

Over the next few weeks I wore a path to my letterbox. I waited patiently, then impatiently. I tossed and turned at night. Nothing came. Jenny was right—Maggie was tough.

Six months later, I wrote again. Maybe I'd got the tone wrong in the first attempt. This time I'd be chattier. I didn't want to be a pest, though. This was going to be the last letter.

> I thought you might be away or that the address was wrong. Either way, I presume that you did get the letter and don't know what on earth to say to a person who is virtually a total stranger . . .
>
> Believe me, I just want to communicate, to say hello and, by the way, where did I come from?!? My girlfriend, Kate, and I

are madly saving for a holiday in Europe . . . Do you have any big plans for summer? . . .

I hope this note has put you at ease a little more . . . I'm a happy, normal and well-adjusted thirty-year-old guy. I'd love to hear from you soon.

Once again, no reply. Jenny's instruction to leave Maggie alone was beginning to look like sound advice. I went back to Jigsaw. They were able to dig up some useful information from the Registry of Births, Deaths and Marriages Victoria and voting records. From those, I discovered a new address. It appeared that Maggie had recently moved to an exotic-sounding beachside suburb of Sydney. I was elated. She wasn't ignoring me, and she hadn't thrown my letters in the bin—she didn't even receive them!

I pictured her suburb looking like an old Elvis movie set in Hawaii. I imagined Maggie living a carefree, sun-shiny life overlooking the harbour while I was stuck in drab, conservative Melbourne. I resisted the urge to drive up and sit outside her flat, to breathe in the warm, salty Sydney air. Four days before Christmas 1991, I wrote a third letter.

Two weeks later, I received an envelope with 'M. Becker' written on the back in a tight and efficient script. In a wave of relief, I said aloud, 'At last!'—the wait was over. I held the unopened letter for a few moments and told myself that Maggie's second rejection must have been distorted somehow in Jenny's telling. There'd been a misunderstanding. It was important to think positive.

I quickly tore open the envelope and saw a full page of my birth mother's handwriting for the first time. Maggie had a steady hand, with understated flourishes. I took a deep breath and sat down to read.

Maggie's letter was to the point. She had received my third letter, she said, but not the previous two. She said she was happy to hear that I was well-adjusted and healthy, and she acknowledged that, while stressful for her, I had a right to some information about the circumstances of my birth. Maggie told me she had been in a serious relationship with a man in Sydney but then had been abandoned by him when she became pregnant. To avoid the judgement of society, she had come to Melbourne to have me by herself and then put me up for adoption, because she thought it would be for the best. She still believed that she'd done the right thing, but asked my forgiveness for any hurt that decision may have caused me.

Maggie said that she and I would never have a face-to-face meeting. This was not a rejection, she added, but as a result of the secret she and I shared. If there were other questions, I was to contact Jenny Abbott. She told me she loved me and prayed for me every day and hoped I would understand. She said she wanted me to be happy and signed off with her love and prayers.

Chapter 10

MELBOURNE, 1992

Maggie said she loved me. But she still wanted nothing to do with me.

My birth mother's letter showed she was an intelligent and articulate woman. She'd acknowledged my plight and demonstrated empathy. But this first letter wasn't something to treasure. I was awash with emotion, frustration above all. A strand of Maggie's tenacity had plainly been woven into my DNA. I didn't regret pursuing her—the response only made me more resolute.

Following orders, I called Jenny Abbott. Jenny's response was icy. She advised that there was no further information she could give me and firmly instructed me to curb my enthusiasm. (Many years later, a church insider told me that the Catholic Family Welfare Bureau saw its role at the time as *protecting* relinquishing mothers from their surrendered children.) While it wasn't the response I wanted, at least I had Maggie's letter. This was the closest I'd been to someone who shared my DNA. It was evidence that I had ancestors, and they were within reach.

After stewing over matters for weeks, I decided I wasn't compelled to follow Jenny's orders. With the help of Jigsaw, I established that Maggie was from a large family in Port Augusta in South Australia. Some of her brothers and sisters were alive and had children of their own. These kids were my cousins! If my mother didn't want contact, then maybe I could somehow reach out to her family. (Or was it now 'our family'?) The problem was how to introduce myself: 'We're related, but I can't tell you how.'

One of Maggie's brothers, Barry, ran a building business in South Australia. It felt good to have a builder in my family tree, builders being resourceful, dependable types. It was easy to find his phone number. Jigsaw's advice was to have a less emotionally invested person make first contact, so I asked Kate to make the call. We thought if Kate rang during the day, she'd more likely reach Barry's wife. A man might be suspicious; a woman-to-woman chat could bring better results. To protect Maggie, we agreed that we had little choice but to fabricate a story. Kate would say she was an old friend of Maggie Becker's from Sydney who'd lost contact and was trying to get back in touch. The next day, during her lunchbreak at work, Kate called my birth uncle's home number and asked his wife for help.

'Yes, of course,' Barry's wife replied. 'You mean Maggie the nun?'

As soon as she hung up, Kate rang me at work. 'Are you sitting down?' My stomach dropped, blood pulsing in my ears. I still have the studio notepad page where I'd written Barry's home phone number, Maggie's name, and in large, bold letters: 'A N U N ! ! !'

Christ, I thought. My mother is a nun.

I was shocked and at the same time strangely thrilled. I'd often daydreamed that my birth parents would be special or out of the ordinary in some way—but never this. Maggie's second rejection instantly became easier to comprehend. How could a nun ever tell anyone that she'd surrendered a child? A pregnant nun! How ridiculous. It sounded like something from the irreverent *The Dave Allen Show*. In the world I was brought up in, nuns were revered. They were also virgins.

Roy and Bet held nuns in the highest esteem. How could I now tell them that my birth mother was a bride of Christ? Their faith would be shaken. It was a scandal. I was a scandal. Keeping the secret from them seemed appallingly two-faced, but that's what I did.

Since learning her name two years prior, I began to feel genuine sympathy for Maggie. Back in 1960, when I was conceived, Australia was a conservative and deeply repressed Christian society. If Maggie had kept me, she would have had to endure the shame of not only being an unwed mother, but also the unimaginable social taboo against breaking her sacred vows of chastity, celibacy and obedience.

Two months after receiving Maggie's first letter, I wrote again and enclosed a photo of Kate and me: maybe she'd see something of herself in me. 'I fully understand and accept your decision those thirty-odd years ago to have me adopted,' I wrote. Then I added, 'From what I gather, you were or are a Catholic nun. Is this true? I'd give anything to know more about you, what you've done, what you are doing . . . What about my father? I'd love to know more about him . . . Love, Brendan.'

There was no reply.

It was clear I was an object of some industrial-strength shame. It appeared that my mother's sole priority was to protect her reputation. But what about me? I'd convinced myself that I could accept never meeting her, but I felt I had a right to the basic details I was seeking about the family's medical history. I was about to start a family of my own, and I wouldn't allow Maggie to deny me facts that could protect my children. I had to know about potential health complications, particularly given what we'd learned about

Kate's problem with anaesthesia. As the months passed, Kate and I read numerous pregnancy and new-parent books full of information about genetics and ailments likely to recur in offspring. The more I read, the more incensed I became about Maggie's lack of cooperation.

Eighteen months after my last contact, I wrote again. It was time to put my cards on the table. I didn't want to die wondering, but this had to be my last attempt.

The letter didn't ask for help—it was a crude blunt force:

> Sorry, I've tried to put you and the associated questions out of my mind, but try as I do the great unanswered chapter of my life keeps rearing its head . . . I certainly harbour no ill will . . . In the least I would like biological information, possible illnesses or disorders that may be a problem to our kids. At best I'd like for us to be friends.
>
> Aren't you intrigued? I've got a turned left eye with low vision. Which side of the family is that from? What about my father? What did he do? Was he Australian? . . . I'm here and I'm in need of your help . . . Will you choose to give in and pull the shutters again because of something that happened 33 years ago? . . . the most self-centred course available to you is to deny the biological fact that is ME. I would hope you feel an obligation. It did happen. Please write.

There was no reply.

I was knocking on a deaf nun's door; my birth mother wasn't going to be pushed into doing anything she didn't want to do. My effort to provoke a response through guilt failed. Though thrown off balance, I was determined that this denial would not define me.

I'd hoped that by now I'd be impervious to these repeated disappointments, but it wasn't any easier this time. I had to accept I was never going to find my father or have a relationship with Maggie. In effect, both of my birth parents were dead. It was a strange bereavement, as at least one of the people I was grieving for was very much alive.

The struggle for an adoptee is to convince yourself of the paradoxical notion that your parents loved you so much that they gave you away. To mourn in public is to be ungrateful; the only place for grief is within. I marinated in angst for too long, and months passed as I struggled to accept that the hunt was over. But I just couldn't get past it; bogged in confusion, I thought I might be depressed.

A long six months after Maggie's letter, I spoke to a therapist I'd been referred to by my GP. I'd already done an enormous amount of reading about bereavement, adoption, ethics and the trauma of familial rejection, and ploughed through a gaggle of psychological self-help books and dutifully done all of the recommended therapies: exercise, sleep, journalling, socialising, nutrition, etc.— everything except talking to a professional. I went half-a-dozen times. Therapy was exhausting but incredibly valuable. Eventually I went from depressed to a smidge sad to life is just fine and dandy. The past had been consigned to the past.

Chapter 11

WHYALLA, SOUTH AUSTRALIA, 1954

Father Vin was on his way south, thumping down the dusty track back to Whyalla. The 52-year-old priest had been away on a lengthy contemplative retreat. He was at ease. He'd made a life-altering decision and was about to deliver a letter to his bishop informing him of his plans.

Officially, he was the assistant priest of the Whyalla diocese. The reality of the role was that he was either trekking way up north to the outback missions or following the east–west rail corridor from Broken Hill to Port Pirie. Granted, the travel had been something of a relief, an escape from the suffocating neediness of the Catholic communities of Whyalla, Port Augusta and Port Pirie. But this damned east–west rail corridor, where he'd spent the past six years, was such a barren, lawless stretch: 250 miles of godless mining towns and barely viable pastoral allotments—some of them the size of small European countries.

Over the past decade he'd tried several times to transfer to a diocese back in Sydney. This would allow him to involve himself in family matters more closely. But the bishop wouldn't hear of him leaving South Australia. Hope of an escape had been offered just once, after the Americans had dropped atomic bombs on Japan. The bishop had entertained Vin's written request to be transferred to Japan as a missionary. Vin was encouraged to learn Japanese and everything he could about the culture. He bought language guides and began his studies. Unfortunately, after months of searching, the bishop was unable to entice a single priest to relocate to the northern desert. Vin's Japanese appointment was cancelled.

One of the few advantages of constant travel in the desert was that Vin could swap his priest's garb for overalls and earn quick cash building shearers' quarters and sheds on the outback stations. The skills acquired during the decade he'd been house building in Sydney would always come in handy. The Shiel family back home were at times in need of financial support. He assisted favourite brothers, sisters, nieces and nephews during the thirties and forties.

And he was, of course, obliged to continue sending cash to his brother to help cover the costs of the baby boy he'd deposited there four years back. In truth, the situation in Sydney was all a bit of a mess. His brother had already retired from work; he was unwell and had limited resources to support the child.

Father Vin had been rattling around the scrub trying to keep a tiny flock of Catholics on the straight and narrow for too long now. Half the time he felt as though he was on the wrong side of the confessional box—that he was the one who should be seeking absolution. Temptations were threatening to bring him undone. He'd bet on the neddies every chance he got, often winning big. But on occasion he'd lose more than he had, and it was necessary to get back on the tools to settle debts. There'd be hell and fury to pay if word got back to his bishop.

In his sermons on a Sunday, Father Vin would often relate the biblical story of the temptation of Christ. After Jesus was baptised, he fasted and wandered the desert for forty days and nights. During this time, the devil worked hard to tempt Jesus toward sin. On three occasions he returned to lead the weary Jesus astray, but Christ resisted temptation each time. It wasn't a big stretch to draw a parallel between the wandering Christ of this story and Father Vin, or indeed a number of his desert constituents, many of whom wrestled with personal demons of their own. Unfortunately, their disillusioned priest felt incapable of being an exemplar to his congregation.

Sometimes, when conducting a mass in one of these outpost churches, he'd catch sight of a handsome married couple and think to himself, if only they knew that their priest once, back in his twenties, had been engaged to be married. A priest with a sexual past—or any sexual life—would be unthinkable. At the time, Vin had been in love with his fiancée and sex was a perfectly natural expression of that love. Vin and his fiancée had shared every intention of marrying and raising a family, but it was not to be. Instead, he had answered the call of his Lord and made his mother the happiest woman in Balmain. When he finally became a priest, well into adult life at thirty-eight, he'd believed his previous romantic experience would stand him in good stead when counselling couples whose marriages were under strain. (The great majority of his fellow priests were entirely naive in matters of the heart, but that never stopped them dispensing advice to those experiencing marital problems.)

Father Vin conducted regular visits to hospitals, gaols and schools, anointed the sick, visited the elderly and checked in on shut-ins. He was also the first person called when a family lost a loved one. He'd witnessed many ghastly acts in the desert. The cruel treatment doled out by the nuns running Catholic orphanages was particularly disturbing, as was the wailing of Aboriginal mothers when their babies were forcibly removed. He was also troubled by the permanent change he saw in the young girls he'd sent away to give birth and surrender their babies for adoption. But this was a part of his role as the wise parish priest, to find a 'good Catholic family' to adopt the unwelcome infants.

When Father Vin was completely honest with himself, he acknowledged he still craved intimacy with a woman. A carnal appetite had been awakened when Vin was a young man. He prayed often that his calling would act as a form of divine intervention, quelling his mortal desires. It didn't. Rather than rising to meet his congregation's expectations of him, he found their demands somehow pushed him away from them.

He'd been thinking increasingly about the most inspirational period in his training. He had first entered a seminary in 1935, in Italy. When Germany threatened to invade Rome, he fled the Continent and continued his studies in a Trappist monastery in Ireland. The monastery at Mount Melleray Abbey was operated by a community of Cistercian monks. Those years, living a secluded, monastic life in Ireland, were when Father Vin was most at peace.

On his arrival in Whyalla, he delivered his letter to Bishop Bryan Gallagher.

He asked for permission to leave the diocese and enter the Cistercian order. He pointed out that over the previous thirteen years he had served the diocese entirely at his own expense and asked for the bishop's blessing in allowing him to pursue a life devoted to contemplation as he was certain this was where his genuine vocation lay.

Chapter 12

MELBOURNE, 1994

Though the highs far outweighed the lows, this was one of the most stressful times of my life. Whenever Maggie appeared in my thoughts, I knew instinctively that I had to get busy and push my perplexing ancestry from my mind.

In 1994, Kate and I welcomed our first child into the world. The euphoria that accompanied the birth of our children was unlike anything I'd ever experienced. The single smartest thing I've done in my life is to have children with Kate. Still to this day, each time I hear the first notes of John Lennon's 'Beautiful Boy (Darling Boy)', I'm transported to the morning of Pat's birth and the unparalleled elation of welcoming the first person I'd ever laid eyes on who shared my DNA.

Birth was to be the first and last time Pat arrived bright and early for anything, a worrying six weeks premature. This meant he spent his first weeks in a humidicrib, with few opportunities for us to touch and hold him. The fact that he was underweight, and so fragile, made him all the more precious. I would visit the neonatal intensive care unit daily and talk quietly to him in his sealed plastic crib. I knew he would recognise my voice from his months in Kate's belly—I hoped I could make him feel at ease in his strange new surrounds. Peering at him through the plastic, I scanned his face for my eyes, nose or mouth. I would do anything for this little boy and his mother.

I had a family, my family. It felt as though my life had at last begun. I'd spent far too many hours angsting about identity and my denied ancestry in the preceding years; I was determined that my children would forever feel secure and loved.

Our second child, Nell, arrived a couple of years later. Like a true sprinter, she was fast out of the blocks and has made every post a winner ever since. A boy and girl, one of each—we were complete. I've never felt more optimistic than when our two children were born.

Roy and Bet could not have been happier and revelled in their role as doting grandparents. In the fog of raising young children, building a career and whittling down a whopping mortgage, I didn't have much time to think about their third grandmother, Maggie. But on occasion I caught myself contemplating how unnecessary it was that she was missing out on these perfect grandkids. I sent her infrequent birthday and Christmas cards; none was ever reciprocated. Sometimes the most brutal punishment is silence. I wavered between pity and anger. She was ignoring not only me but her new grandchildren. Frustration grew in me like a weed.

The year Pat was born, my much-loved job at the recording studio blew up. Virtually overnight, digital technology obliterated analogue recording. Our studio had invested everything in analogue technology, and we couldn't adjust quickly enough to what the market demanded. I then accepted a role at a hand-to-mouth public radio station, thinking it'd be an interesting, slow-paced role that would give me more time for the family.

I accepted a big pay cut. Though the station was a Melbourne institution, it was on its knees financially and needed painful interventions. The upside was a number of fabulous gigs, albums and broadcast events; the downside was dealing with some hardline broadcasters who struggled with the reality that even uber-cool not-for-profits had to sell ads to pay the bills. We saved the station, but I was at the pointy end of initiating unwelcome change, so it was no party.

To add to this friction at work, a couple of years earlier Kate and I had purchased a 'renovator's delight' that was burning every cent I'd earn. I came home from every haircut with a crop of new grey hairs exposed. Maybe because of my adoption, or Maggie's second rejection, or whatever programming was wading in my gene pool, I was obsessive about providing a secure, loving and stable home for my family.

I still hadn't shared the truth about Maggie with Roy and Bet, the people I owed the biggest debt of gratitude. Maggie's need for secrecy made me resent her very existence. I tried to ignore her, deny her, tell myself I was not hurt and that I had everything a man could want. The truth was that I was floundering.

Chapter 13

MELBOURNE, 2002

Over the previous several years, Bet's knees had become increasingly painful. By this stage she couldn't get out of bed without painkillers. According to the specialists, the only solution was two knee replacements, but as she was nearly eighty and had advanced diabetes, we couldn't find a surgeon prepared to perform the operation. Due to the immobility, she gradually put on several kilos, and things then went from bad to worse: the pain increased; she could barely walk; and the diabetes went haywire. After weathering an early-life hysterectomy, a brain tumour and late-onset diabetes, it looked like something as innocuous as failing knee joints was going to dissolve the glue that held our family together.

When I was a teenager and still living at home, I'd often been roused by a near-hysterical Roy in the pre-dawn, insisting I get up and help 'bring her back'. His response to Bet's frequent diabetic comas was to frantically repeat, 'Drink the orange juice, Bet!'

'She's bloody unconscious, Roy—she can't hear you!' I'd snap at him as I groggily entered their bedroom.

I'd always been Roy's backstop. Usually a wad of honey to coat the inside of her mouth was enough to bring her to a semi-lucid state, but there were a number of times when we had to call an ambulance. Bet's lax attitude to blood-sugar regulation kept Roy on a hair-trigger. His anxiety rose as her health deteriorated. As I had my hands full with my own family, there was little more I could do but offer encouragement from the sidelines.

When Roy's mother passed away in 2001, my parents inherited a few dollars. They weren't millionaires, but for the first time in their lives they could tick off a couple of items on the bucket list. As mobility was the most immediate issue for Bet, it was decided they'd take the Ghan from Adelaide to Darwin. Bet could sit the entire time and enjoy the vista of the red deserts of South Australia and the Northern Territory. (Little did I know what significance those remote deserts would hold for me in years to come.) Roy arranged for me to arrive at their place at 6 am on 12 June 2002. I was to deliver my parents to Spencer Street Station (now known as Southern Cross), where an Adelaide-bound train would set out to hook up with the Ghan that evening. I set the alarm and went to bed early.

I don't know what time Roy's call came through, but it was pitch black outside, and by the time I hung up the hair on the back of my neck was standing on end. Roy's voice half-demanded, half-pleaded: 'It's Bet. You have to come now!' He slammed the phone down.

I sped to their house. In the car, my legs shook and my stomach rolled. Roy and Bet's home was five minutes away.

I knew this was a disaster.

Don't think. Drive.

As I pulled into their driveway, all the house lights were on, drawing me inside. I bolted through the front door and came to a halt in the lounge. Roy was slumped on the couch. He looked tiny.

'Where's Bet?'

Our eyes met, and he crumbled. 'She's dead.'

Though we hardly ever touched, we now hugged tightly. 'I'm so, so sorry,' I consoled him, as we both gave way to a deluge of tears. I've never cried as intensely, before or since. To share this trauma—and emotional release—with my dad was one of the great honours of my life.

Roy said Bet had had trouble sleeping the previous week. Her left arm ached, so she'd been sitting in the TV room upstairs with it propped on a pillow and dozed through the night. She didn't want to go to the doctor before the Ghan trip—the doc wasn't dispensing any good news in those days. The aching arm, of course, was a textbook red flag that her heart was giving out. They should have known, but my parents weren't particularly curious people.

Roy said I should go upstairs to see her. I'd never seen a dead person before. Entering the modest TV room, I saw my mother sitting upright in her chair, eyes closed. Both palms faced upward on the pillow. It was still dark outside, but the dawn was close. The first birds of the new day had begun to stir. I sat down and told my mother I loved her, regretting not having said it often enough when she was alive. Nobody accepted me as completely as Bet.

Kate appeared, having arranged for a neighbour to mind our kids. As undertakers wheeled my mother out the front door of her home for the last time, I stole a glance out of the corner of my eye; I couldn't force myself to witness the scene head on. My brother, Damien, was overseas; it was time to get word to him that our mother had died.

Roy had lost his anchor. Attempting to take control of the chaos, he insisted we have the funeral directors attend immediately to make arrangements. Still barely able to speak, he told me it was my job to choose the coffin and make plans for the funeral. It was all too soon . . . Kate and I then began working through Roy and Bet's Teledex, spreading the ripples of shock and tears. I offered to stay the night but my dad wanted to be alone.

I'd driven to Roy and Bet's home before the sun rose and was now leaving Roy's place as it set.

The next few years saw my father carry on with surprising fortitude. I was convinced he'd fall in a heap, but I got that totally wrong. Roy-boy made me proud. He stoically insisted on remaining in the family home and used few of the home supports available for the elderly. Bet had died at seventy-nine, so Roy decided he was going to get to eighty. He was a man on a bloody mission.

He was pretty average at looking after himself. Bet had prepared virtually every meal for fifty years, and though they had a reasonable variety of veggies, they ate meat most days, drank too much booze and enjoyed 'sometimes foods' on a near-daily basis. I still wince at the thought of Roy in the backyard, in the middle of winter, charring snags and chops on his barbecue, a halved 44-gallon drum. (He hated the washing-up when he cooked inside.) He'd barbecue his Weeties if he could get away with it.

A year or so after Bet died, he was diagnosed with bowel cancer. He then developed lung and heart problems. It all turned to crap. Roy insisted on taking every single drug offered by every single specialist. He endured merciless doses of chemo. He was fighting, because that's what old blokes were programmed to do. Always a social animal, my father began to enjoy being in hospital—there was no food to prepare, no washing-up to do, and plenty of people showing an interest in his old footy stories.

Though Roy and I were different in most respects and had few day-to-day common interests, other than sport, we cherished our shared history. We spent a lot of time together, particularly at mealtimes. I'd visit at least once a week, and every couple of weeks we'd have him around for Sunday roast, or pasta and a couple of reds on a Friday night. We'd talk on the phone most days. I'll always feel that I didn't do enough for him. The older I get, the more I appreciate what he and Bet gave me.

He got to eighty, but only just. The photos of him celebrating the big day, sitting in our lounge room surrounded by friends and family, show him reduced to half his prime-Roy size. The only part of him unaffected by the cancer and chemo were his ears, and they were bloody magnificent. He kicked that eightieth goal, but there was nothing much for him on the other side of it, not without Bet. I'm certain having Damien and me in his life had provided both purpose and pride, but he'd done his dash, and soon the health dramas caught up with him.

'How are you Roy-boy?' I'd ask.

'Well, let's just say I'm not buying any green bananas, Bren.'

By February 2007 he was in palliative care when a nurse called early one morning. 'If you're coming to see your father today, you should do it soon.' Thank god Kate came with me. It was profoundly disturbing to see a person in such distress kept in a conscious state. I repeatedly pleaded with the nurses, 'Can't you please give him something?' Roy's last hour was simply cruel—it will forever haunt me. The medical profession let him down that morning.

I'd known Roy had been raised by his mother, with no father-figure. Many years after his death, we would find out that Roy's family had kept devastating secrets from him about his own paternity, a heartbreaking tale that in some ways paralleled my own.

This poor disowned man had given me the greatest gift of all: unconditional lifelong love and acceptance. I hope he heard my final words as I held his hand at his death: 'I love you. Thank you, Roy.'

The following week, back at work, one of the older members of the board, thinking he was making a profound remark, said, 'Well, son, now you know what it feels like to be an orphan.' I didn't let on.

Chapter 14

MELBOURNE, AUGUST 2008

Fifteen years after my last letter to Maggie—a hot-headed appeal—I decided it was time to revisit the family tree. Roy had died in 2007, and we'd lost Bet five years earlier. The weight of secrecy and guilt about going behind their backs had evaporated. I was forty-seven; it was time to get a move on.

My two children had their own individual personalities right from the start, despite growing up in the same household with the same parents. Watching them grow up, I was regularly reminded of how little I understood about the origin of my own traits and inclinations. The joy of fatherhood was unsurpassed by any other role I'd had. I operated a small business and consulted, and we created an arrangement where I could be closely involved in the kids' lives, and Kate could have time for her art and teaching. We'd extended and then largely DIY-renovated our ugly-duckling house into a much-loved family home. My family was, and is, everything. But like a floating cork that eventually finds a shore, I couldn't prevent my thoughts returning to my ancestry.

The kids were no longer toddlers, I had some time on my hands, and Maggie wasn't getting any younger. If I was ever going to act, it was now. Thankfully, the internet had arrived, making research far easier. Using Google, Kate and I sifted through church publications, electoral rolls and other online materials to learn all we could about Maggie. The first question: was she still alive?

She'd be seventy-four now, but Maggie could have passed away way back in 1993, the year of my last letter. (It struck me as incredibly heartless that adoptees aren't notified when a birth parent dies. Surely, if you really wanted to know—as I did—then you should be able to tick a box on a government website somewhere and receive a notification.) The first site I visited was Births, Deaths and Marriages NSW, where I was promptly blocked from searching for a death certificate for my birth mother as I wasn't deemed to be 'family'. Then I searched in newspaper funeral notices. No result. So far so good.

Kate and I quickly found that the church does a poor job of making records of its nuns searchable online. Our research was hampered by several websites duplicating information, some displaying incomplete records, and most riddled with broken links. There is no central register of all things Catholic. I located an independently operated wiki-listing of convents, orders and nuns. Maggie Becker's name was missing from the database. Why wasn't she listed as a nun?

We then explored Trove, operated by the National Library of Australia, a database that holds over six billion digital records of Australian artefacts, curiosities and stories. Family history nerds treasure Trove (get it?), because it gives them free access to historical newspapers and publications. While searching old newspapers, Kate found an article published in the mid-fifties, about seven years before I was born, which noted my mother's admission to a convent in Sydney. It confirmed that she was originally from South Australia, and said that she took the name Sister Vincent.

Priests and nuns often take on a new name when they join an order. I wondered why Maggie chose Sister Vincent? What was the significance of the name?

Next task was to locate her. Bingo, the online White Pages confirmed she was at the same address I'd written to fifteen years earlier. That address had always struck me as odd—a flat in the suburbs, not a convent. I assumed that nuns might have an option of living independently, or maybe the church owned the flats—or was she caring for an elderly relative? Regardless, it was excellent news. My mother was alive, and I knew where she was.

There was no trace of Maggie on any social-media sites. In fact, other than a phone number and some decades-old newspapers, she'd escaped the internet age completely. It was clear that if I wanted more information, it would have to come from her. I asked Kate if she would call. I hoped her sensitivity and powers of persuasion would allow her to establish a rapport. Kate is naturally outgoing and open, and people warm to her quickly, particularly the older ones.

There was, of course, another reason I asked Kate to make the call. I didn't want to expose myself to a third traumatic rejection.

The night Kate made the call, I had to leave the room. In fact, I felt like leaving the country. Kate had a list of the general topics I wanted her to ask about, as well as some specific questions. High on the list were enquiries about my birth and the days following. I desperately hoped I hadn't been left alone in a foundling home or orphanage. The Catholic Family Welfare Bureau had told me back in 1990 that I was born at the Vaucluse Private Hospital, East Brunswick (now Brunswick Private). But where was I sent next? How long before Roy and Bet came and saved me? Kate had further questions about my father, potential health issues, siblings, whether Maggie gave birth to me while she was a nun—there was so much that I wanted to know.

I tried to distract myself in front of the TV but was incapable of registering a word. The call took forever. I paced the room until finally Kate emerged carrying the phone, a writing pad and several pages of scrawled notes. She looked uncharacteristically shell-shocked, drained. I handed her a large glass of wine.

'Well, she was awfully unprepared for that call. But it was okay, she wasn't angry, and she eventually opened up—a little. I suppose she must have known the call might come one day . . . Maggie isn't a nun anymore. She served in the convent for twenty-five years and resigned twenty-one years ago.'

'Huh? What? Wait, so she wasn't a nun when I wrote to her at the start of the nineties?' I was thrown. Why didn't she tell me? was my first thought.

When Maggie's sister-in-law had described her to Kate as 'Maggie the nun' way back in 1992, I'd pictured a slow-moving, slightly stooped woman in a full-length black habit, backlit by a stained-glass window, going about her good deeds in a convent, a vague scent of incense in the air. But now I'd been told that she hadn't been a nun for more than two decades. I couldn't process it.

'Maggie had an extremely difficult time in the convent . . . so she eventually just up and left. Apparently they can resign. She was locked away from the world in a notoriously strict order. For the first twelve years, all contact with family was banned. She wasn't allowed to use a telephone or read a newspaper. Crying was forbidden.

'As it turned out, I did most of the talking. I told her about you, about us, our family and Roy and Bet. She really was caught off-guard—we have to take things slowly. She was cautious, holding back. I'm afraid I didn't get many of the answers you were after.

I think she needed to see what I was like—and what you want. It's the first call—you'll need to be patient.'

'So what about my father, who is he? Where is he?' I asked.

'No, no, she wouldn't go there. No way.' Kate had tried to get Maggie to talk about the nature of her relationship with my father, but she was having none of it and had tactfully steered the conversation toward benign chat whenever my father was raised. 'She only skimmed the surface of your questions,' Kate said. 'She's firm but elusive. She is nice . . . but she's no-nonsense. Maggie is direct—just like someone else I know! You!'

Maggie told Kate she'd had very limited contact with men during her time in the convent, though she'd also said that men occupied every position of authority within church hierarchy and that the nuns were completely subservient to the male clerics. She hadn't enjoyed a good relationship with her father, either. As Kate reported, 'Her dad—your grandfather—was a cold and distant man. Men are strange beasts, in Maggie's estimation.'

It was so fortunate that Kate made the first call. It sounded like a man, even her own son, wouldn't have had much of a chance with Maggie.

The final question Kate put to my birth mother was about the circumstances of my birth. Did Maggie see or hold me after I was born? I knew those first hours and days immediately after birth are highly significant in a developmental sense. I'd studied a unit of psychology at university and was fascinated by the research of American psychologist Harry Harlow. His 1958 paper, 'The Nature of Love', completely debunked conventional thinking about mother-and-child relationships. Up to that point, the accepted proposition was that babies became attached to their mothers simply because they provided food. Harlow conducted experiments in which baby rhesus monkeys were removed from their mothers and presented with a choice of two inanimate 'surrogate mothers'. One was made of wood and wire and offered food. The other was covered in foam rubber and soft terry cloth—but it had no food. Harlow found that the baby monkeys chose to spend the vast majority of their time clinging to the foam and terry-cloth mothers, even though they provided no food.

The experiments presented the first empirical evidence of the primacy of the mother-and-child attachment. The study underlined for me the significance of touch and stimulation of the senses by a mother for the healthy development of her newborn. Monkeys deprived of sensory stimulation and attachment often emerged depressed, antisocial or aggressive. Harlow's findings were documented just three years before my birth. He also filmed everything. We were shown the footage at uni, and fragments are still with me: anxious, rocking, motherless, isolated baby monkeys, never able to find their place in the world. I didn't want that to be me.

Kate said there was no emotion in Maggie's voice as she described my birth: 'He was bundled up and rushed out of the room by nurses. I never saw him . . . I wasn't allowed to touch him . . . The next day I was told he was a boy.' Two days after giving birth, my mother was back home in Sydney. She said she'd never told another soul about me and had never seen my father since.

When Kate asked Maggie if she was prepared to talk with me, she said she'd think about it and let her know. At the end of the call, my mother asked Kate to tell me that she had prayed for me every day since my birth.

A while after I first made contact with Maggie, I'd read Nancy Newton Verrier's groundbreaking book *The Primal Wound*. It's still one of the most oft-quoted publications in adoption literature. I ploughed through it, thinking, 'Bloody hell! I'm not bonkers— I'm just adopted!'

Verrier adopted her much-loved daughter in 1969 and faced challenges as her daughter grew older and started acting out. These behaviours led Verrier to write her master's thesis on adoption. During her research she became 'more and more convinced that adoption, which has long been considered the best solution to relinquished babies, was not the panacea that it was hoped to be'.

She discovered that although adoptees in California represented around two to three per cent of the general population in 1985, they represented thirty to forty per cent of the individuals found in residential treatment centres, juvenile detention and special schools. She also found that adoptees 'demonstrated a high incidence of juvenile delinquency, sexual promiscuity, and running away from home [and] had relatively consistent symptoms, which are characterised as impulsive, provocative, aggressive, and antisocial'. Verrier concluded that the two most extreme responses of adoptees to separation from their birth parents were to 'act out' (by testing their adoptive parents) or to become 'pleasers' (who were acquiescent, compliant and tended to withdraw).

I'd always been a 'good boy', a pleaser who aspired to be worthy of adoption. This trait often goes hand-in-glove with a highly developed need for independence, organisation and self-sufficiency. I also identified with one of the most often-cited responses to adoption trauma: hypervigilance.

Verrier found that the children who 'acted out' were easily identified, which meant their issues could be addressed. Those who withdrew (us pleasers) frequently internalised their grief; it often presented as stomach aches, eczema, allergies, stuttering or other 'internal' delinquent or antisocial behaviours.

The most haunting sections of The Primal Wound describe surrendered newborns screaming in outrage as they lie alone in hospital nurseries, and how they were often sedated. These same practices occurred in Australia—it's likely I was sedated, too.

It's been proven that premature or dangerously sick newborns, or those withdrawing from addiction, recover much faster if they're regularly held and spoken to by volunteers. *The Primal Wound* highlights what we intuitively know: that the moment of birth, the first skin-to-skin contact with our mother, the first hours, are incredibly important. I'd always wanted to know if Maggie held me, caressed me, fed or cared for me when I first emerged into the world. Now I knew she didn't. My only thought was of the anxious monkeys clinging to their wire mothers in Harlow's film. Because Maggie wasn't prepared to discuss my father, I also worried that my conception was the result of a sexual assault.

The next day I read online accounts of the experiences of Australian mothers who'd surrendered babies in the 1960s. In the days, weeks or months before giving birth, many travelled far from home, often alone, lying to friends and family about where they were going, and why. Maggie had travelled all the way from Sydney to Melbourne. Had she been on her own? In the perinatal period, she'd have been administered powerful drugs for pain relief, as well as sedatives, and also hormones to suppress lactation. It's unlikely she'd have been aware of what was happening as I emerged from her womb. Where was my father? Did he know where she was, or what had just taken place?

The following week, Maggie said she was willing to talk to me.

Chapter 15

MELBOURNE, SEPTEMBER 2008

'Hello, Maggie? It's me, Brendan.'

I'd rehearsed the conversation, or at least what I was going to say, each night after I went to bed.

Confidently, she replied, 'Well, hello there, Brendan. How are you today?'

At forty-seven years of age, I was speaking with my 74-year-old birth mother for the very first time. 'It's so nice to hear your voice . . . after all these years,' I said.

We small-talked weather, Melbourne vs Sydney, politics . . . and eventually Maggie brought up her twenty-five years as a nun. 'A number of nuns from my order all resigned at a similar time to me. Several have moved close to one another here in Sydney, and we continue to support one another.'

She sounded proud of her decision to walk away from the church; it was as though she wanted me to understand that she had a rebellious streak. She was equally pleased that her superiors in the convent were shocked to receive her resignation. '"But you never complained!" they said.'

Is she a 'pleaser', too? I wondered.

I asked, 'Maggie, how would your friends describe you?'

'I don't suffer fools gladly, and I get things done,' she quickly replied.

'Ha! That's me to a T!' I said. 'That's absolutely me!'

But there was no acknowledgement from Maggie.

I kept trying to establish a connection, pointing out similarities in our personalities and preferences, but she greeted each of these attempts with silence. It was obvious she was an extremely sharp woman, but one who spoke cautiously. She had been expecting my call, too, unlike Kate's initial call, so she'd had time to prepare. She didn't exactly open up to me, but there were some details of her life that she wanted to share. 'I sing in a community choir and had an excellent voice some years ago. We perform in hospitals and old people's homes.'

'Fabulous. But I'm afraid I can't sing to save myself,' I replied.

She talked a lot about the choir and how she helped old people. 'After the nuns, I still do a lot of charity work—it's very important to me. I nurse several elderly people in the neighbourhood. I'm never home, and I'm interested in everything!'

I hadn't expected that she'd want me to view her as a good citizen, but I supposed it made sense. There were plenty of pauses in the chat, each of us wanting to see who'd steer the conversation to more challenging topics.

Maggie confirmed that she became pregnant with me when she was twenty-six and described my father as 'a handsome man who wasn't totally honest with me'.

'He didn't want to know me after the pregnancy was discovered. I called his number several times, but shortly after the line was disconnected.'

'That must have been awful,' I said. 'How did that make you feel?'

'I didn't have time for thinking about my feelings, Brendan,' Maggie replied curtly.

She came to Melbourne when the pregnancy began to show. Nobody but my father knew that her journey south was to have a child and to surrender it for adoption.

She told me that she entered a well-known convent two years after my birth. This seemed to contradict the newspaper article that Kate had found on Trove, which said that Maggie had joined a completely different order and that she'd done so several years before my birth. I was puzzled. Was I getting the truth? I didn't want to have her think that I'd been snooping, looking into her past on the internet (even though I had). I let it go.

Maggie confirmed that I was her only child and that she didn't know if my birth father had other children.

When I probed for more information about my father and their relationship, Maggie cautioned me: 'That's it, Brendan. That's all there is.' She wasn't going to go back and relive one of the most psychologically wounding experiences of her life. When I asked about my birth, she dropped her voice and said slowly, 'I told Kate—ask her.'

'Okay, I'm sorry, Maggie. I'm just curious. I've thought about these things for so many years.'

She volunteered, 'I came to Sydney as an eighteen-year-old. A dear friend helped me leave Port Augusta. I'm the black sheep of the family, you know! Most of my family is still in South Australia.' I wondered who the 'dear friend' was. I should have asked but had been put on the back foot.

I explained about Kate's issue with anaesthetics and my interest in inherited health complications that the kids or I might be vulnerable to. In a boastful, upbeat voice, she declared, 'You'll be happy to hear that there's no major sickness or crime in my family.' That made me feel bulletproof, but in the next breath she explained that two of her siblings had died in recent years, and another had advanced Alzheimer's. As an afterthought, she added that she had high blood pressure. 'So do I!' I exclaimed. But again, there was no acknowledgement from my mother.

Maggie's responses to my questions were delivered in a clinical, almost dismissive manner. She was at times impatient, sounding confounded that the answers could be of any interest to me. Kate's words rang in my ears: 'It's early days—take it slow.'

Plucking up courage, I asked, 'Your parents, my grandparents, are they still alive?'

Maggie said that her parents were German-Irish and her father had worked on the railways all his life. 'Both of my parents are long gone.'

It felt surreal. Maggie had acknowledged that she was my mother, but she didn't appear to be capable of acknowledging that *her* parents (and siblings) were also *my* relatives. It was as though we had been uncoupled—as if my relationship to the Beckers ended with the cutting of the umbilical cord. I later read that many mothers who surrendered children, particularly in closed adoptions, would go on to suffer dissociative disorders as well as an array of psychological disturbances. Was my mother of sound mind?

She went on to tell me that after leaving the convent two decades earlier she'd worked as a nurse until she retired.

I was astounded to be told that the flat she lived in had been left to her by an elderly woman whom she had cared for while she was a nun. 'I was incredibly fortunate, as I was given only $2000 by the church when I resigned after more than two decades of service.'

Maggie also said she loved sport.

'Me, too!' I responded.

And that she was captain of her junior basketball team.

'I've played basketball for thirty years!' I said.

But again, silence from Sydney.

Maggie made no enquiries of me, although she did volunteer, 'What a lovely young lady your Kate is.' And then, a bombshell. 'I have never told a single person that you exist, and that's the way it must remain. I did tell your father I was pregnant, as I explained earlier, but he has since died.'

I'd lost him.

The second half of my story was gone. I didn't know how to respond. Maggie added that she couldn't remember anything about him—not even his name. I bit my tongue. Rubbish, how can you not know my father's name?

Maggie emphasised that that she would 'forever maintain the secrecy'. The unspoken expectation was that I also had to keep my mouth closed. I sensed that, even though she'd consented to this conversation, there'd be no more discussions—this was it.

'Okay, are there any other questions?' She was keen to wrap up and get off the phone. There was no need for her to say the words—my mother wanted me to vanish back into thin air.

As we wound up the call, I made one final request, and Maggie agreed to mail me some photos of family. I thanked her and hung up, then went to find Kate in the lounge room.

'Christ! Aren't nuns supposed to be God's dispensers of charity and compassion?' I asked. 'I've felt more connection to strangers at a bus stop.'

Kate reminded me that Maggie and I shared some similarities in how we communicate. 'This may be a long process,' she said.

'She didn't ask a bloody thing about me or the family . . . Oh, and she said my father is dead.'

Maggie's and my connection had been terminated long ago. I'd naively hoped that when we spoke it'd be like putting a power plug back in the socket, situation normal. Kate reminded me, 'Maggie Becker is the opposite of Bet Watkins, in every way it seems. She is under no obligation to tell you a single thing, but it does feel like there's something else going on, I know.' It was true, but a hollow consolation at that moment. I wasn't feeling grateful. My brain was like a snow dome, and it'd take weeks for the flakes to settle.

A few days later, when replaying parts of the conversation in my head, I remembered that Maggie had told me she had Crohn's disease. I'd neglected to scrawl it onto my notepad. She said that it didn't cause 'enormous discomfort', but occasionally it would flare up and 'really play havoc with the plumbing'. (She was such a tenacious woman, more like an ex-sergeant major than ex-nun.) I'd read a little about Crohn's and knew it was an inflammatory bowel disease. Many in the online adoption community suffer recurring stomach and bowel issues, so I found it interesting that Maggie did, too. I certainly have a sensitive stomach, and at times of stress experience significant changes in the workings of my gut. My stomach is the barometer of my emotional health.

I have since found research papers that link sudden trauma (including adoption, rape, sexual abuse, etc.) to subsequent post-traumatic stress disorder and a range of knock-on inflammatory gastrointestinal disorders in both children and adults. Many adoptees trace their health issues back to the trauma of separation from their birth mother and the denial of maternal touch. The trauma is magnified if the child is abandoned in a hospital for several days or even weeks before adoption. And it's not just adoptees who experience the trauma of separation—mothers who surrender their children are often traumatised by the experience, leaving them vulnerable to similar health problems. Maybe Maggie wasn't as tough as she made out? Was her Crohn's linked to our separation, her body, like mine, quietly keeping score?

After our first-ever conversation, I followed up with a letter.

It was terrific talking the other day. I've included a random array of family photos . . . I found this an odd experience, selecting a dozen or so shots to encapsulate my life . . .

I fully understand and empathise with your decision to relinquish me. I'm well aware that in those times single mothers, and their offspring, were up for an extremely difficult time . . . I only want to enjoy a friendship. I'd really like to get to know you. Feel free to ring me at any time . . . Looking forward to seeing some of your pictures.

I couldn't wait to see the photos she'd said she would send. I hoped to salvage some sort of relationship with this ever-pragmatic woman who gave life to me. And I wanted to learn about my father.

But there was no reply and no photos from Maggie.

Chapter 16

SYDNEY, 1959

'Evangelicals, ha! That Billy Graham is nothing but an attention seeker, a bloody show pony!' Father Vin shouted down the table to a startled nephew. It was Christmas Day, the lunch plates cleared, Vin was holding court and decided it was time to put an impertinent gasbagging teenager in his place. The Shiel family had eaten until their bellies could take no more. Vin, sitting at the head of the table, decided to have the last word on the feted minister.

Unprompted, he then raised his voice to a new level, and everybody seated around the adults' table had little choice but to pause and listen. 'Son, I do accept Jesus Christ as my personal saviour—as Graham proposes—but *he has the wrong son of God*! It is *our* most holy *Catholic Jesus* that we pray to, not that false prophet American hot-gospeller!'

'But, but, with respect, Father . . . he must be doing something right. He got 130,000 people to the Melbourne Cricket Ground, and another 150,000 went to see the Graham Crusade at the showgrounds last May—one million Australians listened on the wireless . . .'

The room hushed. The warm, sticky aroma of plum pudding hung heavily in the room. Father Vin's eyes darted to the father of the lad, who in embarrassment then looked to his lap, as if in prayer. Vin stood up and glared at his nephew. 'Respect. You show respect, laddy. I won't be spoken to in that tone by a bloody upstart eejit like you. Do not question Our Lord and saviour! Or me! I'll hear no more about Billy Bloody Graham!' And with that, the priest theatrically dropped his napkin on the table and marched out the back door.

As the flywire door strained on its hinges, he heard the boy softly exclaim to his father, 'What did I say?'

Sitting on a bench on the back porch, Father Vin was immediately joined by the always-smiling twenty-five-year-old whom he'd helped to flee Port Augusta: Maggie Becker.

Six years since leaving Port Augusta, Maggie was now living with the family of one of Father Vin's sisters. Seated close, she said, 'He means no harm, Father.'

Though she hadn't spoken with the priest for close to eighteen months, she chatted with an easy rapport. Maggie gushed about the beauty of the harbour, the hustle and bustle of the city, her delight in this opportunity, so far from the strictures of Port Augusta. 'Thank you so much, Father. Thank you for arranging my journey and accommodation.'

A young woman with an unselfconscious enthusiasm, Maggie was unaware of the way she drew people to her. Father Vin, a little taken aback at her high passion for plain old Sydney town, looked her square in the face.

'Please, Father, I've heard so much about your travels. I would give anything to visit Europe and America! We've read in the papers about the stone church you relocated to Kimba in South Australia, and the church you built in that outback mining town.

Please tell me everything . . .' And with that they chatted for two long hours.

The pioneering builder-priest was a man at the peak of his powers; the Far North Catholic Inland Mission at Radium Hill was his first appointment as priest-in-charge. After completing the construction of a church and school at Radium Hill, he was celebrated in newspapers, as well as from the pulpits. He then embarked on a twelve-month tour of England, Ireland, Italy and America. In Rome he had an audience with the Pope. He travelled largely with an American cousin, the Reverend Father Murty Shiel. (Based in Washington, Fr Murty had recently retired after fifty years as a priest.) During the tour, Vin also met the famous American Archbishop Fulton J. Sheen, on whom the Australian made a lasting impression.

'Maggie, I did have some issue with Bishop Gallagher—you may recall His Eminence from South Australia? I wasn't entirely forthcoming about my intentions with my recent trip. I'd asked for twelve months' leave in England, and it was denied. He said it was too long—but I took a year anyway!' They both laughed, the priest slapping his knee.

'Gallagher wrote to me demanding I return to Australia. He said, "I pray that you've not deceived me, remember I am your bishop!"

'You see, Maggie, he wrote to me in England—but I replied from the USA! It was not a deceit—just a slight error of omission!'

As one, they leaned back and roared. Everyone inside stopped to listen to the hilarity outside, quietly wondering what could possibly be so amusing.

While regaling his wide-eyed audience of one with his stories of international travel, their legs occasionally touched (he was her friend as well as her pastor) and then suddenly, noticing the silence inside the house, and realising he'd been talking endlessly, he said, 'That's enough about me, young lady. Tell me about you. You withdrew from the convent a few years back? I believe you'd studied for more than two years? Why did you resign?'

Maggie hesitated, then began with a shaky voice, 'I thought I wanted a life as a nun. But I was not ready, no . . . no, that's not right . . . Father, I think, in truth . . . I was so inspired by your reverence, your commitment to those in need. It's why I chose the name Sister Vincent, you know—that I wanted to follow you. But it seems I was not made for that life. I'm sorry. I don't know what's next, I feel I need to experience more of what life has to offer. All I've done is odd jobs and working at *Reader's Digest* since leaving the convent. I very much looked forward to your return, to seek your counsel.' Maggie glanced across to Father.

He took her hand and patted it. 'There, there, Our Lord picks imperfect vessels—I should know.'

They then both looked silently to the garden, geraniums bursting with blood-red flowers as Vin enjoyed the warmth of Maggie's palms and fingers. He squeezed her hand and placed it back on her lap. They sat in the early-afternoon summer heat, the most agreeable time of the day, admiring the still-piercing quality of the summer light. A harbour ferry blew its horn as it docked down in Balmain.

'Maggie, I'll share a secret with you. It's in confidence: I trust you will never repeat it?' Without waiting for a response, he continued. 'I was tested in the Outback, you see my nerves had been dashed during the war; it wasn't a weakening of my faith, but I did question my *purpose*. I was lost.

'My instinct said to return to the one place I felt at peace, the Cistercian seminary in Ireland. And so, five years ago, I wrote to my bishop and told him it was my earnest desire to seek perfection as a Trappist. It was where I was certain I could be saved, in a contemplative order. But the bishop was shrewd and had other plans for me. He didn't refuse my request but appealed to my sense of adventure. He offered me the opportunity to build my own church and lead the Catholic community at Radium Hill. So you see, Maggie, I can empathise with your leaving the convent. There have been times when I've had my hesitations—we are more alike than you may think.

'I have an idea. My next leave is due in May. What say I take you to the Blue Mountains? I've been interested in making my retirement up in the hills—I know it's years away—but I'd like to look at houses. There's a beautiful cafe in Katoomba, too, with the most delicious chocolates, the Paragon . . . lots to do up in the mountains. Your thoughts will be clearer in the open spaces, the fresh air a tonic. What do you say?'

Maggie leapt with excitement. 'All I've seen are postcards of the Blue Mountains—I'd love to—thank you!' A flame had been lit.

'All right, that's settled. I'll make plans upon my return to South Australia. Now, one small point—I think it best you travel under the name of my sister, we don't want to give anybody a topic for scuttlebutt. This holiday will just be between you and me, agreed?'

'Yes, Father. I'll keep the secret—on God's word.' She winked.

Chapter 17

SYDNEY, 2009

On 24 March, at precisely midday, we pulled up out the front of Maggie's block of uninspiring 1950s flats. It was hardly the cosmopolitan beachside vista I'd imagined all those years earlier.

The sun in the cloudless sky was beaming as I stood flat-footed on the nature strip strangling a bunch of flowers. Getting out of the car, Kate and the kids were wearing the only 'presentable' clothes they'd packed for the road trip. From the corner of my eye, I saw an elderly lady in a blue and white striped t-shirt striding toward us.

We'd decided to take the kids out of school for a few months and go on a driving adventure: Melbourne to Cooktown. We were so proud of our little family, and it made sense to attempt to introduce them to Maggie along the way. My mother might see that our children were an extension of her, and in meeting them be more inclined to open up about her life and my ancestry. Who knows, she may even want to get to know her only child?

I left it to Kate to persuade Maggie to meet with us when we headed through Sydney on our way north. After a couple of calls, she succeeded in arranging a day to have lunch at Maggie's flat.

During their conversations, Maggie had stressed that when I was conceived, in 1960, she was not a nun—that detail was important to her. There was something mysterious going on, as an old Trove article we'd discovered said she'd entered the convent in 1954. But Maggie told Kate she joined a very different order a year or so after my birth (being 1962 or 1963). If that was true—I'd always assumed she resigned because of the pregnancy—why had she entered a convent and then resigned? I guessed it was to be with my father. It was a frustrating exercise extracting the truth from Maggie, who was a master of diversion. Maybe today I'd learn the truth. Maybe today I'd find out who my father was.

The kids were fourteen and eleven. We'd explained about my adoption years earlier and also told them Maggie had been a nun. As we weren't religious, the fact that I was the son of a nun was no big deal. 'Nobody can replace Nanna and Pa and Grumpy and Grandma,' we told them. 'They're your grandparents.' But it was tricky explaining that 'technically' Maggie was their 'birth grand-mother'. Like most children, they'd judge Maggie on merit rather than on anything we said. They had no idea what to expect from lunch with the old ex-nun lady that was Dad's mum but wasn't really, and nor did we.

Without Kate's cautious establishing of trust, none of this would be possible. I was grateful and apprehensive in equal measure.

That morning, as we had to be out of our motel early, we filled in time with a visit to the site of James Cook's first landing at Botany Bay, a strange parallel to my first arrival at Maggie's. It was hard to believe that Maggie's and my relationship—if you could inflate it to that—had stayed on track after the arduous path that followed her first letter of rejection seventeen years ago.

'It's her!' Kate called, a little too loudly. I was taken aback, too, subconsciously expecting my mother to be wearing a nun's habit, not a striped t-shirt.

All of my well-rehearsed small talk evaporated into the ether. We hugged, but I was not emotionally embraced. It felt forced. Maggie was quick with a smile—not at all what I'd anticipated. I don't know how I expected her to look—like me, maybe— but more importantly, I expected I'd recognise my mother, but I didn't. I was wrong-footed that she'd left the safety of her flat to meet us out in the open, on common ground. It was a large block with plenty of nosy-neighbour windows facing out. As Maggie had made it abundantly clear I was to be 'a secret forever', who would the neighbours think we were? At lunch she told me that she'd timed our visit to coincide with a day her closest neighbour was away visiting family. 'Clever,' I said with a nod. She replied with a wink.

Maggie's flat was tidy, light-filled and homely. The still air offered the scent of lavender and generously deployed cleaning fluid. Nothing was familiar in my mother's home. When she shared that she'd recently 'very much enjoyed' painting the flat, Kate and the kids joked that painting was a task I was happy to do and they all hated. Searching for common ground, I asked, 'Did you use a ladder, or a roller on a pole to do the ceiling?' (Gawd, get a grip man!)

The mantelpiece held photos of young children. Curious, I crab-walked closer. Were these my relatives? Reading my mind, Maggie said, 'No, they're the children of a neighbour.' I was disappointed that none of the photos I'd sent had made it to public display. Maybe they were in her bedroom? It was unsettling to not immediately feel drawn to this woman who had carried me in her womb for nine months. She could have been anyone, though she did keep stealing sideways glances.

Maggie sat us all down in the lounge and retreated to the kitchen to bring out lunch. I was specifically directed to a large single-seat sofa in the corner. She appeared to be a well-practised host. Kate jumped up and went to lend a hand, and a moment later Maggie emerged, smiling, and handed me a beer (it was the 1950s again!).

Though I'd been seated at the head of the table for lunch, my mother firmly steered the conversation. She talked sport, TV, politics, travel, gardening—anything but my ancestry. Over a light chicken and salad, she revealed new details about her life in the convent.

'There was great disappointment among nuns and priests that Vatican II had failed to drag the church into the twentieth century. It was the younger nuns who resigned during the seventies and eighties, to build new lives. Some of us had work-ready skills— teaching, nursing, cooking and housekeeping—which meant we could earn money to pay for a roof over our heads; I cooked and cleaned. The older nuns, and those less qualified, had little option but to stay in the convent. The church made it clear there'd be no ongoing support for those who left. Deserters would not be tolerated. I didn't want to end up like the wretched old senile nuns, locked downstairs, away from the sun—it was cruel. Those most affected by dementia were strapped to their beds, only getting the most basic care. Awful!'

For most of her years in the convent, she was forbidden to drive a car, read newspapers, go to the cinema or enjoy modern conveniences. On one exceptional occasion, she was allowed to visit her dying mother in Port Augusta. As she approached the family home, her father met her at the flywire door with the words, 'Your brother is waiting for you—in the cemetery.' She had no idea he had died. Maggie had no kind words for my grandfather.

'I found God after I left the church,' she said.

Puzzled, I asked, 'What do you mean by that?'

She looked at me and then at the tablecloth. For once her face did not exude confidence. 'It was a tough life. A lot of good can be done, and kindness shared, outside of the convent.' It was another loaded statement, and one that I thought a lot about afterwards . . . but she kept moving the conversation, bounding forward.

She watched rugby league and admired Sydney right-wing shock jock Alan Jones (which would have pleased Roy, at least). 'Alan says it as it is!'

As the afternoon progressed, when conversation slackened, Kate would help Maggie with good-natured stories about our family—leading her to neutral topics. My mother clammed up whenever I asked too many questions, and looked to Kate for a diversion. There were no disclosures about my father, though I tried.

Maggie showed only a passing interest in her two grand-children. I couldn't help thinking that if it was Roy and Bet having us for lunch, all of the early focus would be on the kids. There'd be gifts, special food.

After lunch, without me having to ask, Maggie went to a bed-room and returned with eighteen photographs. Most were of her, the rest of assorted family groups. One showed my mother as a young woman in a nun's habit. With her hair fully concealed in a headdress, she could easily have been a twenty-five-year-old me. I blurted, 'The likeness is startling: chin, eyes, mouth—the works! I looked exactly like you at this age. We're dead ringers!' At that moment, though she'd rarely held my gaze for long since arriving, she couldn't help but grin back and the physical similarities were astonishing.

'So now I know what I'm going to look like in my mid-seventies!'

Kate and the kids giggled, but Maggie squinted, unsure of my humour.

One of the images was of my grandfather, Len. He was a nuggety unit with tightly crossed arms, tattoos on both forearms, and a sour look on his face. Len was the bloke you instinctively knew not to accidentally bump in the pub late in the evening when he was carrying a beer. In another shot, Maggie (in nun's habit, again looking just like me) had her arm around Len, but he was having none of it. She beamed, but Len was expressionless. Maggie had previously said she had little time for him, and I decided I didn't either.

After going through the photos together, I asked if I could photograph them. I can still remember the dismissive wave of her hand: 'No, no. Take them, have them—they're yours.' Then she added, 'They're the only pictures I have.'

'Oh, that's fantastic—thank you! You've already got copies for yourself?'

'No. I'm not sentimental,' said Maggie. I looked across and saw that even Kate struggled to suppress a look of puzzlement.

I wondered what happened to the photos I mailed to her. Did she throw them away? It stung. While I've meticulously archived thousands of images of family and friends—trying to anchor my place in the world—here was my mother anxious to scour away all trace of the past. She shared few happy anecdotes, no funny stories of her growing up or incidents from her life in the convent, or the years that followed. I felt I knew nothing about Maggie. She had asked so few questions. She didn't want to know.

As it was getting time to leave, Maggie repeated the story she'd told us on the phone of 'the kind old lady I nursed who died and left me this wonderful flat'. And there was a second benefactor. Somebody had left her money to allow a trip to Russia at the end of the year. When I responded, 'What incredible good fortune—but you can't be much of a nurse!', everyone laughed, including Maggie. Was she thawing, or just pleased the visit was at an end?

It was an amiable first meeting, but little more. I think I hugged my mother at the front door, but I can't be sure. On the doorstep, I asked if we could drop in a couple of months later on the way back from North Queensland. She let the question pass without response.

The moment we got in the car, the kids talked excitedly about how curious it was to see a grandparent-aged person who looked similar to me. It had dawned on them just how physically dissimilar were Roy, Bet, Damien and I. Maggie was my flesh and blood, but even the kids could see she didn't want to get to know me. It didn't make sense to them, but I didn't show my hurt. The chatter in the car gently subsided, my passengers lost in thoughts. Heading north from Sydney, driving under a wide-open sky, my window open, I knew it was too late to claw back what had been lost with Maggie.

Later, as the sun approached the horizon, I kept replaying in my head words I faintly heard Maggie say to Kate while they were in the kitchen preparing lunch: 'I would be mortified if my friends or family found out about Brendan.' Did she consider for a second how those words might sound to my ears? I fled Sydney feeling more abandoned than when I'd arrived.

Now, in the night, stars shimmering above, we bolted toward the Queensland border. I could've driven all night. As my family slept, I put on Lucinda Williams's *World Without Tears*. In 2003, Damien had given me an air ticket to New York. I'd been waiting for the release of that CD for months. When it came out just a few days before the flight, I bought it and, with an abundance of Catholic delayed gratification, told myself I wouldn't play it until I got on the plane. That album never fails to ameliorate. It became the soundtrack of that solo life-affirming NYC escape, a big-hearted gift from my steadfast brother.

Chapter 18

MELBOURNE, 2010

Summer holidays always found me contemplating family. While I always looked forward to Christmas, it was a completely new proposition without Roy and Bet. Some of the lustre of the season had been erased. Magnifying my focus was the fact that two friends' parents had died, and others had begun caring for an ill mum or dad. I became increasingly conscious that when Maggie died, so did my father. We lost both Roy and Bet when they were around eighty. Maggie was now seventy-six. Nine months had passed since our face-to-face meeting. I wrote.

> The reason for this letter is to ask for details of my father . . . I'd like to know his name, how he died and anything else you know of him. I may well have half-brothers or sisters. I don't think anyone—other than those in the same situation—can under-stand what it's like.
>
> Formulating a true 'sense of self' can be challenging. Knowing that you have this information, and may possibly deny me, is difficult . . . I'd never wanted to say this . . . you owe me this

information. This knowledge is a birthright. I want to know who both of my parents are.

I hit a nerve. The response was immediate.

She said things had been very different in that time, and that I had no right to be angry. There hadn't been any government supports, it had been considered a shameful thing to be pregnant out of wedlock, and society had dictated that she must put me up for adoption—she challenged me to think about how it felt for her when at my birth she was prevented from seeing or touching me.

I was stunned when she said that I had been told my father's name, Paul Hayes, from Northbridge in Sydney.

She went on to explain she had never been to Paul's home but after discovering the pregnancy there had been two more meetings with him. My father had flatly refused to assist on both occasions. Soon after, she panicked and called his number repeatedly—until his line was disconnected. She was angry at him and with herself. Abortion was abhorrent; she stressed that only God had the right to end a life and so she had decided to carry me to term and have me adopted. She had been boarding in Sydney and did not tell anyone, keeping the situation a secret she shared with God alone.

After a couple of years she decided to do something useful with her life and entered a convent. It was far from easy. As the years passed, other convents relaxed their harsh rules, but not hers. She decided that twenty-five years' service was sufficient and resigned, and around fifteen other disenchanted nuns left at a similar time. Life on the outside was overwhelming—computers had been invented, she hadn't managed money for many years and on top of that she had to contend with the new decimal currency.

In wishing me the best she reasoned that the mysterious ways of the world cannot all be understood and encouraged me to be satisfied with the wife and children that I had been given.

Days later, I was still stumped. What the hell? Maggie had never told me my father's name or where he was from. It was a bizarre development. Did she dream she'd told me? (Did I forget?) She said in our first call that my father was dead, and now this. Is he dead, or alive?

As the news sank in, I felt a rush of adrenaline—I still have a chance to meet my father! My original birth certificate revealed Maggie had named me Paul Becker. And now I'd learned that my father's name was Paul Hayes. One twenty-year mystery had been solved—I was named after my father.

But who was he? Where is he? Maybe my father would want to know his son. If he was alive, he'd probably be around eighty, so there was no time to mess about. I immediately hired a private detective to find a Paul Hayes who once lived in Northbridge, Sydney.

In April 2010, after eight weeks of searching, the private detective confidently reported that there had been no Paul Hayes of the right age residing in Sydney between 1955 and 1965. There were only 180 'prospects' in the whole of Australia, and the detective had written to or called every single one with a connection to New South Wales.

Not good enough. This was my one shot, so I wrote back to him: 'No matter the cost—keep hunting.' After several emails and calls, the investigator lost patience and angrily set me straight: 'Look, I've done plenty of these types of investigations, Brendan. You've got to understand, mate, quite a number of these birth fathers just don't want to be found. Many of the names they used are invented. I'll happily keep sending you invoices if you want, but I really don't think he's out there. This is a wild goose chase.'

I'd been jolted back to reality. The search had already cost me a couple of thousand dollars. Time to stop throwing good money after bad.

I wrote in my journal: 'I've been speculating recently that these may well be the best days of my life. We're all healthy, Kate's fulfilled creatively and work-wise, the kids are adorable, work is good (or as good as this job will ever get!), money is coming thru the door . . . millions would swap their lot for mine.' Nonetheless, every cell in my body told me Maggie was withholding. Every contact was like pulling an eel from a fast-moving stream. I shared the results.

> Well, after spending a couple of months trying to find my father via a private detective, it's time to write again. Firstly, I need to clear the air, there have been some misunderstandings. You are who you are, and you did what you did. I don't judge you poorly for my adoption, I'm grateful you didn't choose a termination. I'm also extremely thankful you eventually agreed to have some contact. I recognise that I am a fortunate individual and am happy in my life . . .
>
> So, Paul Hayes, we can't find him. It seems there was no Paul Hayes living in Northbridge, Sydney, between 1955–65. Is there anything else you may know that could help me locate my father? His age? Employer name? Street name? If he died, when? The advice I've received is that he can't be located with the detail I currently have. Did you say he was a friend-of-a-friend? Could they help? I realise he may not have used his real name . . . yes, I am clutching at straws, but I owe it to myself to make a serious attempt to resolve this once and for all.

A few weeks later I received a reply. It was short and sharp.

I was surprised to read that she was delighted that I'd hired a private detective.

It proved what she'd thought all along: my father had been dishonest. He not only abandoned her, but he abandoned me, too.

She said that at the time of her pregnancy it was only her faith in God that ensured her survival, and then she went on to inform me she'd had enough of going over the same facts repeatedly with me and that I'd found out all that I could—in other words, to move on. To value what I already had, and to ask for God's help if these matters still troubled me.

Maggie and I had been dumped. I surrendered.

Part Two

LIES

Part Two

LIES

Chapter 19

MELBOURNE, 2015

Ten years earlier I'd created an annual reminder in my Outlook calendar: 'Check that your mum didn't die ☺'. I'd trawl the online death and funeral notices each year, the only way I was going to find out for certain when Maggie passed. Only then would the whole exhausting saga be over. I hoped her will included a letter for me, something that explained why she'd kept me at arm's length all my life, identified my father and explained their relationship. A decade earlier Maggie had told Kate, 'I've instructed my lawyer. Brendan will be notified when I've passed.' I resented the ease with which she dictated terms. But trust had long ago evaporated; I searched online, half-hoping my mother was dead.

I'd succeeded in crowding Maggie from my mind over the previous five years. Now in my early fifties, I figured if I was ever going to get serious about financial security, it was time to make hay. The industry peak body I ran demanded long hours; there was little opportunity to navel-gaze, even if I'd wanted to. In essence, my job was to make rich men richer. The longer I stayed the less I enjoyed it, but I was bloody good at it, and generously rewarded. We lived in the leafy suburbs, the kids were well provided for, we travelled—what more could I want?

Once or twice a year I'd fly to Sydney for work. Maggie lived close to the airport, and on occasion, as we circled before landing, I'd peer down and spy her block of flats. Though I knew she was taking my secrets to her grave, being so physically close always led to contemplation. From the moment she signed my adoption papers, the only right I had was to learn her name, birthplace and age on the day I was born. She wasn't compelled to tell me a single thing.

I don't dream often, and it's rare I remember them. But one night I woke from a deep sleep startled that I could vividly recall attending my mother's funeral. The opening sequence was me seated mid-church among the mourners, observing Maggie's family and friends. I nodded with compassion as I listened to stories praising her many charitable deeds. Speakers solemnly referred to her twenty-five years' sacrifice while a nun. One referenced the vows of poverty, chastity and obedience. They made her out to be a saint.

The second scene saw me striding down the centre aisle of the church and commandeering the pulpit, like some semi-deranged priest. I explained to the bewildered congregation that I was, in fact, Maggie's bastard son, Brendan Watkins. I informed them I'd known my mother for thirty years and for that entire time she insisted I remain permanently hidden. She refused to reveal the identity of my father and had no interest in her two grandchildren. On the rare occasion that we spoke, she couldn't even recall their names. And with that I stalked down the aisle, leaving the speechless Beckers with their own inventory of never-to-be-answered questions. That morning, wide-eyed, I recounted the dream in minute detail to Kate. While I frequently acknowledged my fortunate life, it was clear I would never be free until Maggie was dead.

And then, as if out of some weird-arse sci-fi movie, affordable and from-the-privacy-of-your-own-home genealogical DNA testing arrived. This spectacularly powerful new tool promised a pathway to my father.

I first became aware of DNA testing when news services began reporting on US cases of murderers released from death row after DNA proved their innocence. Genetic testing became the go-to weapon in the arsenal not only of law enforcement but also of professional genealogists and run-of-the-mill amateur family sleuths. Suddenly, anyone could find out if their mum and dad were really who they said they were. The adoption communities I followed online began publishing eye-popping stories of adoptees locating unknown half and full siblings, and joyful family reunions.

I tossed and turned about what to do, but in my heart of hearts I knew I couldn't rest until I'd thrown my DNA into the ring. On 16 September 2015, I sent Ancestry.com my DNA. A spit into a plastic tube promised an email link to a world map that would confidently declare the country and even the local regions of my ancestors. I was excited, but at the same time felt like the kid warned not to look up at an eclipse, where searing pain awaits.

There were four major DNA genealogy organisations in existence at the time. I chose Ancestry.com as it was the largest. It claimed to provide access to approximately ten billion historical records and three million DNA participants.

Back in 1990, when I'd learned Maggie's surname was Becker, I felt that finally I had a cultural heritage to cling to. Kate and I had close German friends, and I gleefully told Heti that I was German, just like her! I was punctual, I liked rules, I was direct, stoic and insured for every conceivable risk. My backup plan even incorporated a fail-safe alternate backup plan. I'd found my tribe. Yes, of course I was German! Later, after we began exchanging letters, phone calls and finally got to meet Maggie, she said her family was half German and half Irish, and was vague about what came before them. And that was only half the story, as it excluded the genealogy of my father. I could be a Heinz 57 Varieties—how exotic!

With zero fanfare, my Ancestry.com DNA results plonked into my inbox a month later. A colour-coded world map proclaimed my 'Ethnicity Estimate': Ireland and Scotland 78%; England, Wales & North-western Europe 16%; Germanic Europe 6%. Hold the sauerkraut, I'm barely German at all? I'm bloody Irish-Scottish! Finally! I'd been stateless for more than fifty years, and I now had an ancestral home. It was science-fact. Maggie can't have corrupted my DNA—I had the truth.

After I slowed myself down and carefully read the fine detail, what I was actually being told was that I was 78% Irish. Kiss me, I'm Irish!

In fact, Ancestry.com was able to situate my forebears within an area of approximately a hundred square kilometres north of Kilkenny. I pulled up a satellite view map of the countryside and scrolled into the green, hilly pastures and villages. I zoomed in to the farms and houses. I smelled the cool, peaty air. I peered into backyards and over side fences. In the centre of each village, I saw an ornate church and cemetery where my ancestors might rest. It was deeply satisfying.

As well as an ancestral concentration in Kilkenny, the map highlighted maternal and paternal origins. It accurately identified my ancestors in Port Augusta, where Maggie was born. Hotspots glowed in Adelaide, where maternal relatives lived. Sydney flamed red. This is where my father is . . . or was.

Elated, nobody could challenge the accuracy of these results. Kate and I celebrated, and when I called Damien and a few close friends, all were thrilled and amazed in equal measure. We began plotting a trip to Ireland. I'd loved Irish comedians. Now I started reading Irish authors, dug out Irish movies, and even gave Guinness a nudge.

After a few months, though, the excitement dimmed. The DNA sample hadn't brought me my father. He was out there, somewhere, possibly closer, but still out of reach. If my father had given his DNA, I would have found him by this stage. The only way to trace him now was through his lineage. We dug in for the long haul.

After a participant provides DNA and receives their ethnicity estimate, emails begin to arrive alerting them to 'new genetic relatives'. You can choose to communicate with the person or load their details onto your family tree. Regardless of how you respond, the branches of the world's largest family tree grow a little closer. The volume of data held by Ancestry.com is both awe-inspiring and disturbing. Many members upload not only family names but health data, employment and education information, and photos. Ordinarily I'd run a mile from such an Orwellian loss of privacy and control—but it was my only hope.

In the first few months, my heart raced whenever a new Ancestry.com email pinged, 'We found new discoveries for Brendan Watkins.' I opened each email, where a bountiful sky-blue font proclaimed, 'You've got new DNA connections!' I'd quickly scan for the familial proximity of the newly minted kin. Even though I received many emails, they were usually third, fourth, fifth or sixth cousins—irrefutably related, but distant, and of no use to my paternity quest.

Kate began digging about in genealogical databases, matching up these new if distant relatives. Unfortunately, every DNA needle eventually disappeared back into the genetic haystack. Kate did the heavy lifting when it came to searching for my father, as I was annoyingly impatient (though I told everyone she did the slogging work because I was time-poor).

I also discovered a kink in my cognition. Since the day I was told I was adopted, back in 1969, a part of my brain switched off whenever someone explained the logistics of a biological relationship. In one ear, out the other. 'He's my auntie's cousin'—don't understand. 'She's my niece'—what's that mean again? I've simply never bothered with absorbing the terminology, because I was on my own. I wasn't sad about it—the jargon simply didn't have a practical use. Kate would spout, 'I found a second cousin, once removed', and it may as well have been Chinese algebra. Plus, I didn't see the point in poring over obscure DNA links to people from a hundred years ago. Fourth to sixth cousins, bugger that, I just wanted to know who my father was. Where Kate loved the journey—picking through the rich seams of long-ago ancestral lines—I wanted the destination.

Weeks became months, months turned to years. The promise of finding my father came and went like the seasons. New leads frequently pinged; I'd be emotionally drained while Kate spent hours trawling the net, often discovering what she called 'your *fascinating* distant relatives'. She excitedly showed me excerpts of their '*intriguing lives*', but I wasn't having a bar of dead old blokes who weren't my father. I got to the stage of refusing to look at these '*amazing characters*'. It caused tension in the home. I went from mildly disenchanted to completely disinterested. I was a pain in the arse.

Fortunately, our 23-year-old son had become intrigued by Kate's research. While I sulked, his enthusiasm encouraged Kate to push on. Pat was eager to learn about his ancestors and even got involved in some of the deep-dive researching of maybe-relatives in Sydney.

On a work trip to Sydney around this time, he called Maggie and asked if he could drop in and say hello. She declined, saying it wasn't convenient. This was the first and last time either of her grandchildren has reached out.

In the end, it took a single email to solve the riddle of my paternity.

Chapter 20

MELBOURNE, MARCH 2018

Early one morning, yet another tiresome Ancestry.com 'discovery' email arrived. It had become tempting to delete them. I didn't open it, just flicked it to Kate and went to work.

That evening when I got home Kate was still in her PJs, furiously punching at her laptop keyboard. Photocopied family trees were spread all over the dining-room table; she was totally in the zone and banging on about that 'first or second cousin email'.

Tilting my head, I looked quizzical.

'It's the closest match we've ever received!' she said. 'Don't you get it? It's just two steps back from your father! He's your first cousin once removed!' Her expression said, 'You know you really are an absolute goose sometimes?'

'Really? I didn't read it. I don't want to get my hopes up again.'

If anyone could unravel the knotted threads, I knew Kate could. This cousin who'd dropped anchor in my inbox was a Sydneysider named Peter Meaney. 'Meaney is an unappealing surname, more appropriate for Maggie I'd reckon. I'll stick with Watkins, thanks anyway.' I went downstairs and switched on the TV.

Sitting on the couch, thinking it through, I fought to stifle my excitement. It's probably another dead end . . . and if it's not . . . what if my father turns out to be despicable? Or, what if he refuses contact, too? Buckle up for the roller-coaster, here we go again.

This email brought to mind one of our kids' favourite early-years books, *Are You My Mother?* Kids books are crammed full with messaging about families, but for adoptees, this one takes the cake. In the story, a hatchling emerges but the mother bird is nowhere to be seen. The only way for the little bird to find peace is to learn its identity and to locate its parent. It wanders and asks a dog, a cat, a steam shovel and a cow if they are its mother. None are. If the hatchling didn't find its mum, it's liable to moo or bark its whole life (or spend the rest of its days searching). A happy ending eventuates, naturally, when parent and child are reunited.

I was always struck that the book doesn't question why the bird has to find its parent; it's accepted that even the youngest reader intrinsically knows the importance of finding our ancestors. Nobody discourages the bird from searching. Nobody says to go home and forget about her forever. Nobody says the bird did not have a right to know, and most importantly, nobody infers the bird is ungrateful for seeking the truth. This is what we teach toddlers about (non-adopted) familial connection. I'd had thirty years of roadblocks. Why was it made so difficult? What was there to hide?

Over the next few days, Kate manually transcribed several family trees, which were then photocopied and grafted, one branch to the next. Limbs of Watkins and Meaneys reached across to Condons, Mulligans, Bloods and more. She then reviewed the generations of bloodlines, hunting for tenuous links to my father. Photocopies of electoral rolls, Trove articles and Births, Deaths and Marriages data reinforced the raw genetic evidence sourced from Ancestry.com. Discreet calls to distant relatives provided valuable cross-matching of intelligence. The task, of course, was made that much harder by Kate's commitment to concealing Maggie's identity.

I'd return home from work to find my loved one buried under a swelling pile of A4 folders, sticky tape, staplers and sliced-and-diced family trees spilling over the dining-room table and onto the floor. Rejected rellos had been relegated to screwed-up balls of paper for Artemis the cat to tap-tap around the room. Holly, the forlorn hound, sat under the table looking like she needed a feed.

I still don't fully understand how Kate went about ruling out the various sepia-tinged prospective fathers from sixty years past (her investigative savvy is far superior to mine) but finally the evidence pointed to a large family from Sydney by the name of Shiel. Several Shiels were quickly added to the parental 'unlikely list', due to living interstate or being too young at the time of my conception. In a laborious process of elimination, Kate began to narrow the field of prospective fathers down.

I'd told myself my father had been dead for many years. It was easier that way (the thought of him still alive was too painful). Assuming he was the same age as Maggie when I was conceived, he'd be eighty-four now.

With cross-matching to electoral-roll data, Kate established several overlapping addresses for Maggie Becker and one particular Shiel male: Vincent Bede Shiel. Kate fished out a newspaper article about Vincent in Trove. It had a photo. I didn't think he looked like me. And anyway, he was much older than Maggie.

A week later, the paternal candidates had been whittled down to Vincent Shiel and his nephews, Sean, Daniel and Connor, the latter three being closer to Maggie's age. My birth father was one of these four men, Kate was certain.

But what to do next? Finding my father was going to be tricky if we were to continue to withhold the identity of my mother. We agreed to lie to protect her.

This insta-cousin of mine, Peter Meaney, was easy to unearth on the net. I found him on both LinkedIn and Facebook. I wanted to check him out and get a phone number for Kate, rather than take the easy Ancestry-offered contact option. Always three steps behind, as Kate picked up her phone to call Peter, it dawned on me that he would almost certainly have known my flesh-and-blood father (I've never claimed to be an intellectual). A large part of me refused to accept that the answer to decades of questions could be resolved at this very moment.

The phone rang—Peter answered. Kate explained that she was researching family history and saw that he and I were brand-new cousins via a DNA match. She said I was adopted and had been searching for my birth father for thirty years. Peter sounded hesitant. By this stage Kate knew generations of the Shiel and Meaney clan by heart. She could recite any one of half-a-dozen associated family lines, and name siblings and parents with confidence. Peter had just retired, was well advanced in his own family history research, and was able to verify all that Kate had discovered. She then began to gently probe around Vincent, Sean, Daniel and Connor Shiel.

Peter had known all four possible fathers and had plenty of stories to share. Kate and he hit it off, chatting like mates. He was generous with his time and knowledge, and, as the conversation progressed, the reality began to dawn on Peter that one of those four men had a secret child. A scandal was unfolding.

'Peter, I noticed several shared addresses between Vincent Shiel and someone named Maggie Becker? It looked like an interesting friendship . . . ?' Irrespective of Peter possibly knowing Maggie, it was treacherous terrain. If he was going to get cold feet about assisting Kate, now was the time.

'Yeah! I've got vivid recollections of both Vincent and Maggie. As a young lad I visited her at the convent, I called her my Flying Nun! She was wonderful, warm and fun. We played basketball!' As with everybody else, the thought that a Catholic nun could have been my birth mother didn't occur to Peter. Nuns didn't have children: Maggie's secret was safe.

Peter and Kate wrapped up the lengthy conversation, agreeing to research in tandem and share findings. 'Your cousin, Peter, is terrific and outgoing, and has a super-strong connection to Ireland—you'll definitely like him. He's got photos and all sorts of ancestral records . . .'

The following week, Kate urged me to call. It was the strangest feeling: Peter knew both my birth father and birth mother, even if he didn't realise it. As we chatted, he was irreverent and jovial, without being over-friendly—and after hearing about my secure and happy family life, he made it something of a mission to help solve the riddle of my paternity. When he asked directly who my birth mother was, I was vague. I blocked and steered the conversation away. (I'd been taught by an expert.) 'Peter, I'm sorry, she's still alive. She insists on remaining anonymous. She's shamed by all of this—I just can't tell you.'

Meanwhile, our lounge room was starting to look like a set for *CSI* (the only thing missing was the white tape outlining where a body had been found). I stayed busy with work and exercise; I didn't get involved. At this stage Vincent was just one of four suspects on Kate's wall chart, though the more information Peter shared via email and phone, the more he looked like my father.

In one of several calls, Peter told Kate that Vincent and Maggie were great mates and were very often together: 'You realise, Kate, they'd known each other for decades. In fact, Maggie and Vincent

had lived together for several years toward the end of his life—
she was his housekeeper.'

Vincent Shiel immediately became Kate's number one person
of interest.

Chapter 21

MELBOURNE, JULY 2018

It appeared Kate's ongoing chats and email exchanges with Peter may have unearthed my dad. But there were two impediments to that theory:

Vincent was thirty years older than Maggie.

Vincent was a Catholic priest.

Fifty years of paternity questions had been narrowed down to one of the most unlikely answers imaginable, my ex-nun mother may have conceived me with a priest. Unfortunately, Father Vincent Bede Shiel was unable to assist with enquiries as he had passed away on 14 April 1993 at ninety years of age.

There had been so many false dawns; my first reaction was to disbelieve it was him. I wouldn't allow myself to feel anything until Kate's theory was confirmed, in triplicate.

As I didn't have a sample of his DNA, there were only two ways to confirm the truth. The least strenuous was to have Maggie confirm it, but if she wasn't going to help (I only half-jokingly told Kate) I was prepared to grab the shovel and drive up to the Field of Mars Cemetery in Sydney where he was buried.

Since sending my sample to Ancestry.com in 2015, I'd read of several exhumations to access DNA. While it sounded ludicrous to have to dig up a priest to prove paternity, I was aware of an American priest about to be exhumed to source his DNA. A man called Jim Graham was battling the church to obtain consent to dig up his presumed father—it was big news in America. Surely, we wouldn't have to resort to these measures?

Kate was convinced Vincent Shiel was my dad. Maggie had to fess up. She was now eighty-four (unfairly, she'd outlasted Roy and Bet). I'd resolved to never call or write to her again, and it'd been eight years since our last contact. I looked up her number but for some reason I couldn't find her in the Sydney phone directory. Had she passed? How did I miss it? I extended the searching to Australia-wide and discovered she had moved to Brisbane. A new life in the sun would be a tonic and (consciously or otherwise) her relocation had the bonus of putting another nine hundred kilometres between her and me.

Although a priest and nun having a child and surrendering it was one of the ultimate taboos for Catholics, I didn't care one iota if my father was a priest. What I was uneasy about was the nature of Vincent and Maggie's relationship; Father Shiel may have been an abusive man. He was thirty years older than her, so what could she have seen in him? I clung to Peter Meaney's comment that Vincent and Maggie 'were great mates', as I braced for turbulence.

On 16 July, Kate called my mother and explained how I'd submitted my DNA and what we'd found. She went through the convoluted steps that led us to believe that a man we now knew she'd been close to for decades was, in fact, my birth father. As Kate talked, Maggie did not utter a word . . . proceeding with care, Kate stepped through lists of the Shiel family. She named my new DNA-confirmed cousins, uncles, aunts—relatives with whom we'd just learned Maggie had shared decades of her life.

For a non-computer-user like my mother, this rollcall must have come as a bolt from the blue, a miracle even.

Kate shared some of the electoral-roll addresses that directly linked Maggie to Vincent Shiel. Almost thirty years of obfuscation was being dismantled as she spoke. The fact that Vincent and Maggie had lived together for some years before his death was the clincher. 'Maggie, Brendan is a Shiel. The DNA is irrefutable. We just need to know which Shiel. Please, Maggie, we believe that Father Vincent Shiel is Brendan's father.'

Sitting next to Kate on our kitchen bench, I remained silent, leaning in, trying to make out the response down the line from Brisbane. How could she deny the identity of my father now?

Maggie umm-ed and ah-ed, rolled the question around like a riddle: 'Noooo . . . No, I don't think Father Vincent could be Brendan's father.' Kate left a long pause. My mother didn't fill it.

'I understand this is hard to talk about . . . but please, Brendan is owed the truth. I'd prefer to not contact the other three men's families,' Kate pleaded.

Maggie evaded again. Kate and I locked eyes. This was unexpected. Kate was gentle but direct. They went around in circles for some time, but as there was no progress the call was wound up. 'Maggie, please have a think and give me a call when you'd like to talk.'

Shaking my head, I stared at Kate in confusion. 'Are we too late? Could she have dementia? Do you think she even knows who my father is? None of this makes sense.'

At work the next morning, Kate answered her mobile, and my mother made her confession.

Kate called me at work to relay the long-awaited truth; my journal notes record Maggie's response. 'Yes, Father Vincent Shiel is Brendan's father. Yes, he was a priest. A good man—but long dead. The lifting of this weight is an enormous relief for me, although I am anxious Brendan will think poorly of me and be angry . . . but more than anything I feel so much better that this troubling secret is finally out. I'm sorry for lying to Brendan over all of these years.' Kate said to me that Maggie's relief may bring about a desire for closer contact.

I exploded. 'Really?! After decades? After so many lies? The pointless private detective chase? Maggie bare-faced lied to me for twenty-five years. She's now been found out by the DNA. She was never going to tell me the truth! Now she wants to be friends?'

Maggie had revealed that Vincent was 'a kind and decent man', though 'he was older than me'. She'd known him since she was a teenager, and their friendship had endured until the day he died. She shared some surprising details. He had been an architect, went to university and then became a builder, before becoming a priest late in life. He also designed and oversaw the building of a number of churches in the Outback. He'd travelled the world. She described him as 'a great dancer . . . a charmer'. When she discovered the pregnancy, Father Vincent had arranged for her to travel to Melbourne and stay with a Catholic family in the months before my birth and adoption. He made Maggie promise to keep me a secret forever. 'You must tell no one.'

Maggie had stressed that the truth must remain a secret between the three of us. She reiterated that she had been raised in poverty, her family had rarely shown kindness or love, and without saying it, she was asking for mercy.

Regarding my conception, Maggie said, 'It was just a thing that happened.' What did that mean? I asked Kate. I wanted to understand the nature of my parents' relationship. Had they been in love? It was a jumble of information, and still so many unanswered questions. But as had happened so many times before, Maggie's words had dried up—she'd lost her nerve.

'This is all wrong,' I fumed. 'How can a 57-year-old priest have a child with a 27-year-old? And what does this mean, "It's still a secret"? Does she mean don't tell my own family? My friends? Or her family? Or my birth father's family? They are *all* my family now. She still wants to control this!'

All the cards were finally on the table. We'd got our man (well, Kate had got my man). My overwhelming emotion was contemptuous disappointment in my devout birth parents. A nun and priest, exemplars of the compassionate Catholic faith. I'd been sacrificed for a sin committed against their God. How pathetic.

Once my father was found, I'd thought I'd feel somehow complete, but it was a shuddering anticlimax. I wanted to quit my job, lie low for several weeks, or months . . . the knowledge that my birth parents were a couple and yet still chose to shun me to preserve their holy reputations was such a gut punch. They were the worst kind of frauds: religious hypocrites. My mother spent the majority of her life evading her only son because I had a priest father.

I let it all out on Kate: 'I don't want anything to do with Maggie ever again.' I'd never wanted her to be my mother— there could never be a more loving mother than Bet. All I'd ever wanted was my story. 'A priest-father is such a lame excuse for Maggie to have screwed me over for thirty years.'

From that day on, I claimed ownership of my story. I would be my own narrator. As I digested this news, I recalled a photograph of Father Vincent Shiel we'd found on Trove a couple of weeks earlier. The weary, grey-bearded, old priest stared straight back at me.

Hello, father Father. I'm the son of a preacher man.

I was fifty-seven years old and for the first time in my life I knew for certain who both of my birth parents were. The insatiable curiosity ignited half a century ago when Roy and Bet told Damien and me we were adopted ended on this bleak winter day.

I exhaled as though I'd been holding my breath for years.

Chapter 22

NEW YORK CITY, 1964

Father Vin sat in the sumptuous library in front of a blazing fire-place at St Raymond's Rectory, Castle Hill Avenue, in the Bronx. He was waiting for his friend, Monsignor Gustav Schultheiss, a former secretary to Cardinal Spellman and past chancellor of the Roman Catholic Archdiocese of New York. The clerics were about to drink coffee and enjoy the fine chocolates that Vin had purchased that morning in a rushed trip downtown during a break in the snow. He and Monsignor Schultheiss had made a habit of meeting at the end of the day. The men would often talk (and gossip) for hours into the evening.

The Australian was in New York recuperating from an oper-ation to remove a tumour from his arm. It had been caused by working in the radioactive waste of his Far North Catholic Inland Mission at Radium Hill. The past five years had taken both a physical and intensely emotional toll on the 61-year-old. He was profoundly troubled by a secret that would never be confessed while he was on God's earth. He had a sexual encounter with

Maggie Becker in May 1960. It was unforgivable, a cardinal sin, even though it somehow felt right at the time.

Maggie fell pregnant. Through his church networks, Vin arranged for the birth and adoption of their child. His hard-won reputation was on the line, the young lass was devastated, and he prayed the rosary each day for forgiveness.

In a wild panic, the month after the sexual encounter, Vin tried to flee. The builder-priest wrote to his bishop requesting to be transferred to assist Bishop John Jobst, a pilot-priest, the 'flying bishop' of the West Australian Kimberley. Born in Germany in 1920, Jobst spent close to forty years establishing Aboriginal missions and flying thousands of miles across his vast parish. Drowning in dread, Vin supposed he could assist with building works in the punishingly barren mission—he needed to suffer. The escape would place fifteen hundred miles between Vin and his South Australian bishop and parishioners, and more still between him and Maggie in Sydney. Vin's request letter to the bishop was returned with a scrawl at the bottom of the page: 'Not possible.'

With pin-oak logs crackling in the fireplace, lost in these tumultuous thoughts, Father Vin did not at first notice Monsignor Schultheiss enter the room and sit in his leather lounge chair.

They took up the conversation where they had left off the previous night. 'I overheard our dear Archbishop Sheen telling a visiting African bishop about some of these hilarious regional names in your Northern Missions. Can you tell me some?' asked Schultheiss.

'Of course,' obliged the Australian. 'Now we were reasonably close to Oulnina, Wawirra, Outalpa, Olary, Yunta, Cutana and Oodla Wirra. If you drove to Radium Hill, of course, you'd pass close to Wantabibbie, Nackara and Paratoo . . . take a turn-off and you could endure a treacherous trek through Coolawatinnie and Winnininnie . . . and, of course, how could I forget the real Outback of Waukaringa, Wadnaminga and Teetulpa!' Father Vin smiled. Reciting the placenames was one of his party tricks while on overseas tours.

Schultheiss laughed uproariously.

'Gustav Schultheiss! Could I remind you that your name is something of a tongue twister, too . . . my good man!' smiled Father Vin.

'Yes, you have a point!' replied the Monsignor. 'And what became of the Radium Hill township?'

'Yes, well, that adventure ended three years ago. The newspapers called me a one-man building team! Father Six-in-one: the bricklayer, carpenter, painter, plumber, joiner and plasterer. Granted, I did receive a little community assistance, though essentially, I drew the plans, dug the footings and hand-made the bricks for our beautiful church. Hardest manual labour I've ever undertaken.' Father Vin stretched and rubbed his arm.

'When the mine closed and was abandoned in December 1961, it had operated for just seven years—though it felt like a lifetime.' He recalled the abrupt demise: the contract for uranium, for defence purposes mainly, fulfilled; a community of close to a thousand workers sent packing; one hundred and fifty homes, a hospital, canteens, a swimming pool and even the timber schoolhouse he'd built himself, all demolished or relocated. It couldn't be more different from where they were now relaxing, in this stately library, with New York snow falling outside—the desert heat would peel paint.

He looked over to the Monsignor. 'Thankfully,' he went on, 'I like to think, with divine intervention, a light had been shone on my sweat-soaked church—Our Lady Queen of the World was spared. Pleasingly, it still stands today, jaw-jutted out, defiant to the elements. My schoolhouse was saved, too. It was trucked two hundred miles west to Port Pirie. It's now part of The Lady Fatima School.

'I baptised, christened, married and buried a great number of my flock in that desert congregation: good, simple, hard-working people. Mainly migrants, European refugees, looking for a new life in Australia . . . I miss it terribly. We were a tight community. The few who had money out in the desert, the surrounding station owners, were a tight-fisted lot. All I could get from them was the odd sheep for a barbecue—damn pagans!' Father Vin caught the Monsignor's eye, and the men chuckled.

'Radium Hill was my true calling, Monsignor, where I did my most valuable work.' Transfixed by the glow of the fire, Father Vin's voice trailed off . . . 'I feel I now need to get back to Australia. I've been gone most of this year. I need to see my family, too . . .'

Schultheiss tried to rally the homesick Australian. 'Father, don't forget tomorrow morning we have a specialist appointment. We have to get your arm fixed before you go. The last operation was a disaster—we have the best doctors in the world. The finest cancer specialists are here in New York.' What a shame the tumour had hid under his watch until it spread, incapacitating him for months. He was placing his trust in the experts at the Misericordia Hospital. 'We'll get you right first. Then pack you up for Australia. Try to relax. Tell me about your tour earlier this year with our esteemed friend, Archbishop Sheen.'

Relieved to again be snapped out of his negative thinking, Vin was happy to oblige. 'Fulton showed me a newspaper article just yesterday that claimed, after the Pope, he was the best-known Catholic in America. He has gone from strength to strength, that man! It had a picture of he and I together; I mailed a copy back home to Australia. And do you know that I nearly didn't join his overseas mission? My bishop in South Australia was reluctant to grant the leave, saying I too often overstayed the approved duration. He cited my excuses—cancelled ships or aeroplanes, illness, my apparent confusion over travel arrangements, missed boats, and the odd car accident—like hitting kangaroos. The bishop said, "If I allow you to go is there any certainty you'll come back?" And you know . . . I could hardly argue—because everything he said was true!'

The men hooted.

'But this was to be a tour of a lifetime, so I wrote to my bishop and pulled rank. I told him that no less a man than Fulton Sheen had requested my company on an all-expenses paid trip, *don't you dare refuse me!* I emphasised our itinerary—the Eucharistic Congress in Bombay . . . Egypt, The Holy Land and Rome . . . and, of course, back and forth to America. It would be an astounding, a *deeply enlightening*, experience . . .'

Vin continued more sedately, 'But sadly, Monsignor, I have crossed swords with Fulton, yet again. Yesterday, at lunch, he told me he has begun preparing notes for an autobiography and will highlight the work of inspirational missionaries, including me. But he reminded me that he'd always speculated that I desired a plastic cross over a wooden one—I believe he sees me as a shirker. It makes no sense putting me in a book if that's his estimation of me. He talks in riddles . . . so, I stormed out of his rooms . . .'

'Father, I am sure that's not true. Regardless, can I remind you that you do not answer to Fulton Sheen. It is Our Lord who ultimately judges our devotions and humble contributions. There is only one man you must impress.'

'You're right . . . look, I am short-tempered, my arm is a mess, my health in pieces. I cannot sleep anymore—I am at a crossroad, Monsignor, I don't know what to do . . .' Now glassy-eyed, it appeared the Australian might cry.

Schultheiss stood. 'Would you join me in another coffee, Father? Another of these exquisite chocolates? I'm going to have one more before bed.'

As Schultheiss left the library, Vin pulled himself together, and contemplated the reason for his volatility. He had recently received a letter from his sister in Sydney updating him on family news, she also mentioned that Maggie was a changed young woman. She had inexplicably lost weight and her zest for life had vanished. She'd re-entered a convent, one that was known for its draconian practice. The only explanation offered was she felt compelled to dedicate the rest of her life to good deeds. Maggie had (again) taken the name Sister Vincent. Father Vincent, though honoured by the gesture, wondered what the Shiels back in Sydney would make of her name selection? What awkward encounters would they have to contend with at family events— *here comes Father Vincent and Sister Vincent . . . ?*

Back in Australia, Reverend Bryan Gallagher, the Bishop of Port Pirie, was well aware of Father Vincent's state of mind. He wrote four times that December. He acknowledged Vin's silent suffering, saying he admired him for pushing on with his spiritual and manual work. He had news—he'd posted Vin to a new parish, in Quorn. He said he would now consider Vin's health to be of the highest priority. Quorn was relatively civilised, and it would be a far less taxing role physically. This was to be Father Vin's reward, a parish to recuperate in and enjoy. It was time to leave the desert trails behind.

Father Vin flew back to Australia just a few weeks before Christmas 1964. After surgery in New York, there was further treatment in hospital in Adelaide, and then recuperating with his brother in Sydney, and there was another exploratory operation of the nerves and tendons just above his wrist. The bishop continued to offer support: basically saying that he wanted Vin to return to good health, cool his heels, stay in Sydney as long as he needed. He also emphasised that the Quorn posting was not to be seen as a demotion—it was about taking stock, and putting physical welfare first.

True to form, Vin managed to stretch out his Sydney stay through to Christmas 1965—a full twelve months after his announced commencement in Quorn. He was still receiving therapy on the arm when his brother had a stroke. He was hospitalised for several months, before passing.

By the time Vin commenced in Quorn in early 1966, he was a sixty-three-year-old with several debilitating health issues. He'd spent decades traversing some of Australia's most hostile landscapes, completed significant building works, and seen more of the world than most of his fellow Australians. He was a builder, a gambler and a fool.

And he had fathered a hidden child, a boy now five years old whom he prayed had been adopted by a good Catholic family somewhere in Victoria.

'Nobody will ever find out,' he would console himself. 'Try and get some sleep.'

Chapter 23

MELBOURNE, LATE JULY 2018

I wasn't the son of a mass-murderer after all.

The decades-long apprehension that I was the result of an appalling violent or unnatural act had been dispelled. The relief, however, was soon replaced by colossal questions. Who exactly am I now? Would the news change how others saw me? Should this discovery remain secret? Of immediate interest were more mundane questions—what was the basis of my parents' relationship? Had Vincent and Maggie been in love? Did they consider themselves a *couple*? My mother was firmly evasive on all of these topics, which didn't stop Kate and I speculating on the fine details. Did they share a bed in the years they lived together? We hoped they did, that they held hands in bed as Kate and I sometimes do. What was certain was that my father was a dusty old salesman for God. It brought to mind the Clive James line that 'church is an advertising agency for a product that does not exist'.

One night Kate asked, 'You've had a couple of weeks to roll it around in your head—how do you feel about all this?'

It was a good question, but hard to answer. The first thing that came to mind was the certainty that I didn't want to be alone with the secret this time. And that there were so many emotional and spiritual layers. Though Kate's parents had been raised Catholic, they strongly rejected the church later in life. Kate had been raised in a house that was cynical of the church. She hadn't experienced the intense formative-years indoctrination that I had. 'The fact that I was surrendered is one thing, it's understandable they gave me up, but my story is so warped by their vocations. When a nun takes her vows, she becomes the bride of Christ. I haven't just inherited new relatives—my stepfather technically is Jesus Christ himself!'

I tried to unpack it. According to the Catholics, my father should be burning in eternal flames, roasting because he and Maggie had conceived me. 'You realise that for devout Catholics I represent an abomination of their entire faith.' I told Kate I wanted to explore how many other children of priests are out there. But there was happiness, too. 'I feel relief. I know where I'm from, at last—it's good to say it out loud.'

The next morning I googled 'children of Catholic priests' and found an eye-watering number of results: 68,300,000. Thousands of newspaper articles, personal testimony, videos and what looked like an international support group. There were so many confronting stories: Irish priests who had raped women and forced them to surrender their babies; an Indian nun who was murdered for catching a priest and nun having sex; nuns who had been raped; priests who sold their own babies; priests who fathered multiple children; priests who had children to underage girls. The daughter of a French priest revealed that the children of priests in her region were called the 'Children of Satan'. They were officially categorised with the children of prostitutes and those born of incestuous relationships as *ex damnato coitu nato*: 'born from a damned union.'

The knowledge of my birth parents' roles within the church didn't bruise anywhere near as much as it would have had I been a 'believer'. I'd decided as a teenager that the devil with pointy horns palaver was nothing more than a control device invented by the spin doctors of two thousand years ago. But my Google deep dive underscored the enormous scandal of my parentage, and magnified how disastrous Maggie's pregnancy must have been for her. I didn't tell anyone but a few friends and family what we'd discovered.

Kate and Maggie had developed a bond that had now stretched over close to thirty years. Kate reminded me that Maggie was elderly and alone. My mother had been neglected in her early years, treated poorly in the convent and had a 'relationship' with a powerful, much older priest. I struggled to know how to feel about her.

Kate made a couple of 'welfare check' calls to Maggie over subsequent months. Since her revelation, the familiar tension in my mother's voice had faded. On occasion, at my insistence, Kate nudged the conversation toward her relationship with Vincent, but she only reluctantly revealed details; now that the genie was out of the bottle, she was trying to push it back in. During one of these calls, Maggie told Kate, 'I wasn't shown much love as a child. A little went a long way with me.' More than any other, those words have replayed in my head. Her relationship with my father certainly wasn't a raging love affair between equals.

Vincent and Maggie met when my mother was sixteen in her home town of Port Augusta. He'd been appointed assistant parish priest and was directed by his bishop to get involved with the community. One Christmas, Father Vincent asked Maggie what presents she'd received. She replied, 'None.' The next day he presented her with a jar of sweets. I was instantly repelled when Kate told me. 'That sounds like grooming!' I said. I searched online for references to priests and that clichéd jar of sweets. It turned out they were a standard treat that priests gave to children, a gesture that could have had good or evil intent. That didn't put my mind at rest.

Maggie said Vincent had arranged her escape to Sydney. I found a notice in what was her local newspaper, published in 1951, that said she had gone to Sydney with a girlfriend. They flew on a plane—probably their first flight, I imagine—and would be holidaying in Sydney. Father Vincent had paid for my seventeen-year-old mother's holiday. The following year he encouraged her to leave her unhappy family situation, as he'd arranged accommodation with the extended Shiel family in Sydney. Vincent had bestowed an opportunity to start anew. Maybe he was okay?

Whatever the foundations of my parents' relationship, I was itching to explore my ancestry. I'd only ever had a faux family tree, plastic branches speckled with relatives sharing not a drop of ancestral blood. In reality, the tree began with Roy, Bet, Damien and me. Now there were hundreds of relatives eligible to be added to my tree, though I'd never met a single one, and I didn't know how they'd deal with learning of the hypocrisy of their revered priestly relative.

I began to map the myriad names, letters, certificates, adoption records, conversation notes, electoral rolls, family trees, press articles and photos we'd gathered. Me; Vincent and Maggie; 4 grandparents; 8 great-grandparents; 16 second great-grandparents; 32 third great-grandparents; 64 fourth great-grandparents; 128 fifth great-grandparents; 256 sixth great-grandparents; 512 seventh great-grandparents; 1024 eighth great-grandparents . . . At fifty-seven, to be looking at my genetic family tree for the very first time—its longest branches extending to the 1600s, and not just branches but names—completely blew my mind.

Vincent Shiel wasn't just from a different generation to me; he was from an earlier generation than Roy and Bet. Born in 1902, my father had been ten when the *Titanic* sank, a teenager during World War I, and a young man when the war was followed by a global pandemic and then the Great Depression. He was thirty-one when the Nazis came to power in Germany, thirty-seven when World War II broke out, and he'd lived through the Korean and Vietnam wars since then. War cheapened the value of a life—did experiencing it make surrendering a child easier?

I was just a speck on that vast tree, and I was more than a little overwhelmed. My brain struggled to grasp the new information, and it spilled over into daily life. In a fog I forgot names, keys, the date . . . I was in shock.

Chapter 24

MELBOURNE, AUGUST 2018

Take a moment. Just stop and imagine that you, well into adulthood, learn that this person is your father.

HE IS EIGHT MEN IN ONE!

ADELAIDE—Radium Hill's new Catholic Church-school is unique, thanks to a former North Bondi lifesaver. The architect is a priest, so is the bricklayer, the joiner, the plasterer, the painter, and the plumber! What is more, they are all the same priest—Father Vincent Shiel.

As a member of North Bondi Lifesaving Club Father Shiel personally rescued or had a hand in rescuing more than 100 people. Father Shiel was an architect for some years before he began to study for the priesthood. 'The Southern Cross', a Catholic Church journal, says that he has never let either his ideas or his hands grow rusty. Radium Hill, important SA mining centre, is hundreds of miles from the sea, but, in a spiritual sense, Father Shiel is continuing his 'lifesaving'. He had to

make every one of the 42,000 bricks for the church-school, yet
he took only seven months on the job . . .

The Sydney Morning Herald, 4 November 1956

In 1956, as Elvis released 'Heartbreak Hotel', my father was in a tiny
outback uranium town, building a church for Christ-knows-who.
In the same year television was launched in Australia. The introduction of TV coincided with the Melbourne Olympic Games,
which provided Australians with much craved international recognition—with an identity—a need I understand all too well. A few
short years later, I was conceived—possibly in that same tiny
outback town.

When I googled 'Vincent Shiel', I found two other men sharing
his name, both born at around the same time. One even shared his
full name, Vincent Bede Shiel. He was a lad from Cooma who'd
joined the Australian Imperial Forces in 1914 and succumbed to
diphtheria in Cairo in 1916. Frustratingly, the other was also a
priest. I needed some unique-to-my-father search terms to add to
'Vincent Shiel'. My warm-hearted cousin, Peter Meaney, provided
town names and people. I began to intensively explore the outback
regions where Vincent spent most of his life. His role called for
extensive driving. Each time I found him connected to a new
town—Radium Hill, Woomera, Quorn, Hawker, Renmark—
I'd add it to my search list. I collected dozens of links, articles and
screenshots, and added them to my spreadsheet.

It took weeks of trawling before I nutted out the most successful
search terms: 'Father Shiel', 'Fr Shiel', 'Father Vincent B Shiel',
'Father V.B. Shiel', 'Fr Vin Shiel' and 'Reverend Shiel', having
realised that the addition of an inconspicuous space or full stop
had a great impact on results. I learned to not just rely on his
name. If I searched combinations such as 'Radium Hill Catholic

Priest', Google would offer up material that I knew with certainty was him, even unnamed. The jackpot was to locate a source that included a picture. 'Wow. Do I look like him in this one? Kate, look, he's exactly my age here—the hair, our mouths, they're similar—yeah? Do you think . . . ?'

After spending most of my working life in some interesting creative and not-for-profit organisations, I'd somehow ended up the CEO of a small industry association. There'd been many enjoyable years, but I'd been there too long. In the preceding few years, I'd begun looking for a way out. I'd stacked a little cash away, and now there was this ever-distracting news. What I most wanted to do was immerse myself in the search for Vincent. Maggie was bogged in ocean-deep shame; it felt callous to keep asking her about where I fitted into their story. I wanted to go where he'd been—the Outback.

I had significant responsibility at work. It was a 24/7 role—all in or all out. Maybe it was in my genes, or maybe the result of the mountains of subterfuge in my life, but I'd call out a bullshitter every time. I'd made bonfires at work out of what were a couple of run-of-the-mill spot fires. I didn't want to damage the good I'd done over the past twelve years. I'd only told two people at work that I'd just found out my father was a Father. I was isolated. I was done. So I quit.

'We're all allocated a prescribed number of hours on earth. The hours spent swimming don't count.' I saw that on a sign someplace, and it often pops into my head while following the black line in the bottom of the pool. Nothing could be more elemental, more pure, than the all-of-body sensation of swimming. There are few more pleasurable experiences than slipping into the water on a chilly dawn, steam billowing from a heated pool as rain beats on your back, bliss for $7.20.

My daughter, Nell, and I enjoy many common interests. In recent years we'd begun to swim the famous Pier to Pub Ocean Swim at Lorne with a few friends. We've done a lot of swim training together, followed by an obligatory Bircher muesli and latte at a local cafe. It wasn't hard to convince her that a reasonable way to celebrate my pending unemployment was to head north to the sun and spend a couple of weeks swimming and photographing the ocean pools around Sydney. We'd been sending gorgeous pics of those dazzling pools to each other throughout that soggy Melbourne winter.

The morning after I ended my twelve-year career, my daughter and I headed north before the dawn. The following day I stood at the foot of my father's grave in the Priest Circle of the Field of Mars Cemetery in Ryde, Sydney.

Chapter 25

MELBOURNE, SEPTEMBER 2018

It was now two months since we'd identified Vincent. I'd stood at his grave in Sydney a month earlier and felt nothing. All I had were questions. I was shocked at how difficult it still was to organise my thoughts. Now, not having a job to go to, my complete focus became the Becker-Shiel Spreadsheet.

Kate urged Maggie to write to me. She suggested my mother explain more about Father Vincent, mend the broken bridge. Nothing came, so I wrote.

> I wanted to say sincere thanks for confirming to Kate that Vincent Shiel is my father. It's something I've wanted to know for decades . . . We've already found out a lot of—frankly quite amazing—things about him . . . I'd really appreciate your help in filling in the missing pieces. What sort of person was he? Why did he become a priest so relatively late in life? Do you have any photos? . . .
>
> Maggie, I fully appreciate that 'not keeping the child' in circumstances such as yours was the norm, I don't judge you for that decision or any other that you've made.

Kate said you'd sounded great for having the 'weight of the secret' of Vincent lifted—I'm very glad for you.

Shortly after I received her reply.

She apologised for the pain she had caused and then told me more about my intelligent, hard-headed, but kind father. He was an excellent tradesman and enthusiastic punter. She explained that their last outing was to the Randwick Racecourse on 14 April 1993. Maggie was driving him home when she glanced across and saw that he had died peacefully in the front seat.

Maggie expressed great relief that the truth was now out in the open, and thanked me for my letter and understanding. She said that she should have known that the truth would always come out in the end.

With the letter came the only photo she had of my father, taken on Christmas Day 1992.

I felt there were still clues, hidden truths I might be missing or forgetting, in my growing mass of documents, and I returned to them again and again. I was repeatedly stung when I re-read Maggie's 2010 letter where she fabricated my phony father, Paul Hayes. But the burn of that particular deception paled when, after reviewing the spreadsheet materials as a whole, I realised that *my parents were actually living together* when I first made contact with Maggie in 1990. Vincent didn't pass away until April 1993—it hit me like a train. Maggie said she and Vincent moved in together not long after she resigned from the convent. They were under the same roof for several years. My mother first heard from me in 1990 when Jenny Abbott called on my behalf. My mother knew then that I'd received my original birth certificate containing her name (but not Vincent's) and that I very much wanted contact. She replied to my letters in January 1992—Vincent lived for another fifteen months. For a brief window, I could have met both my parents, then residing in the same flat. For three years—thirty-six long months—Maggie was with my father, knowing that their adult son lived in Melbourne and incessantly asked for information. I was about to start my own family. How could she, or was it *they*, deny me?

Did Maggie tell Vincent that she'd received my letter?

Did they discuss how to respond?

Did one of them want to see me and the other didn't?

Did Vincent even know Maggie had written back to me, or did he read my letters and say, 'Ignore him—throw it away'?

That's when I realised that Maggie's story of an old lady she'd cared for who'd died and left her a flat was probably also a lie. I downloaded a copy of the title to the flat she lived in and now owned: 'Father Vincent Bede Shiel' was recorded as the owner of my mother's flat up until his death. It hadn't been a generous old biddy who gave her the flat, but Father Vincent.

This was the flat where Kate, Pat, Nell and I had visited Maggie in 2009. Another penny dropped. Maybe I'd sat in Vin's chair when we visited Maggie? Jesus!

I distinctly recalled Maggie directing me to sit at the head of the table when we ate lunch that day. Was that where my flesh-and-blood father sat? It must have been. Lies, lies, lies.

This realisation completely reset the picture that I was forming of my parents.

I searched for excuses. The decision to withhold a consequential truth is a mighty one. What you risk, if exposed, is an annihilation of credibility. I'd known for thirty years that Maggie's story was full of holes. In her defence, I'd never said, 'I think you're lying to me,' and I didn't tell her I was hurt. I didn't say that at times I felt isolated and misunderstood or as if I didn't belong. I had, in fact, written glowing letters boasting of what a successful, well-adjusted, bright young thing I was, akin to the cover letters I'd attach to a job application. I squirmed when re-reading them.

Was Maggie mourning Vincent's imminent death around the time that I first contacted her? Or perhaps she felt that after she'd begun telling lies there was no going back. Either way, maintaining her secrets was her sole priority; I was collateral damage. Of course, I'd lied in the past, and I'd lied by omission, too—who hasn't? But there was a mighty scale to Maggie's deceptions. How many more layers of the onion were there to peel?

When my son, Pat, was six, we were driving home one morning and he looked across and asked, 'Dad, is Santa real?' Pat was a straight shooter. Only a *yes* or *no* was going to cut it. Without giving it a lot of thought, I told him the truth. 'No, mate, he's not. Santa's just for the little kids.' He was quiet. I glanced across and saw a self-satisfied *thought so* expression. I was worried I'd made a mistake, but I was also positive any weasel words from me would have come back to bite me later. By the time we arrived home, I'd convinced myself I'd done the right thing.

I told Kate and some friends about Pat's Big Santa Question over lunch that day and was amazed at the varying responses. Overwhelmingly, the consensus was that I'd done the wrong thing. One mother was shocked at what she called my 'utter heartless stupidity'. The most commonly suggested 'better answer' was, 'He is real, *if you believe* he's real.' The next best alternative (usually from the fathers) was, 'No. He's not real. But whatever you do—don't tell your little brother/sister!'

I had researched secrets and lies. When studying ethics at uni, I'd learned that eighteenth-century philosopher Immanuel Kant said that lying is always wrong. Our tutor then smugly presented us first-year students with a range of situations in which intentionally lying to or misleading someone was the only kind or rational response.

Contemporary Swedish-born ethicist Sissela Bok suggests in her book, *Lying: Moral Choice in Public and Private Life*, that lying *is acceptable* if it *'survives a jury of unrelated "reasonable persons"'*. She posits that individuals can't reliably self-assess, as we are all biased toward our own interests. Bok offers a few tests to consider before lying:

> Are there some truthful alternatives to using a lie to deal with the particular problem?
>
> What moral justifications are there for telling this lie—and what counter-arguments can be raised against those justifications?
>
> What would a public jury of 'reasonable persons' say about the lie?

Heather T. Forbes's book, *Beyond Consequences, Logic, and Control: A Love Based Approach to Helping Children with Severe Behaviors*, explores lying in depth. Specifically, she says that lying is not 'personal' and that it 'originates from a state of stress'. What most resonated with me was Forbes's remark that lying 'comes from a state of survival' and there are those who 'must persist with the lie at all costs in order to *survive*'.

I continued researching, and kept trying to justify the actions of my parents. Maggie appeared trapped in a vortex of deceit.

No matter the depth of my reading, I found it hard to accept Maggie's response, especially now that Vincent had been identified—why couldn't she open up and give me the entire story now?

There was also a spiritual context. Didn't their God know that they'd had a child and given it away? God knew my parents were fornicators, and at least one of them had broken sacred vows. Those guilty of fornication, adultery, homosexuality and other sexual sins would not be permitted to inherit the kingdom of God. It was clear in the Bible, in St Paul's letters, repeated over and over, to the Corinthians, the Galatians, the Ephesians, the Colossians.

Did the Catholic Church have rules around nuns and priests having a child?

Could they be saved? Was confession an option?

I needed to find a straight-talking priest.

Chapter 26

MELBOURNE, LATE SEPTEMBER 2018

'Catholic Church rejects its own advice to lift veil of secrecy.' So read *The Age* headline, on 1 September 2018. The article was written by Joanne McCarthy, an investigative journalist I followed:

> The Australian Catholic Church has rejected the advice of its own Truth, Justice and Healing Council and refused to support lifting the veil of secrecy preventing priests from reporting child sex allegations heard in the confessional to police. Australian Catholic Bishops Conference president Archbishop Mark Coleridge strongly defended the church's rejection of a child abuse royal commission recommendation.

Two weeks earlier, on 14 August, the ABC reported that the Melbourne Catholic Archbishop, Peter Comensoli, said he'd 'rather go to gaol than report admissions of child sexual abuse made in the confessional'. It took time to absorb what Coleridge and Comensoli were saying. Had I heard it right? The church will protect child abusers from prosecution? They hadn't used those words, but in effect, that's absolutely what they were going to do. Australian clerics were prepared to go to extraordinary lengths to protect their own. Links to the articles were added to my spreadsheet; it'd be another twelve months before I summoned the gumption to cross swords with Archbishop Coleridge.

I'd put the feelers out to see if anyone within my networks could put me in contact with a down-to-earth priest. It wasn't going to be easy. Though many of my family and friends had been baptised Catholic, not a single one regularly attended mass. Not a single one could recommend a priest, down-to-earth or otherwise.

So, who knew about priests? Type 'Australian Catholic priest abuse' into a search engine and you'll find Broken Rites, an advocacy group, which 'since 1993 . . . has been researching the cover-up of sexual abuse in the Catholic Church', noting that 'too often, the church supported the offending clergy while ignoring the victims'. To date I'd put off saying to a stranger, 'This is going to sound strange, but . . . I've just discovered that I'm the son of a Catholic priest.'

I finally stumped up the courage to make the call to Broken Rites. To have the friendly but heard-it-all-before voice of Anne at the other end shoot back 'Yeah, my closest friend is, too' was a total liberation. We spoke for what felt like hours. 'Brendan, your story—if it was the script for a movie—nobody'd believe it!'

Anne assured me there were a number of Australian children of priests. She'd had contact with around a dozen, though she was sure there were many more, adding, 'If the church knows exactly how many, it hasn't made it public.' While I was initially (strangely) comforted to learn I wasn't alone, it was sobering to hear of the depth of the silent suffering of the mothers and their offspring.

As Anne explained, 'The trauma created by priests having children—and they almost always abandon them—has been overshadowed by the church abuse of minors . . . There's a stereotype of the mother of a child of a priest: vulnerable and younger. Just like your mother. The church has been highly effective in silencing both mothers and children. Victims simply aren't prepared to go public. So many of these people have been severely damaged, are unable, or incapable, of speaking up.'

Anne's final words were delivered to me in a measured voice: 'I'm not sure you want to hear this, Brendan, but I'd put money on Vincent having more than one child. It's what they did.'

The next weeks were spent in the library exploring clerical abuse, or 'black collar crime', as Broken Rites had dubbed it. When feeling frazzled, for (slightly) lighter relief I delved into the booming, life-altering world of 'misattributed parentage' uncovered by home DNA test kits (often referred to as the NPE community: Not Parent Expected). I also skimmed doctoral theses on adoption and rejection, and then reconnected with Vanish, twenty-five years after first contacting them. They pointed me to the just-commenced Victorian Parliament Inquiry into Historical Forced Adoptions, which served up oodles more traumatic materials . . . and without warning, I hit overload. It'd snuck up on me. I suddenly felt at risk of drowning in the betrayals and shame that were the bedrock of my reading. This line from Marilyn J. Sorensen played in my mind: 'Unlike guilt, which is the feeling of doing something wrong, shame is the feeling of being something wrong.' My three-times-a-week swimming routine was stepped up to daily plunges into the Harry Holt Pool, the water never failing to deliver some degree of clarity and lightening of my mood.

A fortnight later, Anne from Broken Rites called. She'd been approached by 'a trustworthy journalist' who wanted to do a story on someone heavily impacted by the church. 'You interested?' Joanne McCarthy had won a Gold Walkley Award

for her Fairfax Media reporting, which contributed to then prime
minister Julia Gillard initiating the 2013 Royal Commission into
Institutional Responses to Child Sexual Abuse. Joanne's *Newcastle
Herald* article on 22 September featured Dr Gerardine Robinson,
an internationally recognised Australian clinical psychologist. In
a submission to the royal commission in 2017, Robinson noted
that Australian clerical sex-abuse research closely replicated the
American finding that 'clearly indicates four times as many adult
women and twice as many adult men are sexually abused than
children'. I was shocked to learn that 'vulnerable men and women'
are the main target of abusive clergy, but research suggests that
at least five thousand men and ten thousand women had been
in secret sexual relationships or interactions with Australian
Catholic clergy over decades. The consequences for some have
been described as 'horrendous'.

Robinson's insights made it glaringly obvious to me: Maggie
might well have been a victim, the target of a predator. My
mother could be holding back a darker truth, to protect me from
my priest father. I began to regret judging her so harshly.

Kate and I debated whether or not I should participate in this
story, and, if I did, whether to do so anonymously. I'd left day-
to-day employment and by this time had shared my discoveries
with everyone whose opinion of me I cared about. But as Maggie
was very much alive up in sunny Queensland, protecting her was
a prime consideration.

Kate, Pat and Nell had lives, too. They were also liable to
experience unwanted attention. And although my adopted parents
were long gone, I realised there could be repercussions for Roy
and Bet's legacy, too. Initially I was gung-ho—the tough guy
coming out in the media with all guns blazing—but I slowly
recognised I might not be emotionally prepared for what could
follow. After all, I knew so little about Vincent. What if he was a

repeat offender, or worse? What if Anne was right and a litter of half-siblings came forward? I was beginning to comprehend the bravery of those who 'come out' publicly.

It took a week to decide. Perhaps I chickened out—I agreed to appear, but anonymously. Maggie's and Vincent's names, images and orders were withheld. A photographer was sent by Fairfax to take a photo of the back of my head.

Published in the *Newcastle Herald* on 21 September, the article, 'DNA and Ancestry.com exposes the lie of the Catholic Church's celibacy rule', gave a thumbnail version of my story and explored the same themes I'd been researching, that only fifty per cent of the Catholic clergy practise celibacy at any one time, and that the church had no intention of changing clerical celibacy laws, despite the recommendations of the royal commission. I was quoted saying:

> To have discovered what I did—double clergy—was a jolt but I would encourage others in the same situation to consider DNA . . . there will be many in the church with big secrets feeling very anxious that DNA may prove them to be flesh and blood, just like the rest of us.

The article went on: 'He led a successful life, in spite of the Catholic Church and its rules, that meant his parents could not acknowledge him as their child. "One of the most significant contributors to my success has been the love and devotion of my devout Catholic adoptive parents, which is somewhat ironic,"' I was quoted saying.

Over coming days, a couple of friends excitedly made contact. 'You'll never believe it—there's somebody else who's had an experience just like yours!'

'Duh! Didn't you recognise the back of my head? It was me!'

The next day I was fish-and-chip wrapping.

I'd taken my first tentative step into the public arena. If change was what I wanted—or at least to bring attention to some of what I was learning—I'd have to bide my time. There was still much to learn.

Little did I know that the article about me had filtered through to a number of prominent children of priests in the US, the UK and elsewhere in Australia.

Chapter 27

MELBOURNE, OCTOBER 2018

*'A priest is a man whom everybody calls "Father",
apart from his own children, who call him "Uncle".'*
—A SPANISH SAYING

I approached Births, Deaths and Marriages NSW and obtained a part-copy of Vincent's will. Though my application included the entire blow-by-blow account of my story and reams of documentary evidence, I was refused the 'inventory of assets' annexure detailing what my father owned, as I wasn't considered to be family.

The will appointed Vincent's 'housekeeper', Maggie Becker, and two Sydney lawyers to act as executors. The document provided for Maggie to live in his flat for as long as she wanted after his death. Then, after she'd 'permanently vacated' the flat, it was to be sold and the proceeds go to a bishop, several priests, the Shiel family church (St Joseph's, Rozelle) and the Mission of Charity in Darwin. Next, I purchased a fully detailed title of his flat. As expected, it showed that after Vincent's death Maggie and the lawyers (who in effect were representatives of the church interest in the property) were listed as joint owners.

Mysteriously, in 2005, before my mother finally agreed to talk to me, the lawyers resigned and Maggie became sole owner. She then immediately took a mortgage and jetted off on her first overseas holiday.

Clearly, I'm connecting dots, but why would the church consent to assign the title of their property to my mother? Was it in exchange for her silence about my paternity?

I made contact with a prominent Sydney lawyer, Dr Catherine Lynch. Catherine is an adoptee and president of the advocacy group Adoptees Rights Australia. Before calling, I did my usual background checks. She wasn't backward in coming forward, and she had a lot to say about inter-country adoption and forced adoptions. On adoptee inheritance (from birth parents), she said in an online interview (ipsify.com): 'Can you remind me why tiny babies are disinherited? It was something to do with not wanting bastard children to profit from their ungodly situation, I suppose.'

Catherine confirmed that there are only two groups in Australia who can be legally disinherited by their parents: criminals who murder their parents, and adoptees. 'But that's the last thing on adoptees' minds when they go searching. To know who you are and where you come from is a universal need. What adoptees seek is truth, recognition, knowledge of origins and ancestry, and to heal the trauma caused by maternal separation after growing up in the closed records system.'

I'd learned thirty years earlier that as an adoptee I had no right to be notified of my mother's death or to claim a single memento, not even a photograph.

I'd read that many adoptees striving to claim their rightful place in the world—as well as numerous children of priests— want both of their birth parents listed on their birth certificate and their own name added to their parents' death certificates. While

I identified with the sentiment, I felt that as Vincent didn't want me at birth, and my mother had been the single most reluctant participant in my life, neither of them were worthy of sharing a certificate with my name on it. That honour would put them on equal footing with Roy and Bet—I'd never let that happen.

The more I spoke with Catherine, the more I saw the most Reverend Father Vincent Shiel's hypocrisy for what it was. He'd gotten off scot-free; his funeral was attended by bishops, no less; he was buried with his reputation intact and would have been lauded for leaving a windfall to the church. Maggie was left to deal with the repercussions. I began to sense that the church receiving my venerable father's estate was perpetuating a cynical Catholic heist.

So, what does clerical celibacy have to do with money? Plenty, it would seem. I learned that several popes had fathered children (why wasn't this on my school Religious Instruction curriculum?) and that in the eleventh century, Pope Benedict VIII, in response to a decline in clerical morality, introduced a church law that specifically prohibited priests' children from inheriting property. As acclaimed French economist Thomas Piketty described in *Capital and Ideology*, priests could marry and reproduce up until the twelfth century, but then celibacy was introduced and family influence on priests waned. Of far greater significance, celibacy avoided wealth passing from priests to dependent families. Unsurprisingly, the church then boomed for several centuries. It could offer ordination as a legitimate means out of poverty for the impoverished. Stopping priests from (officially) procreating gave the church enormously increased revenues, which in turn enhanced its political influence. This funded an unprecedented church-building program, which helped attract waves of aspiring priests, nuns and brothers. I wasn't convinced by the counterview promoted by the church, that the original motivation for clerical celibacy was to reduce distraction and therefore make priests more available to God.

As a general rule, nuns take vows of poverty, chastity and obedience, but, unsurprisingly for the male-centric Catholic Church, most priests don't take a vow of poverty. Quite a number of children of priests feel cheated that their father died and left nothing to them or their mother; others are angered by a general lack of opportunity in life caused by the strained financial circumstance of their upbringing. While it's difficult to locate any official data, it appears most priests leave their estate to the church.

Though a priest's periodic stipend is small, some enter the seminary with considerable assets. (How many would join if the church stripped assets at the door?) A number will also inherit from parents, siblings and relatives during their tenure. As it happens, my father was already a successful businessman. In his civilian life he'd amassed a reasonably large estate. He had once owned three houses in Sydney. The estate was left to the church. To be clear, I do not want his money, but I am his only child, and as far as we know, my children are his only grandchildren.

An article in the US *National Catholic Reporter* titled 'Celibacy advances the priesthood's culture of compromised truths' hit the nail on the head: 'Celibacy contributes to a culture of mendacity [a tendency to lie] in the priesthood.' It quotes the 2016 novel *Strange Gods: A Novel About Faith, Murder, Sin and Redemption*, co-authored by Catholic priests John F Myslinski and Peter J Daly, in describing how 'Celibacy leaves a wound . . . Some priests drown their sorrows in alcohol or pills. A lot of them overeat and get obese. . . . Some guys travel all the time to escape. Others take secret lovers. Some redecorate the rectory over and over again. That's a classic clerical tradition, decorating. Just look at all the frescoes in the Vatican. It's a kind of retail therapy that has been going on for centuries.'

A few weeks had passed since learning about Vin's will, and I kept researching, ruminating on how to clear these roadblocks. Bloody-minded, I made a second attempt to obtain Vincent's inventory of assets, and this time I also requested his death certificate. If he had other children, who may have found him first, they could be noted on the Births, Deaths and Marriages files.

The request was denied. I called and received the most bizarre of bureaucratic waffle-slaps: 'In the eyes of the law you are not your father's son.'

I made a formal appeal of the decision. Two weeks later, the appeal was declined. They wanted DNA evidence that I was related to a man who was six feet under in the Priest Circle of the Field of Mars Cemetery.

I stopped to ask myself what I was hoping to achieve. My conclusion was that I hated the feeling of invisibility, of being locked out. I wanted acknowledgement. As the product of a closed adoption, denied contact by my birth mother, and DNA then leading to a priest father—and a cavalcade of lies throughout—I decided it was my time to be let in, even if I had to kick the door down.

I asked Kate to call Maggie. Did she put aside a memento of my father for his son? Maybe his watch? I wanted to know what became of his personal effects. There must be more photos, papers, his driver's licence? I hoped Maggie had tucked away some keepsakes, perhaps his chalice or crucifix? I'd been pestering Maggie for contact in the years immediately prior to Vincent's death—she must have realised I'd appreciate a remembrance of him? She could easily have arranged for her lawyer to send me something after her passing: assuming DNA didn't identify my father.

'Everything is gone,' Maggie told Kate. 'The only possession that remained of Vincent's was the single photograph of him that I mailed to Brendan a month or so ago.'

Vincent had changed his will three months before his death. Maggie said 'he'd assumed that even though the church was going to receive the lot', they'd allow her to remain in the flat after his death. She was fifty-nine when he died. She had no assets. She'd have had to rely on the generosity of others to supplement her small income as a housekeeper, and bide her time until eligible for the pension.

At this time, a close family member had cast doubt on Vincent's confidence about Maggie's access to his flat, and so a late revision to the will was made, only weeks before his death. A relative had put it to him straight: 'You need to do the decent thing. You'd have been dead years ago if it weren't for Maggie looking after you!'

The new will provided lifetime accommodation. But not the title to the property.

Chapter 28

SYDNEY, 20 DECEMBER 2018

I made a quick stop at Gundagai to grab a double-shot latte. Kate and I were on the Hume, heading south to Melbourne after a few days in Sydney. Coming down from a giddy high, I needed the caffeine to get us back to Melbourne in one piece. We'd just met the first of my paternal relatives: Peter Meaney and two new insta-cousins, Sue and Louise.

Over recent months, conversations with Peter had become increasingly candid. It had been a one-way flow of photos, stories and secrets—he revealed everything, while I had little to offer, except the truth. 'Pete, I'm not going to ask that you keep it a secret—secrets created this debacle. But you need to understand the magnitude of Maggie's shame. We must respect her privacy. I don't know what to think about her. Anger is the too-easy default.' The truth did not come as a shock to Peter.

We'd agreed to begin our day at the place where my father's illustrious journey ended, his burial plot at the Field of Mars Cemetery. After a bear hug in the cemetery car park, Peter pressed into my hands a professionally printed hardcover photo album chock-full of images of Vincent, Maggie, my paternal grandparents and assorted relatives. I cherish it, but equally, I am forever grateful for the sense of acceptance I felt on that day.

Fully caffeinated, I jumped back behind the wheel. Kate returned to her slumber, reclined in the passenger seat. My mind drifted to the photo album and one image in particular: a sepia-tinged Shiel family portrait, proudly posing on the deck of the SS *Oronsay* on 17 August 1935. The ship, docked in Sydney Harbour, would arrive in London in five weeks' time, and 33-year-old Vincent Shiel would disembark. Vincent had a letter in his pocket from Bishop McCabe of Port Augusta, South Australia, addressed to the Reverend Rector of Mount Melleray Abbey, a Trappist monastery on the slopes of the Knockmealdown Mountains in Ireland. It stated that Vincent Bede Shiel wished to become a priest, and due to his advanced age, had agreed to pay all expenses necessary for his studies, travel and accommodation. McCabe believed Vincent would benefit from Theology and Philosophy education in Ireland. He requested the support of the Reverend Rector to ensure Vincent's success.

In the remarkable bon voyage portrait of the Shiels, McGoogans, Meaneys, Halls and Mulligans, the sun is high; a shadow is cast over some of the twenty-four well-wishers. All are dressed against the winter air in buttoned-up Sunday-best suits, coats and hats. Keeping with the tradition of the era, no toothy smiles are visible, though the group does radiate an unmistakable pride: the youngest of the Shiel clan is the first in the family to offer his life to the Lord.

Vincent is the tallest. Dressed in a sombre black suit, he wears a large, broad-brimmed, felt hat. Vincent's headwear is distinctive, even flamboyant, and identical to his father's. He is flanked by his parents, Margaret and Francis. Margaret stands closest to her son. 'We were more attached, and I was always the loved one,' he wrote of her.

My grandmother's death notice in *The Southern Cross*, 31 January 1947, recorded:

> It was the most illustrious day of her long life when she was able, in 1942, to enjoy the pleasure of attending the offering of his first mass in Australia by her priestly son, Fr. (Vin) Shiel, celebrated in the family church of his baptism and confirmation, upon his arrival back home after his ordination at St. Mary's Cathedral, Kilkenny, Ireland.

Though Margaret's heart swelled with pride on the deck of the *Oronsay*, Vincent was despondent. Not wanting to leave his ageing parents and close-knit family, he'd hoped to study for the priesthood in New South Wales. Unfortunately, no seminary in Australia would accept a man of his 'advanced years'. Regardless, grand things were expected of Margaret's golden child. England, Ireland and Italy beckoned—to sea he must go.

Margaret was born in Callan, Kilkenny, Ireland, in 1859. As a young woman, she chose to take a perilous voyage in the sailing ship *La Hogue* to reach Australian shores. Shortly after arriving, she married Francis Shiel, who had also immigrated to Sydney from Ireland at a similar time. Over the next twenty years they produced fourteen children, a number typical of the era, though only half survived to adulthood. Francis was a dynamo. He landed in Sydney Harbour as a twenty-one-year-old and headed inland to Orange. It's thought he succeeded as a gold prospector, or on the railways, as he returned to Sydney only a few years later and purchased land in Rozelle, where he built what's referred to as 'the family home' in Oxford Street. Working as a

coal and wood merchant, he went on to purchase thirteen properties in and around Sydney. By the time the Great Depression had
ended, he'd lost most of them.

My great-great-great-grandfather was Murtagh, born in 1760.
He was convicted of horse theft during an Irish rebellion, and
though married with six dependent children, was sentenced to life
in the colonies. Placed on a ship in Cork Harbour, he set sail for
Port Jackson in 1800. After several years in Sydney, he was granted
a conditional pardon by Governor Lachlan Macquarie. He lived
as a free man and had a son, the first Shiel born on Australian
soil, James. Murtagh died at seventy-five, having never seen his
wife, children or beloved Ireland again.

As the *Oronsay* eased from the pier at Woolloomooloo, Vincent
waved to his mother, her face glistening with tears. Though
she was despondent he would not sire children of his own, she was
certain he would bring respect to the Shiel name for generations
to come. As he stretched and craned to wave, Vincent caught a
final glimpse of his father, Francis. It was the last time he set eyes
on his dear dad.

Gathering pace, the ship glided alongside the Royal Botanic
Gardens to Mrs Macquarie's Chair on the shore. Did Vincent
know that more than a century earlier it was Mrs Macquarie's
husband, Lachlan, who had granted freedom to his great-great
grandfather, Murtagh?

Over the previous two decades, World War I, a global pandemic
and the Great Depression had inflicted previously unimaginable
suffering. Although the masses craved peace, further calamity was
in the air. The mighty *Oronsay* was destined to run the London–
Sydney–Melbourne route until World War II erupted four years
later, and would be hastily redeployed as a troop carrier until
torpedoed by an Italian submarine in 1942.

As the ship built up steam, it entered Sydney Harbour proper. With seagulls swooping and squawking above, Vincent saw on the port side the remarkable Sydney Harbour Bridge, completed three years earlier. It symbolised the hope of a modern Australia. The *Oronsay* then turned east to the Pacific Ocean and then north, headed for Europe. Vincent's destiny lay ahead.

Damien, my big brother (right), and me in 1961. Our family was more forgiving than the majority of my friends' families who all shared DNA—did we unconsciously try harder?

School days, 1975. The upside of adoption was I felt limitless. There was no compulsion to follow footsteps as there were none to follow.

Beatrice (Bet) Watkins, my mother, 1950s. Right up to the end she possessed a deeply empathetic smile.

Roy Watkins, my father, 1950s. He could talk with anyone, remembered jokes and loved nothing more than spending time with family and friends.

Sailor boys with Bet, 1963. It has only recently struck me how often my brother and I were dressed identically as young kids.

First Communion at Immaculate Conception Church, Hawthorn, 1969.

Damien and me, 1970s. Guess who got PJs for Christmas?

My boyhood friend Mitch, girlfriend Kate and me on the back step of the family home, 1990s.

Strongly influenced by books as an adolescent, I was keen to visit the home of W. Somerset Maugham, in Cap Ferrat, France, 1988.

Left: In a Paris photo booth, 1992.
Above: Kate and me about to fly to Europe, 1992.

Kate's parents, Marg and Brian, with our young son, Pat, 1994.

Roy with Pat in his
first Richmond kit,
1995.

George Pell conducts the 50th wedding anniversary mass for Roy and Bet, and many others, at St Ignatius Church, Richmond, 2001.

My daughter, Nell, and her grandfathers, Brian (left) and Roy, 2003.

Bet and Roy, likely after a long family lunch, 1980s. This is how I always remember them.

A few months after discovering my father in 2018, I quit my job and committed to spending a year investigating him and the children of priests. One year became five.

Vincent Shiel, my birth father, as a trophy-winning ballroom dancer, 1920s.
Courtesy Shiel and Meaney families

Vin Shiel's passport photograph, 1935. The Sydney house builder sailed to the United Kingdom and entered an exclusive late-vocation Roman seminary. Courtesy Shiel and Meaney families

Vin (second from left) and family as he prepares to sail to the United Kingdom, 1935. Courtesy Shiel and Meaney families

. ADELAIDE, Saturday. — Radium Hill's new Catholic church - school is unique, thanks to a former North Bondi lifesaver.

The architect is a priest, so is the builder, the bricklayer, the joiner, the plasterer, the painter, and the plumber!

What is more, they are all the same priest— Father Vincent Shiel.

As a member of North Bondi Life Saving Club Father Shiel personally rescued or had a hand in rescuing more than 100 people.

Father Shiel was an architect for some years before he began to study for the priesthood.

"The Southern Cross," a Catholic Church journal, says that he has never let either his ideas or his hands grow rusty.

Radium Hill, important S.A. uranium mining centre, is hundreds of

HE IS EIGHT MEN 'IN ONE!

miles from the sea, but, in a spiritual sense, Father Shiel is continuing his "lifesaving."

He had to make and lay every one of the 42,000 bricks for the church-school, yet he took only seven months on the job.

His efforts saved the parishioners £6,350. The actual cost was £2,000.

4 November 1956 *The Sydney Morning Herald* article about my birth father's exploits as a priest in Radium Hill.

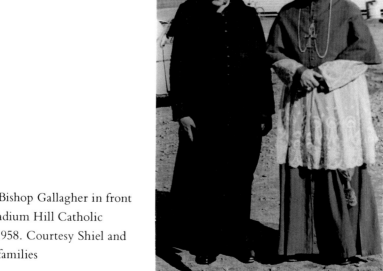

Vin and Bishop Gallagher in front of the Radium Hill Catholic School, 1958. Courtesy Shiel and Meaney families

Father Vincent Bede Shiel, 1960s. A man with a secret: a hidden son. Courtesy Shiel and Meaney families

THE SOUTHERN CROSS

● ORGAN OF THE CATHOLIC CHURCH IN SOUTH AUSTRALIA

THE OTHER MEMBER OF YOUR FAMILY

Established 1889

Published Weekly

VOL. LXVII, NO. 3445   FRIDAY, OCTOBER 26, 1956   Registered at the G.P.O., Adelaide, for transmission by post as a newspaper.   PRICE SIXPENCE

RADIUM HILL'S UNIQUE CHURCH

● **THE Church-School blessed and opened at Radium Hill on Tuesday evening, Oct. 2, by Mgr. M. B. Clune, Vicar-General of the Port Pirie Diocese, in the absence of His Lordship Bishop Gallagher, must be unique amongst all the churches of Australia.**

FATHER SHIEL

The architect was a priest; the builder was a priest; the brick-maker was a priest; the carpenter was a priest; the bricklayer was a priest; the joiner was a priest; the plasterer was a priest; the painter was a priest; the plumber was a priest. That would be sufficient to make it unique. But there is more to it than that. The architect, the builder, the brickmaker, the carpenter, the bricklayer, the joiner, the plasterer, the

(BY OUR SPECIAL REPORTER)

ing of two rooms, bathroom, laundry and kitchen, is of concrete solid returns. It has a hip-skillion roof, and "all mod. cons." are included—electric light, water laid on; hot and cold water, septic tank. The bricks were all 9 x 4 x 3½, as the nature of the ground (alluvial limestone) made it necessary to erect a particularly strong building. The main part of the building is 65 ft. x 20 ft., with a vestry 20 ft. x 14 ft. 6 in.

SEVEN MONTHS A'BUILDING

The church-school-convent was only seven months from drawing-board to opening. All of the 42,000 bricks were made on the premises, Fr. Shiel working all day and every day—apart from necessary parochial duties. He carted the sand for the bricks, made them, and then, with his own hands, laid every one of the 42,000. He made the doors and windows, did the plastering and the putty-coating, put the roof on, and painted the building. At the weekends he received great help from

ADMIRATION AND AMAZEMENT

No wonder, then, there was joy at Radium Hill on the night of the opening, and joy the next morning on the feast of the Little Flower, when the first Mass was celebrated in the newly-blessed church by Mgr. Clune. No wonder Mgr. Clune expressed admiration and amazement at the unique achievement of Fr. Shiel.

From the financial viewpoint alone Fr. Shiel's efforts saved his parishioners £6,350. The cost of building had it been erected by contract would have been £8,350. The actual cost was £2,000.

Fr. Shiel expressed particular gratitude to Mr. Terry O'Connell for absolutely unfailing help after work every day and at every weekend, to his other constant helpers, Mr. Ted Colligan, Mr. Tighe Fleming, Mr. Frank Kelly, Mr. George Milling, Mr. Marco Pradel, Mr. Angelo Trettai, and Mr. Angelo Leßso, and to all others who assisted him.

10 NATIONALITIES

Fr. Shiel's congregation, though

A newspaper article describing my birth father's church as 'unique amongst all the churches of Australia', 1956.

Vin's cross and hand-stitched book of Latin rites, a thoughtful gift from one of Vin's devout supporters, 2020.

The destination of our failed 2019 trek, my father's hand-built church,
Our Lady Queen of the World, Radium Hill.

Friends I've known for decades, Frank, Sandy and Mitch, with Kate and me in Quorn, Easter 2019.

At the Immaculate Conception Church, Quorn, Palm Sunday, Easter 2019—everything changed on that day.

Chapter 29

MELBOURNE, 21 DECEMBER 2018

'Do you look like your cousins? Do they look like us?' Back in Melbourne, Kate and I sat down for breakfast with the kids (hardly kids now, one twenty-four, the other twenty-two). They wanted to hear every detail of my first paternal family meeting.

'Well, not really,' Kate told them, 'but they said that your dad very closely resembles Maggie at a similar age, and he has lots of expressions and mannerisms *exactly* like Vincent. He stands and carries himself just like his father.'

'It was a jolt really, to feel accepted by birth family,' I added. 'They welcomed me with open arms. That's never happened before—I've always felt like I was imposing myself with Maggie.'

Passing the photo album around, we pointed out not only my paternal ancestors, but theirs as well. 'What's perplexing is knowing Vincent and Maggie didn't want the people in the photos we're looking at to ever be my family . . . or our family. I feel I've forced entry into this group of strangers . . . I let myself say "my mother" and "my father" when talking with Peter, Sue and

Louise, but I couldn't bring myself to say "my grandparents"—I'm not sure why. I think I'll always feel like an interloper.'

The fact is that Francis and Margaret Shiel, my grandparents, would have been appalled at the appearance of Father Golden Child's Bastard Son. The contrast with our little family was so stark.

'Though I share DNA with these people, we don't have a single shared experience.'

'What was fabulous, though, is I got a much better sense of Maggie and Vincent's relationship. From what we heard, they really had larger-than-life personalities back in their day. And they went everywhere together. Even though Maggie was officially referred to as his "housekeeper" or "carer", it's obvious there were lots of raised eyebrows. There was even a family drama once when an uncle said out loud—after Maggie moved in with Vincent—"She's shacking up with her de facto!"' It was an outrageous thing to say about a priest and ex-nun—but it said a lot about their relationship, and how it was perceived by some of those closest to them. Cousin Louise even confided that she'd always seen Vincent and Maggie's relationship as 'a great secret love story'.

I tried to boil down the main impressions, and the common views held by my cousins. 'All three adored Maggie and were either ambivalent or cold toward Vincent—Sue idolised Maggie. She said Maggie was friendly. Fun. Sporty. They were so sad to learn I'd never seen that side of her.' I couldn't help adding, 'And so am I.'

According to Peter, I told them, Father Vincent played favourites, and Peter wasn't one of them. 'He was bossy and dogmatic, but Maggie softened his rough edges. He always expected to get what he wanted.' He'd become financially successful in the building game when he was in his twenties. The family theorised that that's what made him so comfortable wielding power, and after ordination, he used the authority provided by his religious robes to dictate terms.

'Vincent did enjoy spending time with nieces and nephews,' I went on. 'Sue shared a story of visiting him at Radium Hill when she was about thirteen. She and her sister loved travelling the desert tracks in the back of Vincent's ute—there was little more than red dust for hundreds of kilometres. One day in the middle of nowhere, he pulled off the track and told the girls it was time they learned how to shoot. He stomped off into the scrub and stood a few bottles up on a rise for the girls to blast away at.' Sue had gone first. Under instruction from Vincent, she purposefully took her stance and pointed the big shotty at the bottle glinting in the sun. Unbeknown to her, she'd placed one foot on a bull ants' nest. Realising in panic that the somehow familiar (but hard to immediately place) sensation on her legs was angry ants, she'd thrown her arms heavenward and the shotty discharged. Fortunately there was no need for Father Vincent to administer the last rites.

They had been wide-eyed reminiscing about the excitement that'd buzz through the families whenever Father Vincent announced he was coming to town. 'He'd invariably call from some South Australian outpost, barking orders to my cousins' parents: "Pick me up at the airport tomorrow at 6 pm. And I feel like roast lamb for dinner! And iron a shirt! We'll all be off to the races at Randwick on Saturday!"'

It seemed every visit included racing, be it dogs, horses or the trots—whatever was going. Before leaving for the track he'd conscientiously change his clerical robes for civvies. Though they'd been happy to share it with me, the family insisted they'd never mentioned his duplicity at the time.

'Father Vincent bet big money, and he'd bet on every race. He gave the kids money to gamble with, too! They said it was always a time to remember when Vincent returned home from the desert.

'When he'd gone back to South Australia and the commotion had died down, they'd theorise about where the money came from to fund his gambling.'

They were stumped as to how he managed to gain permission—not to mention the finances—for his European and American jaunts.

'It's funny,' I found myself speculating, 'I thought they'd have most of the answers, but the family have plenty of unanswered questions of their own.'

They had spoken fondly of working-class Rozelle and Balmain, where some of our mutual ancestors' first homes were. Balmain had once been the heart of Sydney's working-class culture. It's where the Australian Labor Party began. Now gentrified, Rozelle and Balmain are the class equivalent of our Richmond, the inner-city working-class suburb where Roy, Bet, Damien and I were from. I at least shared this cultural connection with the Shiel clan.

The Shiels and Meaneys also shared an intense connection to Ireland. There were many references to Guinness, Irish whiskey and stories of a huge Shiel family reunion that'd been held in Ireland three years ago. I found the Irishness impossible to relate to: Roy, Bet, Damien and I didn't share any reminiscences of any 'old country'. In place of ancestral mythology, we'd made our own traditions. My cultural heritage began on the day I was born: I was a Tiger from Richmond, end of story.

Kate took up the story. 'The Meaneys had lost touch with Vincent some years before his death . . . that was in 1993. Maggie had also drifted away from the family around this time—I explained that was when Brendan had made first contact with Maggie. Both Vincent and Maggie were alive and living together then, and the Meaneys had made attempts to contact Maggie over the past twenty-five years—they were so fond of her—but they had been flatly rebuffed. They hadn't known why, but now they knew about Brendan, they told us it all made sense—back then they'd had no idea Brendan existed and now they couldn't fathom how Maggie and Vin had wanted nothing to do with their son. The secret was now out. Their overwhelming emotion was pity for Maggie.'

Both kids were silent but wide-eyed; the magnitude of the complex emotional journey we'd just returned from was slowly seeping in.

I summed up the visit as bittersweet. 'The trip underlined more differences than similarities.'

I'd certainly been buoyed to hear of the respectful relationship my parents had shared. Maybe they'd even been 'in love'—I'll never know. But as wonderful as it was hearing these tales, I felt like a bystander, on the outside looking in. I was enormously thankful to learn about my parents, but these weren't my family stories.

Vincent Shiel had entered a seminary at thirty-three and had remained a priest until his death at ninety. Nobody would know more about my father than the church and the surviving clerics and parishioners who knew him. I decided to tell the Catholic Church that their Father Vincent Shiel had a son.

Chapter 30

COOBER PEDY, OCTOBER 1983

Sipping black tea in the cool of the underground St Peter and Paul Catholic Church, Fathers Adrian and Frank awaited the arrival of Father Shiel. The now retired priest was making a flying visit to his old stomping ground and was keen to inspect the expansion works being carried out to the otherworldly church.

'Those were the days, Adrian—the roughhouse life of an outback diocesan priest will never come again. My parish included Ayers Rock and extended to the borders of WA, the NT, Queensland and New South Wales. Massive!'

Father Adrian nodded, content to listen to this oft-repeated reminiscence.

'Can you image me overseeing the church excavations here back in the sixties?' Father Frank said. 'They didn't know what to make of a missionary priest. I spent many a year sitting with opal miners, fettlers and road gangs smoking my pipe, talking about the neddies, mining and God. I didn't live underground till the church and presbytery were complete. I'd be in my tiny shed in dust storms and 100-degree heat for weeks on end—they liked it

that I could rough it. I finally won them over when I persuaded
a parishioner with a grader to carve out the racetrack—suddenly
the famous Coober Pedy Races were born! A few others and I
got things going in 1969, but I confess they never really took off
until we built the bar . . .'

The men nodded with knowing smiles.

'Of course, as soon as he got wind of the Coober Pedy Race
Day, Vinnie Shiel was drawn like a fly to a barbie. He'd stand on
the other side of the track thinking nobody'd know the lumpy,
bearded punter was a priest. Goose, everyone knew!

'Vinnie and I are a rare breed, Adrian. We'll die leaving these
remote houses of worship behind, and no more will be built.
I wrote to him the other day, and shared a story. I was heading
across to Andamooka to perform a funeral when two flat tyres
delayed my arrival by a couple of days . . . When I arrived, the
mourners were hastily reassembled for the burial, and we did
the job quick smart, nothing exceptional as it was stinking hot.

'Afterwards, over a cup of tea, a pimple-faced copper sidled
up to me and whispered that the corpse had been exposed to
the weather for too long and begun to decompose—there's no
refrigeration at Andamooka, of course—so they'd buried the poor
blighter before I got there. I looked the young copper in the eye
and asked, "So who or what have I just blessed and buried, my
boy?" It was a couple of bags of cement!'

The priests shook their heads and laughed.

As the chortling died down, Father Frank looked about,
muttering to himself, 'What's the time? Vinnie should be here
soon, hard to know if it's day or night down here. Yes, it's
3 pm . . . plane from Sydney will be in soon . . .'

'So, Adrian, what do you know of Vinnie Shiel?'

Walking back from the urn, Father Adrian carefully balanced
his refilled cup. He'd settled on the edge of a discarded crate left

by the builders. 'We both studied in Rome. I wasn't in Collegio Beda, where Vin was, but there was always much to chat about, comparing our European years and how removed it was from the experiences of the Fathers of the Desert—that's what he calls you lot. Vinnie is a determined man, an architect and builder, not your typical priest, as you'd know. Certainly not the serene, cautious type: discretion isn't his thing. Though he upset some of his bishops, he is a good man. I suppose he'll always be best known for the Radium Hill buildings.' He took a sip, lingering in thoughts. 'Awful country over there. Even though they told him not to, he built a brick church . . . instead of timber . . . he seemed to change around that time, after they shut that mine.'

For a few moments, silence filled the church, then Adrian went on, 'I admire that he taught himself to paint in recent years. Some good ones, too. I raffled off one . . . I believe he bought a house and lives there with a housekeeper. He says she's his niece. And he told me recently he now makes chocolates, too. What next?

'I'd heard he was engaged to be married before answering the call, but I'm not sure. He plays his cards close to his chest . . .' At that moment the thud of the entry door closing reverberated into the underground church chamber. A flash of light from above set stars in the eyes of the clerics. They rose as one and went to greet Father Vinnie, gingerly hobbling into the church proper.

'It's fortunate you showed up, Vinnie, your ears must have been burning.' said Frank. 'But first, happy birthday! Eighty years young! . . . I was just about to tell Adrian that tale of you visiting Archbishop Sheen in New York, remember? When he asked you to give a talk on his behalf in Los Angeles, as he was ill . . . ?'

Father Vin, full white beard, overweight, hair like a bird's nest, dressed in cream slacks and a short-sleeved white shirt, a small gold cross pinned to the collar, took the baton excitedly. 'Oh yes! You see, a car pulled up to collect me at the airport. An attractive woman in a mini skirt got out, opened my door, and said she was there to chauffeur me to the venue. I thought, Well, well! I've landed on my feet here, boys! Now, what was astonishing was on the way to the mass, and the later speaking engagement, I learned the woman was a nun! Sister Bernadette!' The three clerics guffawed as one.

'And then, after my speech, when walking back to the car, Sister Bernadette tugged at her short skirt—to stop it riding up you see—and she remonstrated to me angrily, "If the cap fits, wear it!" The message being to stop ogling her legs!' Vin let out a great snort at the thought. 'Now, when I got back to Archbishop Sheen in New York, I told him everything and he and I had a laugh about my big day out with Sister Bernadette. The mass I conducted was recorded and is occasionally played on TV in some parts of America on a Sunday.'

'That's the visit where the archbishop gave you his chalice that you used in the Far North?' asked Father Adrian. 'Do you still have it?'

'Ahh . . . it's a long story, gents. I believe the chalice is now in India,' responded Vin with a straight face. Fathers Frank and Adrian glanced at each other, puzzled. Vin chose not to elaborate.

Frank then explained to Adrian how the recently published autobiography of Archbishop Sheen included a profile of Vinnie. Again, Father Vin, with a mile-wide grin, jumped in to finish the story. 'Yes, yes, I've told some whoppers in my time, lads; I did say to the archbishop that due to the punishing heat all the miners up this way worked naked—I was half pulling his leg, half making a point about the heat! But sure enough, the book was published— all over the world, mind you—with me claiming our opal miners ran around town without any clothes!' Laughter again echoed up through the front doors of the church.

Nothing moved on the surface of Coober Pedy. The occasional far-off BOOM of gelignite was the only sound. Father Frank's old blue heeler, Nessie, lay in the red dust shaded by the church entrance. She raised an eyebrow at the merriment emanating from below, then returned to her daydreams.

Frank let a few moments pass, before more seriously enquiring, 'And have you received your stipend safely each month?' Frank managed the Sick Priests Fund, of which Shiel was a recipient.

'Yes, thank you,' Vincent reassured him. 'Though I've had issues with some Pommie bastard at the Social Security office. It's none of his business that I receive a pension from the diocese! I told him so, and he set the investigators on me. Why is it their business what I receive from my Broken Hill Investments? It's my money, and none of their business! Now, Frankie, can't you just deposit my regular stipend into my TAB account? I'm serious. Who'll know?

'My main source of pleasure these days is the races. The other week I had a big wager on a horse ridden by a roughie, a gal no less. Once she got out of the barriers my jockette was away. She hit the lead and kept it till the end—winner!' The old priest's eyes glistened, lost in his thoughts.

Frank shook his head. 'Tread carefully, Father Vinnie . . . idle hands are the devil's playthings.'

Later that evening, over dinner at a nearby hotel, it was apparent that Vin was not at ease. 'The church is going belly-up, lads. We've got more churches, convents and seminaries than we know what to do with, but we haven't anybody to run them. The sisters at Ryde orphanage are now talking of selling up— no orphans. You know, I was even admonished by my bishop for dispensing pastoral advice. For twenty years I've advised new grooms not to allow their bride to take the contraceptive pill: it leads to them wandering, having affairs with other men—I was told to keep my thoughts to myself!'

All three clerics looked in separate directions. The men could not conceal a sense of dread that their once mighty church, and indeed their own incontestable identity within society, was at a crossroads.

After dinner, apropos of nothing, Father Adrian asked Vin, 'Do you ever regret not having children, Father Vin?'

Chapter 31

MELBOURNE, CHRISTMAS 2018

I kept reminding myself: the sins of my father weren't mine. The child of a thief is no more guilty of a parent's crimes than is a stranger on a train. It was Father Vincent who impregnated a woman who was in his spiritual care and thirty years his junior. Father Vincent who arranged for my birth and adoption in Melbourne. Father Vincent who had Maggie swear never to never tell another soul.

We all crave love. Denial of physical touch, and sexual expression, is a twisted torture, and my parents were human. I could forgive them, two consenting adults, having a child. I could also forgive them surrendering that child—as hundreds of thousands of Australians did back then. What I really feared was my father being involved in the church sex-abuse scandals, news of which was swirling in the media. After reading some of the royal commission testimonies, it felt like every second priest was an abuser of some kind. I could have stopped my sleuthing at any time, but I was drawn to the truth, no matter the cost. Maybe

I was even looking for reasons to disown Vincent, as he had disowned me.

One night, I sat at the computer and googled 'Vincent Shiel' with the words 'conviction', 'abuse', 'allegation', 'guilty', 'crime', 'paedophile' . . . I held my breath as the verdict unspooled. Though hardly conclusive, it was a relief when there were no matches. But what if he'd been accused of crimes that hadn't progressed through a legal process? What if the church had paid off accusers, as the royal commission demonstrated it had done repeatedly?

Trust in institutions, politicians and those in positions of authority has been damaged like at no other time in modern history. The most vulnerable in Australian society have been exploited on an industrial scale. In the last three decades we've seen royal commissions into: Aboriginal Deaths in Custody, Institutional Responses to Child Sexual Abuse, Aged Care Quality and Safety, and Violence, Abuse, Neglect and Exploitation of People with Disability. Of all the time-honoured figures of respect, none have fallen as far as our religious leaders, particularly the Catholics.

In late 2018, I approached the Catholic Church. After several calls and emails over five weeks, during which I felt I was being given the run-around, I was eventually directed to Dr Tanja Stojadinovic, Director of the South Australian Catholic Professional Standards Office. As anticipated, the church requested exhaustive evidence that their Father was also my father. I forwarded the letters between myself and Maggie, in which she confirmed his identity, my original birth certificate, adoption records, DNA data, photographs and Kate's genealogical roadmaps. Communication went back and forth in the weeks leading up to Christmas. There was no doubting Vincent was my father, but as I didn't have a sample of his DNA, I wasn't anticipating cooperation.

My estimation of Tanja was she was open-minded and empathetic. (Ominously, LinkedIn revealed that her previous role was with the Survivors of Trauma and Torture.) She heads up an 'independent' agency, though fully funded by the church, which was established after the royal commission to provide those making complaints against the church with a way to be heard. Not surprisingly, survivors of church abuse don't want to make complaints about priests to fellow priests (as had been the case previously).

Tanja called. She opened with these words: 'Father Vincent Shiel has never been involved in, or alleged to have been involved in, inappropriate behaviour. Nor has he fathered any children— aside from you, Brendan.'

My father's records were clean—I was euphoric. She also relayed that the church recognised Vincent as my father. Though it came as a jolt every time, I was chuffed that Tanja, and priests I later connected to, always referred to Vincent as 'your father'. Tanja had read the church records in their entirety. She said that in most of the letters Vincent received, and nearly always when my father wrote to others, he was referred to as *Father Vin*.

'Okay,' I said to Kate that evening, 'from now on *Vincent* becomes *Vin*.'

The 'not guilty' news, of course, was muted, as my father had still broken his vow of celibacy and done so with a vulnerable woman. As Maggie was reluctant to give Kate details of my birth, other than to say Vin 'arranged for me to stay with a very poor family in Melbourne', I asked Tanja how Vin would have known who to contact in Melbourne to arrange Maggie's accommodation. How common was it for priests to organise for women to travel interstate, lodge with a 'discreet' family and then quietly give birth without anyone finding out?

Tanja had no idea. We kept up communication. Talking to her had a restorative value. When I told her about my reams of journals, spreadsheets and news articles about my complex ancestry, she exclaimed, 'There's a book in it!'

In our chats, Tanja kept referring to 'Vin's file'. It was where the character of my father would be revealed. With her support, I wrote to the diocesan bishop and asked for the file. Two weeks later, much to my astonishment, Tanja called; the church had agreed to provide full access. 'No Catholic diocese in Australia has ever agreed to a similar request,' she told me. 'This is unprecedented.'

There was a certain irony that while the Catholics were being vilified regularly in the media for secrecy and unconscionable behaviour, a remote branch of that church had just agreed to open its vaults on one of its own failed clerics. I was about to receive hundreds of my father's letters. I didn't have to employ a lawyer or threaten to go to the media. I was astounded.

Access to this father-lode of material was approved by the bishop of Port Pirie, Greg O'Kelly. As it turned out, in June 1935 my father had been adopted (church terminology) to study for the priesthood by one of the most progressive dioceses in the country. Without O'Kelly's consent, I would have had only glimpses of Vin's life through published materials and information from relatives. Much later I learned that the diocesan ethics committee that considered my request had recommended that all sensitive material be withheld or heavily redacted. But O'Kelly overruled them, directing that all documents be forwarded to me without restriction—there were no confidentiality agreements and no contracts. I will be forever grateful to Bishop O'Kelly. This wise man had learned from the mistakes of his predecessors.

On 23 January 2019, a large zip file with almost three hundred scanned PDFs pinged into my inbox. A few days later, a full set of printed copies arrived via registered mail. Those dusty old letters may have been the best Christmas present I'd ever received, a life-changing bounty.

The records span Vin's life from 1935 through to his final handwritten letter sent in 1992, nine months before his death. I marvelled at his correspondence, most of it in longhand, telling the story of a complex individual who'd spent the majority of his years in some of the most inhospitable parts of Australia.

Kate and I lounged in the sun in the backyard that summer, reading and discussing newspaper clippings, gazing at photos and poring over letters to and from my brand-new father. The majority of the letters were between Vin and assorted bishops and priests. The postmarks included America, Europe and—thanks to his seven years studying for the priesthood—Italy, England and Ireland. I was transfixed by his correspondence from outback South Australia: Coober Pedy, Woomera, Roxby Downs, Cook, Leigh Creek, Andamooka, Iron Knob, Quorn, Lock, Cleve, Hawker, the Nullarbor and what appeared to be his own sacred site—the Far North Catholic Inland Mission at Radium Hill.

We gradually became proficient at deciphering the distinctive quirks of his handwriting and language. The letters identified many new and intriguing people and locations, which opened abundant new avenues of online investigation that kept us busy late into the night.

Kate had done most of the hard yards over the past three years—it was my turn now. If it were not for Kate, I would have died without knowing who my birth father was. Few people have the chance to give that gift. She gave me our two adored children, my father, and maintained the most fragile of relationships with Maggie.

My life has been full. I've done a few out-of-the-ordinary things. But my exploits have been pedestrian compared to those of Father Vin. For a working-class lad from Balmain to have travelled the world and had such extraordinary experiences was startling. I would have been happy enough to learn that my new-found father was a bland suburban padre sitting mouse-like for fifty years, watching the footy before keeling over at a ripe old age. But what I'd got was the all-bells-and-whistles, windswept-and-interesting, broody holy man.

An intoxicating new chapter of my life had begun. The first task was to put the church correspondence into chronological order and incorporate it into the Becker-Shiel Super Duper Excel Spreadsheet. I then linked each PDF to a retyped summary cell. Click any cell and the source document popped up. The rapidly expanding spreadsheet created a shape, an outline, of my father. It also afforded a much-needed sense of control over him.

I then sat down and read my father's life story from thirty to ninety years of age. Hundreds of letters, thousands of words.

Maggie's name did not appear once.

Chapter 32

MELBOURNE, JANUARY 2019

There are 82,000 Google results for 'Archbishop Fulton Sheen', a name that recurred throughout Vin's letters, and just thirty-one for 'Father Vincent Shiel'. Roughly half of Vin's results relate to Sheen's autobiography. Hoping to find a mention of my father, I bought *Treasure in Clay: The Autobiography of Fulton J. Sheen*. It didn't disappoint.

AUSTRALIAN DESERT

Another friend of mine, who worked among the primitive people [*sic*] in Australia, was Father Vincent Shiel. This missionary, slightly beyond middle age, came to my office with this story. 'I am a missionary in the desert district of 125,000 square miles in Australia. Only two classes live there: sheepherders and opal miners. The opal miners are naked and live underground, cutting holes in the walls for places to sleep. I have no rectory, other than my Volkswagen. The heat in the desert averages about 125 degrees. Almost the only kind of food I can carry are cans of peaches. It seems that any other kind explodes in the desert.

'I asked my bishop if I might become a Trappist; he refused. I then sought his permission to visit you in America, to tell you why I wanted to become a Trappist, namely, because I felt I had failed some of my people in the desert.' The bishop agreed that if I saw in him a vocation to the Trappists, he might join the community to do penance for any remissness in pastoral duties.

When I asked him to describe his life to me further, it developed that, in crossing the desert, he would sometimes be 350 miles or more from a single human being. In one crossing, a stone flew up and cracked his battery, making further journey impossible. The limit of life, he told me, walking in such heat without food and drink, would be less than a day. There was nothing to do but pray for help or resign oneself to death. As he leaned his head over the steering wheel, making his act of resignation to God, he heard the rumble of a truck in the distance. The truck was carrying a spare battery and thus his life was saved.

After hearing the unimaginable sacrifices he was making for his people, and learning that he would often go down into the opal mines to read Mass for his people and instruct them, I said: 'My dear Father, I think that you are looking for a plastic cross instead of a wooden one.' By that I meant that there was no sacrifice he could make in an ascetic community which could equal the sacrifices he was making in the desert. Just a few moments before, I had given him a personal check to buy a new Volkswagen (Kombi), since he had told me that the one he owned when he left was swept away in a flood. But he tore up the check and left, showing considerable resentment against my reference to the 'plastic cross'.

A few weeks later he came back and apologized, saying: 'You were right; I am fleeing from a difficult mission. I shall return and give my life.' This he has done, and to such a noble

extent that it is difficult to find anyone who will take his place
in that desert mission.

I read it once, twice and again. That hot-headed desert missionary
in Sheen's elaborate account was my father. Months earlier, in a
tone of reverence, Maggie had confirmed Vin and Sheen were
close. He had visited the American several times. The archbishop
paid for some of Vin's international travel. I had no clue who he
was, but it turned out my father's admirer was one of the world's
first televangelists.

In the 1950s, Sheen boasted a weekly TV audience of thirty
million. It's easy to view episodes of *Life Is Worth Living* on
YouTube. He entertained presidents, royalty and celebrities. He
was an A-lister who'd appeared on the cover of *Time* magazine,
written seventy-three books and won two Emmys. He was a
decorated theologian and philosopher . . . and my dad's mate.
Why? I couldn't imagine the Father Vin I had in my head,
a cantankerous ex-builder with a gambling problem, rubbing
shoulders with this slick showbiz character and his cronies. Had
I jumped to conclusions too early?

Sheen was renowned for quotable quotes. 'Hearing nuns'
confessions is like being stoned to death with popcorn' was one
of them. Clearly, he hadn't taken confession from my mother. (Or
my father, for that matter.) Millions of Americans idolised Sheen,
and in 2002 the US church began the process of nominating
Sheen for canonisation. Pope Francis personally approved Sheen's
purported miracle. The beatification, however, has not been
completed; it has recently been suggested Sheen's lax investigation
into a priest's sexual misconduct case, back in 1963, could cast a
shadow over his elevation.

I read Sheen's autobiography in amazement; my vow-breaking
father hung with a now-in-question maybe-saint. What next?

Vin's letters showed how he leveraged the friendship with Sheen to obtain approval for lengthy time away from his stultifying desert parish. At one point he wrote to his bishop reporting that Sheen had offered to bring him over to the United States, all expenses paid. He joking-not-jokingly advised his bishop that he'd answer to God and risk his reputation with Sheen if he didn't let Vin go to America, and then closed off respectfully.

How could the bishop refuse?

In 1979, only weeks before Sheen's death, Vin was in New York. He sent a postcard of the Empire State Building to his bishop in Australia. It opens with a one-liner comparing the architectural magnificence of the toilet block he'd built at Radium Hill to the iconic New York landmark. He then relayed news of Sheen's declining health. Nobody was allowed to visit, though an exception had been made for the Australian padre. He'd bought his 'very close friend' a sheepskin bed rug that delighted the archbishop. The reference to the bedding indicated a certain intimacy, something else that didn't fit with the man in my head.

From my reading, Sheen was firstly a celebrity entertainer, and secondly an evangelical priest. A salesman for God, expert at painting persuasive word pictures. In Sheen's account, Vin is portrayed as some sort of crucifix-wielding Indiana Jones. How much of it was embellished? Is that who Vin was, or who he pretended to be?

What correlated closely to Vin's own letters, though, was Sheen's picture of a driven, hot-headed individual. Did Vin need to suffer for his sins? After the hardships of the desert, why would anyone want to become a Trappist, rather than insist on a transfer to Sydney, or resign?

If my father was a man who had to atone, what was his crime? Maggie? Me? Something, or someone, else?

Chapter 33

MELBOURNE, APRIL 2019

I didn't want to embrace Vin for fear of him breaking my heart.

Maybe I was jumping at shadows, or maybe I had too much time on my hands, but due to my research, and the comment from Broken Rites, I feared Vin may have fathered other children. And I still wasn't convinced he wasn't involved in church sex-abuse issues. Like many of my friends, I felt that most priests were either guilty or complicit in some way.

What was happening in Vin's and Maggie's lives in the 1950s? I dug out Vin's letter from 1954 requesting a transfer to the Trappist order: the perfection of contemplation. There's no record of a response from the bishop, but as Vin continued in the Far North for decades, the request was obviously denied.

In August 1953, Vin had tuberculosis and travelled to Sydney for assessment. The next letter, six months later, shows him still in Sydney, recuperating. Three months after that he writes asking to be transferred to the Trappists. What brought about this decision? It was a momentous pivot, a full five years before I was conceived.

Was it his failing health, or had something happened between him and Maggie?

I went to Maggie's file. A newspaper clipping from the mid-fifties celebrated an intake of new nuns. 'The South Australian Postulants who received the habit were . . . Vincent (Maggie Becker) . . .' Did my parents have, or want to have, an affair in 1952 or 1953? At that point, Maggie was just nineteen, Vin forty-nine. Did they both take flight, she to a convent and he to an order of contemplation? Whatever the motivation, Maggie entered the convent in 1953 and recognised my father by taking the name Sister Vincent. Sister Vincent and Father Vincent.

She resigned when a second-year novice. I was conceived mid-1960, well before she entered the later order. My knee-jerk response was to disbelieve her story. When she entered the second, far stricter order, my mother chose the name Sister Vincent a second time. She remained in that order for twenty-five years, an extraordinary act of penitence. Shortly after leaving the convent, she received my first letter.

After decades of deceit from Maggie, I wasn't going to take anything about my birth family at face value. Despite my genuine respect for Tanja, I wanted further proof that Vin's file was 'clean'. It was unavoidable—inevitable—that I would scratch the dirt in Father Vin Shiel's South Australian desert diocese. There must be people out there who knew my father. What secrets would the desert offer up?

While packing for the trip, I pondered what to bring. The bed was covered with the gear I'd need. The first things I packed were Vin's letters: our roadmap. I contemplated what I'd learned so far. My newly ordained father had been forty when he received his first clerical appointment. Like all late vocation priests, he was an oddity; he'd lived a full civilian life and was ten years older than other first-year clerics.

As for me, I was now approaching sixty. I placed multiple t-shirts, shorts and jeans on the bed. I held up some shorts. Were his the same size as mine? He was solid, and taller than most in the pictures we'd seen. There was no denying: physically, at least, we were similar.

The first thing Vin learned after returning from seven years in European seminaries was that his dad was dead and his dear 83-year-old mum had fallen and broken a hip. World War II had been raging while Vin was in Europe; his family hadn't received a single letter that he'd sent during the years abroad. All they'd been able to do was pray. He left Australia in 1935 and was ordained on 8 June 1941 in St Mary's Cathedral, Kilkenny, the church of his aged mother in her girlhood days. He arrived home in late 1942 and celebrated his first mass on Australian soil at the family church, St Joseph's Church, Rozelle.

During Christmas 1942, Bishop McCabe advised Vin to report for duties on 7 January 1943—he'd been appointed assistant priest at St Therese's Renmark, South Australia. He carefully packed his new robes, Bible, chalice and crucifix. He probably included some favourite tools, too; maybe a trusty hammer and saw had made their way back from Ireland? During his forty years as a priest, his letters suggest he did just as much building as preaching. He was proud of the building works, remarking on them frequently. Strikingly, there's not a single paragraph communicating any joy in performing the role of spiritual leader of his congregation.

We aimed to visit several of the locations noted in the June 1991 *Witness* magazine article titled 'Father Shiel, a mighty craftsman for our Lord: His foundation stone is Jesus':

> Father Vincent Shiel is one of the real goers of the Church
> in Australia . . . Fire devastated the Cathedral at Port Pirie,
> so he was sent there to assist in its repair . . . [He] built the

church of St Martin de Porres at Lock . . . [and was sent] to build the church, school, convent and presbytery of Our Lady Queen of the World [at Radium Hill] . . . He supervised the stone-by-stone removal of the church at Gordon to Kimba, more than 120 miles away. Thanks to him the old churches at Hammond, Burra, Booborowie and Mount Bryan [have undergone restoration]. At Crystal Brook he completely renewed the underground sewerage system and repainted the buildings . . . Vincent Shiel has been a mighty tradesman in the craft of saving souls. Not bad with a plumbline, trowel, paintbrush, hammer and chisel either.

The majority of Vin's letters emanate from these out-of-the-way parishes. For four decades my father preached the word of God in the second-largest diocese in Australia, maybe the world.

My mind conjured squint-bright landscapes, vast plains of red dirt and little else: scrubby spinifex, eucalypts and native grasses. I imagined a cobalt blue sky capable of swallowing a man, and small towns with locals who may just be able to recall the old Catholic priest, Father Vin Shiel.

I was fine. All was well in my world. Kate and I enjoyed a wonderfully supportive family life and a close-knit network of friends. With minimal assistance from Roy and Bet, I was financially independent. No matter what I was to discover in South Australia, it wasn't going to change the course of our lives.

However, little did I know that after an Easter Sunday service, standing red-faced in Vin's humble church in Quorn, everything I hoped to be true about my father was turned on its head. In 1950 Vin had committed to a cataclysmic decision. Nearly seventy years later, I walked onto unexploded ancestral ordnance.

Part Three

THE ROAD

Chapter 34

MELBOURNE TO RENMARK, 10 APRIL 2019

We were on the Hume Highway at 5.30 am—I love getting a jump on the day. I'd talked up the Ouyen Mallee Bakery, home of the World's Best Vanilla Slice, to Kate as our first stop. In the 1990s, Victorian premier Jeff Kennett proclaimed Ouyen the vanilla slice capital of the world. For three decades, the assertion has been fiercely debated in rural Australia, giving subeditors plenty of rope: 'Great Australian Vanilla Slice festival battle turns unsavoury'; 'Ouyen loses appetite for vanilla slice contest'.

Heading north, Kate re-read some of Vin's letters while I contemplated the flood of information collected since identifying my birth father eight months ago. I was fifty-eight, the same age Vin was when I was born. No matter how many positive stories I'd heard, the thought of me, at my age, having a child with a twenty-seven-year-old creeped me out. Yes, times were different, but while Maggie was alone in Melbourne giving birth to me, Mr 'Eight Men in One' was being lauded for building a church and school in a wildly remote outback uranium mining town. There had to be a few people in South Australia who could help explain whether that vow-breaking absentee father was worthy of being considered my children's grandfather.

Five hours up the Calder Highway, we pulled into the Ouyen Mallee Bakery. Two of the fabled slices appeared. Mid-bite, Kate's face told me all I needed to know: I'd oversold the reputedly unsurpassed snot block. The food focus I'd conjured proved to be a strategic stroke of genius, however, as it allowed me to distract her with chat about the bakery as we flew past detour signs promising 'local produce' and 'unique artworks' from Patchewollock to Chinkapook, Tittybong, Quambatook and Tooleybuc. I'm a when-you-drive-you-don't-muck-about-with-non-essential-stops kinda guy; if Kate can take six hours for a three-hour drive, she reckons it's been a good day.

We would have three of my closest friends joining us in a couple of days. Worried we could uncover unpalatable news, I'd tried to dissuade them—'We probably won't learn anything new about my father, and anyway, who wants to look at falling-over churches in the middle of nowhere?'—but they'd insisted.

Kate and I arrived in Renmark midafternoon. Dropping our bags at a cheap motel, we walked straight to St Therese's in the idyllic-sounding Our Lady of the River parish. In 1943, Vin found himself in the citrus-growing hub of South Australia. He'd sailed several thousand miles, from one side of the globe to the other, at the height of World War II (his voyage from the United Kingdom included a pursuit by German U-boats) to find himself posted to this sun-bleached backwater.

At midday, 6 January 1943, Father Vin's bus had pulled into Renmark. His senior, Father Hughes, was waiting. The newly minted priest received the grand tour, the baked summer landscape a striking contrast to the lush green of Kilkenny. A letter from Vin said that the temperature got to 111 degrees but after all of his years in Ireland and England he liked the heat and appreci-ated God's gift of the sun. He quickly settled into the routine of a rural priest. The first task was to undertake a census of Renmark per bike. In 100-degree heat my father knocked on every door in town, and then headed out to the farms, to record who was Catholic and who needed persuading.

Things were to take a turn for the worse, however; the following January he wrote to his bishop advising he'd visited a doctor in Berri who had diagnosed him as suffering severe anxiety linked to his experience of the bombing raids in England during the war and prescribed three months of complete rest somewhere outside South Australia and in a cooler climate. My father had PTSD. Not long after Christmas 1943, Father Hughes wrote to the bishop saying he didn't understand Vin at all. He observed that on one day Vin appeared contented, the next in a mournful state, and he assured the bishop that he hadn't been hard on Vin as he knew he'd gone through a lot during the war.

Walking in the brilliant sunshine to St Therese's, I had misgivings of my own. I'd been trying to convince myself that this was a self-indulgent family history holiday, but there was a tension in my stomach. As Kate and I approached St Therese's, we encountered Kathy, who turned out to be a long-serving church volunteer, hand-watering the lawns. Kathy was delightful and eager to share information, and was happy to show us inside the church and sacristy: 'Go on, it's fine to stand on the riser. There, behind the lectern—you can look out to the pews, just like the priest does . . .'

The sun streaming through the gold and red stained-glass window warmed my face. I closed my eyes briefly and contem-plated my father standing in this exact spot seventy-five years earlier. I was open to enlightenment, but I felt nothing.

'What was I expecting?' I asked Kate, later. 'Moses passing down Vin's story on a stone iPad? I felt zip. He was just an assistant here, I suppose, and it was a short stay.'

'Father Vin was well before my time,' said Kathy. She'd heard the name, but nothing more. I'd rushed through, fudging the details of my relationship to Vin, but Kathy was keen to know more. 'So, you've driven all the way from Melbourne to visit churches in South Australia . . . ? He must be close . . .'

I was polite, but vague. 'Father Vin is a great uncle—we think—but we're not exactly sure of the connection. I did a DNA thingie . . . we're still looking into it . . . he just seemed to have an interesting story so we're doing some exploring.' Kathy's face said she wasn't convinced. It was awkward, the lying. In my recent past life as a (small-time) CEO, I was unused to continued probing after overtly fobbing off questions. I wasn't anticipating my non-explanation of our trip to be confronting. As Kate steered the conversation away, I stood in the late afternoon sun thinking, He's your father, what exactly are you trying to hide?

It'd been a long day. We adjourned to a pokie-pub on the riverbank for dinner. Wandering back to our motel, a sign by the river reminded us that Vin's time here coincided with the internment of Japanese-Australians in Renmark. As World War II became increasingly brutal, anyone suspected of compromised allegiances was put under lock and key. Those of Japanese origin were rounded up and placed on a paddle-steamer bound for the Loveday Internment Camp. Though I found Renmark dishwater-dull, it was a reminder of the calamitous backdrop of war during Vin's time both here and abroad. Wanting to bring an end to the war, the Americans dropped two atomic bombs in the middle of 1945. News of the catastrophe spread slowly, and Vin wrote to his bishop in 1947 asking to commence a missionary posting in

Japan. Though the request was declined, it was Vin's first foray of a forty-year campaign to flee South Australia.

Sixteen months after Vin arrived in Renmark, a devastating fire destroyed much of the cathedral in Port Pirie. His building skills were deemed of use, and he was transferred out.

Lying on a lumpy motel bed, my mind raced. I was elated this journey had begun, but troubled by issues swirling in the media that gave it a new and powerful relevance. Firstly, there was a growing number of stories of people who'd been rattled by unexpected DNA discoveries—I was magnetically drawn to them. Though we'd located Vin through AncestryDNA, there were three other major commercial DNA databases: 23andMe, MyHeritage and Gene by Gene. The most committed had submitted their DNA to all four agencies. I hadn't. I hesitated. The only news the DNA sites could deliver was bad. How would I feel if I discovered half-siblings?

Secondly, the 2013 Royal Commission into Institutional Responses to Child Sexual Abuse had initiated a car crash in slow motion, and although the five-year commission had drawn to a close in 2017, spin-off court cases regularly percolated onto the news media sites. A 6 February 2017 Associated Press article said that seven per cent of all Australian Catholic priests (since 1950) had been accused of abuse. Between 1980 and 2015, 4444 people reported they had been abused at more than a thousand Catholic institutions across Australia. The average age of the victims was ten for girls and eleven for boys. The commission didn't investigate adult abuse, which was predominantly where the children of priests would (presumably) have originated. I found myself regularly compelled to switch off the radio reports and shut down web pages. Being Catholic, adopted and exclusively educated in

Catholic schools—and now with a secret ex-nun mother and priest father—it was too close to home.

Casting a shadow over all of this was Cardinal George Pell. Initially, Pell welcomed the royal commission. He said he hoped an investigation would stop the 'smear campaign' against the church. Our family had a tenuous link to Pell. Roy's fifty-year involvement with the Richmond Football Club meant he became friendly with the aspiring ruckman when Pell first signed with the Tigers in 1959. The cardinal didn't progress beyond the reserves, but Roy was outgoing, could tell a joke and bonded easily with men sharing similar interests. He made countless friends at Tigerland, including 'Big George'.

When I was a teenager and Pell had advanced to become the most prominent Australian Catholic, Roy would flag the friendship and tell me what a 'good bloke' Big George was. Whenever Pell's face would grace the TV news, Roy would proclaim, 'He's a good Richmond man, you know!' This was Roy's highest accolade. The Pell association continued through to 2001, when the cardinal conducted a mass at St Ignatius, Richmond, to celebrate the fiftieth wedding anniversary of couples who'd been married in that church, which included Roy and Bet. This mass was a Very Big Day for the Watkins family. A picture was taken of our family and Pell.

After Roy's death, we began clearing out his house. I saw the picture quietly collecting dust on the mantelpiece. Under the gaze of a stony-faced Pell, who is gripping Roy's hand, my dad beams up in awe from a front-row pew at St Ignatius. But Pell's and my eyes are locked. He clasps Roy's hand, but peers directly at me, sitting beside my dad. The cardinal looks both almighty and bored. (The child sex crimes he was to be gaoled for, though later overturned, related to events occurring only three years before the picture was taken.) I squint at Big George with both suspicion and determination on my face—I'd heard the rumours about him. Bet and the rest of our family in attendance (three females) look uncomfortable in Pell's presence: pained smiles, eyes averted downward, as if waiting for it to be over. Pell is imposing, and so was his dad: George Snr was a goldminer, captain of the Perth Lifesaving Club and heavyweight boxing champion of Western Australia. What would Roy and Bet have made of it, if they'd lived to know of Pell's child-abuse charge? I'm glad they never had to wrestle with that dilemma, or my new discoveries.

Trying to sleep in the airless motel, I tossed and turned with the thoughts of my new identity as a McTaggart, Gaelic for son of a priest. I'd never fully come out as the twice-rejected child of a Catholic nun, a truth I'd revealed to just a tiny number of confidants, and now I was also coming to terms with being the son of a priest. It was clear there would be more awkward moments, more being untruthful to elderly parishioners as to why I wanted to be let into their churches, photograph the unremarkable scenery and ask questions about a long-dead priest. I thought I could wing it—I'd been flying by the seat of my pants for decades—but didn't these nice old ladies deserve the truth?

Keeping secrets meant I had to repeatedly lie.

How was I any different from my parents?

Chapter 35

RENMARK TO BURRA, 11 APRIL 2019

I'd met Kate on 17 February 1984 at the Albion Hotel in Carlton. Neon Leon and the Speed Kings had a residency. Mitch and Frank, two mates from primary school, and I loved the band. We were there two or three nights a week. Mitch and Frank know my stories, and I know theirs. It was only fitting that they would soon join our South Australian journey.

It was obvious on that sweltering night in 1984 that Kate was everything I wasn't. She was going to be an art teacher. At 19, she'd punched her ticket. I had no idea who I was or what I wanted to be. I was calculating, introverted and strategic; she was creative, a free spirit . . . chaotic. I knew I needed more of that devil-may-care in my life. It was obvious she was a keeper when half-drunkenly she lit the wrong end of her cigarette. I would have been mortified, attempting to disguise the blunder, but she fell about laughing as though she'd just told the most hilarious of jokes. We've been together since that night.

Late on the afternoon of 11 April 2019, Mitch and long-time partner Sandy pulled into Burra. They'd left Victoria the same day as us, but as they live next to the Otway National Park, they'd followed the coast westward, then north to Burra. The four of us enjoy an all-too-rare couple relationship where each shares deep connections with the others: we 'just click'. We checked in to the Burra Motel, over the road from St Joseph's, the reason we were in town.

Burra was once the second-largest town in South Australia, cute as a button and well-geared for tourists. The town centre is well-maintained and green, but venture beyond the city limits and it's parched, foreboding even. In the evening, we wander through the streets just as most locals sit for dinner. As we stroll, we glimpse other visitors and locals, through open front doors, down darkened passageways, occasionally exchanging a nod.

My phone directs us to La Pecora Nera, the *best pizza in the world* according to Frank. He's a geologist with Italian heritage and he worked around these parts in his uni-student days. Mitch, Sandy, Kate and I find a table. Knowing there'd been a lot of research going on, Mitch and Sandy are keen to catch up. Responding to the Italian flags in the restaurant, I open a letter Vin wrote from Colegio Beda, a Roman seminary founded in 1852 by Pope Pius IX. 'So, Beda was a seminary exclusively for men over thirty. It was prestigious, he was proud of his time there. It had apparently produced four popes, many of the students became bishops, there was even a saint or two, well, so says my father! Vin was in Rome when World War II broke out, listen to this . . .'

I paraphrased some of the key elements. 'He'd only been at Beda for a few months when the seminarians were told to pack the bare essentials and get out. Interestingly the German, French and Dutch were all conscripted, but the English, Irish, Kiwis and Aussies were sent to England. In the dash to Paris, and then England, he lost his luggage and arrived in only the clothes he stood in. He goes on to say that when he was in Beda, Pope Pius XI died (10 February 1939) and he attended the funeral.'

I rounded out the story for Mitch and Sandy. 'Sixty-six years after Vin mourned the death of a pope in Rome, his son, two grandchildren and sorta-daughter-in-law Kate experienced the same phenomenon. In 2005, when we did that house-swap with the Italian family. We were sitting in a pizzeria and Nell was staring at the ubiquitous restaurant television when she turned to Pat and asked, "Who's the dead dude, Pat?" Kate and I looked up to see ashen-faced reporters broadcasting from St Peter's Basilica. Italy was about to commence a lengthy period of mourning and, just as my father had experienced, his son visited the Vatican while the body of John Paul II lay in state. Queues of mourners snaked over St Peter's forecourt to view the corpse as we arrived.'

And with that, four mouth-watering pizzas arrived at our table. 'Anyway, I'm running off at the mouth. I wanted to say—it's great to have you two join us. I just hope it's not a non-event. Let's hope something memorable happens.'

Chapter 36

BURRA TO CRYSTAL BROOK, 12 APRIL 2019

Father Liam Ryan, of the Adelaide diocese, had texted me the phone number of several regional diocese priests and nuns: 'I've worded them up to assist as required. Safe travel. Cheerio.' Liam was one of the first people I was directed to after discovering who my father was.

I'd been shunted around to several clerics with what must have sounded like a way-too-hot-to-handle claim. Before we left for South Australia, Liam asked if I was going to tell the people we met that Vin was my father. I considered the topic at length. It would undoubtedly disturb some of the devout older folk. The news might also somehow get back to Maggie—this was to be avoided. It was also potentially explosive enough to spark the interest of the media. A full disclosure to the people we were about to meet might also temper the things I was told about Vin— I couldn't see an upside. I told Liam I'd keep it quiet, but reserved the right to tell people if it felt appropriate at the time. At no time did Liam or anyone in the church ask me to lie, though there was indisputable relief in Liam's voice when I confirmed: 'I'll just be vague about the DNA links.'

The evening before, I'd called Sister Kerry, the caretaker of St Joseph's, Burra. She was on the road to Adelaide and expecting the call. After explaining where the spare sacristy key was hidden, she asked, half-jokingly, 'Are you sure you're trustworthy?' I wanted to reply, 'I'm the son of priest and a nun. If you can't trust me—who can you trust?!' I wondered later who Liam had said I was. Kerry wasn't at all like the stereotypical nun I recalled from primary school. She was relaxed and irreverent, surely the life of any party. I suspect she wasn't fussing about with that hands-free-phone-while-driving-mumbo-jumbo either.

First thing the next morning, another perfect blue-sky day, Mitch, Sandy, Kate and I located the hidden key and took ourselves on a self-guided tour of St Joseph's. Reflecting the prosperity of this little town in its glory days, it's a substantial construction; perched close to the crest of a ridge, it peers with authority over the township. I unlocked the heavy wooden door. My footsteps boomed in the cavernous space, though we walked lightly. A statue of the Virgin Mary looked down on me with pity in her eyes. Standing at the pulpit looking out at the empty pews, sun blasting through the stained glass for maximum inspiration, I tried hard to imagine my father standing on this spot. But again, there was nothing.

'How weird is this?' I said to Mitch. 'Two long-lapsed Catholic boys and their atheist live-in-sin girlfriends wandering about an empty house of Christ looking for traces of my dead priest dad?'

'Yeah . . .' Was all he could muster. He didn't know what to say. (Nobody ever did.)

•

We pulled off the road and spilled out of the cars for a photo op between Burra and Crystal Brook. I'd spotted the derelict homestead featured on the cover of Midnight Oil's *Diesel and Dust* album. In all probability, the symmetrical simplicity of that stone homestead would have had a roof and lights burning in the windows as Vin rolled past of an evening in his Kombi fifty years earlier.

Father Francis, one of my new ecclesiastical contacts, had arranged for us to meet a local parishioner at the front of Holy Trinity Church, Crystal Brook, at ten that morning. A farmer by trade, Les was a big man with an even bigger handshake. He shared a stream of stories and local knowledge. He'd lived in these parts his entire life and attended the tiny Holy Trinity school fifty years back. After greetings, Les was anxious to show us a book, *Good and Faithful Servants*, a collection of biographies of priests from Port Pirie and Port Augusta from 1888 to 2014. In it was a small picture of my father and a brief recollection of 'Vinnie the Brickie'. A student recounted Vin tossing him out of a class for 'creating a disturbance', noting that 'Shiel was a bit odd with his long white beard and long black cassock.' I was thrilled (but didn't show it).

I was delighted to hear that although Les hadn't seen Vin for three decades, he recalled those days with precision. 'The only time we used a tablecloth, napkins and the good cutlery was when Father Vin made his weekly visit. Sometimes he'd drop in unannounced during the day for tea. Mum would always have his favourite biscuits on hand. He relieved at Crystal Brook several times after his retirement in the seventies and eighties. He'd take his pushbike on the train and happily get about town on two wheels. Your relative, Father Vin—you were never in doubt about where you stood with the man . . . and that's all right, mind you. He was hands-on, practical—people respected that.'

The conversation turned to the royal commission and Pell's conviction for abuse. Les had been rocked by the revelations; he responded, 'It's not over yet.' I felt certain it was, but let it go. As we wandered through the single-room school (a dog-eared Pell poster displayed on a wall), Les pointed to a large clearing behind the school. 'That's where the Sacred Heart Orphanage once stood.' My ears pricked up; orphanages had always both fascinated me and filled me with dread. I'd known for thirty years I could easily have been raised in a South Australian orphanage. Maggie could have elected not to reveal the pregnancy to Vin, gone back to Port Augusta, given birth and left me at this very spot. The hairs on my arms tingled.

The orphanage had been a sizeable building but had closed and then been razed. Sparse weeds now rustled in the breeze. With some reluctance, Les explained the closure. 'An asbestos roof, rising damp, and . . . the last people employed to run it were totally unsuitable—we had to move them on—quickly.' What the hell did that mean? My travelling companions and I exchanged squint-eyed glances. Were the kids being interfered with? It didn't seem right to ask. Les frowned and shook his head. Instinctively, I didn't probe.

Accommodating around 240 children between 1940 and 1979, the orphanage's history coincided almost exactly with Vin's time in South Australia. The children were usually delivered to the orphanage by a parent, relative, police officer or carer and told to play outside to allow the adults speak. Once separated, the 'loved one' often departed through the rear door without explanation, goodbye or final embrace. Though some children were fostered out, the majority remained for years. Brothers were immediately separated from sisters, off to their respective dorms. The nuns (Good Samaritan Sisters) never offered comforting words or an embrace, as physical contact was forbidden. Punishments were swift and brutal; canings were common. Some orphans had been hospitalised with malnutrition after being put on a bread and water diet for the sin of bedwetting. This was the era when my father presided in this region: this was his mindset.

Les explained that the Crystal Brook orphans came from a range of circumstances: parents who couldn't afford to raise children, children that had a parent die or an Aboriginal parent, or children that were 'uncontrollable'.

Running late for our next appointment, Mitch (who is fluent in bloke-talk: tractors, pumps, sharp-tooly-things) had to be dragged away from Les. In our farewells, he invited us all to drop in for dinner and even stay the night on the return journey.

As Les had been so hospitable, I felt a sudden urge to tell him that Vin was my father, and that my mother had been a nun . . . let the whole crazy, jumbled truth spill out. But as it was so complicated, and because I didn't have the answers to his inevitable questions (let alone my own), I remained silent. I hated it; the vows had been broken by my parents, not me. Why did I feel the need to hold my tongue?

On the drive to Port Pirie, I mused to Kate: 'The image that sticks in my mind is Les telling us when Vin stayed here—when the orphanage was still standing but had been decommissioned—that he slept out there by himself. It's such a disconcerting picture, my father, alone in that dank, disgraced orphanage echoing the misery of boys and girls without parents. How could he not lie in that bed at night and contemplate what had become of the child that he and Maggie had given up? How'd he even know I'd been adopted? Did he pray for me? Or Maggie? . . . Or just himself?

'Christ, I hope the next coupla stops this arvo are going to be less confronting.'

Chapter 37

PORT PIRIE TO QUORN, 13 APRIL 2019

I'd arranged to meet Father Francis at the front of St Mark's Cathedral, Port Pirie, at 12.30 pm. As Vin was only here from 1944 to 1946, we'd decided to drop in briefly to meet the young priest referred by Father Liam, before continuing on our way north. I'd previously spoken with Father Francis and his associate, Father Harold, who were both born and raised in the Philippines. Neither had met Vin, or knew he was my father, but as they'd been directed to assist our visit, it felt polite to stop and meet in person.

As I did a U-turn to park at the front of the church, I was puzzled to see Father Francis standing next to a large distinguished-looking man on the footpath. The men stopped their conversation and peered expectantly at our car. As we alighted, I realised that the elderly gent was Bishop Greg O'Kelly, whose photo I'd seen online when researching. O'Kelly is one of the more senior Catholics in Australia. I hadn't expected to meet any high-calibre Micks, or anybody who knew the identity of my father, until we met Father Liam in Whyalla. I didn't feel mentally prepared, my mind raced. Why was the bishop here?

Ever the catastrophist, I feared the church had uncovered new information that they didn't want to put in writing. I felt wired, irrationally so. This moment underlined the risk of the tour, searching for good but possibly finding bad. I quickly took hold of my thoughts and resolved that the bishop only wanted to see if I posed a threat to the church, which sure as hell didn't need more bad publicity. Now out of our cars, we introduced ourselves. I'd never met a bishop before: was I supposed to genuflect? To kiss his ring? (Doubtless Vin would have done this when he first stood on this footpath and greeted his bishop seventy years earlier.)

Bishop O'Kelly was stooped and slow moving. Something about his appearance suggested he'd once been physically dynamic, maybe an ex-footballer. We shook hands. He smiled. The reverence shown to O'Kelly over many decades had seeped into his DNA; when he spoke, he expected to be listened to. It was O'Kelly who ultimately gave consent on behalf of the South Australian church for me to receive Vin's file without redaction, an Australian first. Father Liam and Tanja Stojadinovic from Catholic Professional Standards had both spoken about this bishop with genuine respect. I didn't think I'd ever meet the man. I was pleased, but puzzled.

O'Kelly was concurrently the Bishop of Port Pirie and acting Archbishop of South Australia. In 2015, his predecessor, Archbishop Philip Wilson, was charged with concealing a serious offence regarding child sexual abuse. He was found guilty by a jury in 2018 but was acquitted on appeal later that year. At the time, Wilson was the highest-ranking Catholic in the world to be convicted of that crime. The appalling irony of the conviction was that Wilson had previously earned a reputation as 'the healing bishop' for his handling of abuse scandals.

O'Kelly led us through his stately cathedral, proudly explaining its historical and architectural features. He referred to the fire that dragged Vin away from Renmark. As he spoke and walked, the five of us trailing behind, I noticed that O'Kelly and I mirrored each other's posture. He leaned forward with both hands on the back of a pew, so did I. I folded my arms while placing a single hand on my chin to listen, so did he. Was it deliberate? Who was copying whom?

Our group was respectful and interested, we obviously hadn't arrived to cause trouble, and at the conclusion of the tour we were invited to the presbytery for afternoon tea. Tea with the bishop, strange days indeed.

Due to the presence of Father Francis, Mitch, Sandy, Kate and I effortlessly slipped back into the prickly charade of being on a 'DNA family-tree tour', claiming Father Vin as an unidentified curiosity from my distant past. We chatted about our itinerary, AFL and Bishop O'Kelly's cousin, Margie. Father Francis told us that Margie lived in Crystal Brook and was 'a good friend of your Father Vin . . . she's blind and plays a mean honky-tonk piano'. I knew I had to talk with her, and asked the bishop if he minded if I made contact. He agreed. The bishop had been a decorated educator, and principal of the prestigious Riverview School, Sydney, which had educated Christopher Pyne, Barnaby Joyce and Tony Abbott. 'Well, you can't help bad luck,' I quipped. He said nothing, but he did nod in agreement.

Crowded into the comfortable, though well-worn, presbytery lounge, Kate was taken with the bishop's border collie. Ruffling the old dog's coat, she asked her name. 'Jezebel,' came the straight-faced reply from the venerable bishop. Kate and I exchanged an immediate raised-eyebrow glance. Given the myriad sexual failings of the church, to name a bishop's dog after a 'wanton or loose woman' seemed to have misread the room completely. Catching myself, I wondered if I was being overly politically correct—I knew the Victorian media would go to town if Peter Comensoli, Archbishop of Melbourne, named his pooch Jezebel, Floozie or similar. I made a mental note to find out if Comensoli had a dog.

As Kate and Jezebel bonded, the bishop shared a story from a scorching day the previous summer. O'Kelly had left his bishopmobile running with the air conditioner on to keep Jezebel cool. 'I just ducked into a shop.' On his return, both vehicle and pooch were gone. The police were called, and shortly after, a 170-kilometre-per-hour police chase ensued. Eventually, the holy trinity of bishop, collie and vehicle were as one. O'Kelly explained that a man just released from prison had ambled past the car and 'simply couldn't resist'. He presented a copy of the Port Pirie *Witness*, with a snap of Jezebel in the police paddy wagon. The headline read: 'Jezebel by name, Jezebel by nature'.

With football being the fail-safe conversation for men across the nation, I mentioned to the bishop that my father, Roy, had been the timekeeper at the Richmond Football Club for fifty years; with that, conversation took off like a grass fire. The bishop listened most intently when I spoke of 'my father' and 'my family'—he studied my face as I spoke. Too many assume adoptive families are tinged with unhappiness; I let him know that I'd been adored by my parents. Later, surprised at how I deferred to the authority of O'Kelly's title (my school-days indoctrination more influential than I'd imagined), I regretted not impressing upon him how important it was for children of priests to know our full stories.

Granted, he had given me Vin's letters. It was the wider church that was the problem. I wanted a discussion. Maybe he knew what I was thinking, I don't know, but the polite chat was maddening. Vin's letters changed my life, I wanted to tell him. I realised Vin, like O'Kelly, had spent most of his life retaining the confessed secrets of parishioners. Secrecy is the default, as instinctive as a squid squirts ink. Acting as God's agent, prescribing a collection of hocus-pocus prayers in exchange for a clear conscience.

After an hour of chitchat, we made our farewells. I was keen to get to Quorn before sunset. The roos on the open road at dusk had brought my father undone on more than one occasion. As we made our way outside, I sidled up to O'Kelly and quietly thanked him for all that he'd done for me, and 'the information made available'. He nodded but didn't offer anything more than saying it was 'a topic that had taken some discussions around the committee. I'm glad it has bought you peace.' Then he changed the topic, asking what I did for a living, where I lived . . . any topic but the children of priests.

As we arrived back at the cars, conversation circled back to football; shaking hands, I asked O'Kelly for divine intervention to assist my Tigers. He knew my team had been depleted by injury and was struggling for a win. He replied with a wink and a nod.

As soon as the engine started, I felt a wave of relief. The bad news didn't arrive. Maybe Vin was okay. We scooted to a nearby pub to debrief with Mitch and Sandy. After ten minutes of animated conversation about priests, nuns, bishops and babies, we noticed the table behind us had gone quiet. Glancing back, I saw the back of silent heads craned toward our table. It underscored the surreal nature of our tour.

Mitch and Sandy's presence had lightened the mood, and I was grateful for their presence. As we walked back to the cars to head north, Mitch, my long-lapsed-Catholic schoolmate—showing signs of his own indoctrination—shouted over the bonnet, 'Just wait till I tell Mum. We had tea with a bishop!'

•

Feeling somehow fortified by our meetings in Renmark, Burra, Crystal Brook and Port Pirie, I found the enormous blue sky and warm air rushing through the window as we approached Quorn a good omen. Kate and I didn't talk; there was plenty to mull over.

The Far North accounts for eighty per cent of South Australia's land mass but only three per cent of its population. The most recognisable landmarks are the Flinders Ranges and Coober Pedy, and Quorn, the entrance to the Outback. Quorn, Hawker and Radium Hill have Vin's fingerprints all over them. He presided over these outposts when at the peak of his powers. He also did a lot of building work up there, my father's sweat soaked into the red soil. These were the towns where I hoped to feel his presence and see the results of his labour. If we met a local or two who could recall Father Vin, then that'd be the cream on top.

After an hour, we turned off the Augusta Highway and headed north-east along the Flinders Ranges Way. On our right was the Devil's Peak, the highest point on the southern ranges. When looking back at the quartzite outcrop, it resembled the devil himself, lying back gazing to the heavens. What'd my priest-dad make of Satan peering out over the flock he'd been sent to protect?

Jesus was a carpenter who'd spent forty days and nights in the desert resisting the temptations of Satan. Vin was a carpenter, too. He'd spent forty years in the desert, but he failed his test. Living proof was now cruising into the parish.

As we entered Quorn (population 1200), it was evident times were tough. Ramshackle houses and peeling paint, only a few desert gardens, all parched. Now on a latitude similar to Broken Hill, there'd been just 3 millimetres of rain since Christmas. There was evidence of better days, an undeniable grandeur in the wide main streets, pubs and public buildings. The railway runs along the Flinders Ranges Way, the main drag, and bang in the middle of town is the glorious Quorn Railway Station.

Like Burra, Quorn had once been a critical rail hub. In 1917, it was the crossroads of all north–south and east–west rail travel in Australia. If you were traversing the nation by train, you stopped there. During World War II, more than a million soldiers passed through on their way to Darwin. Quorn's role as a mighty transport pivot was derailed when a standard-gauge railway opened between Port Pirie and Port Augusta in the thirties. Regardless of the arrival of Father Vin Shiel some years later, the town was destined for decline.

As we rolled slowly through town, breathing in the dry eucalypt air, I thought of my father striding purposefully down these dirt footpaths. This is 'ground zero'. After months of preparation, I was exhilarated to finally be here: I could sense him immediately.

Kate and Sandy wanted to stay in no-frills local pubs. Easy, we checked in to the $85 a night Austral Hotel, not a single frill to be seen. Dog-tired from the day, we stumbled into the main bar halfway through the second quarter of the Tigers vs Port Adelaide game. Mitch and I sat at the bar with some friendly locals. Classic pub, the Austral.

None of the media had tipped my Tigers to win. It was always going to be a tough assignment, playing in front of the notoriously feral Port Adelaide crowd, and five of our stars were out injured. It was a cracker of a game. Miraculously we got over the line, by just eight points. As the final siren blew, Mitch and I raised glasses and made a toast. 'To Bishop O'Kelly—we got God on our side!'

Chapter 38

QUORN, 14 APRIL 2019

After the unexpectedly intense start to our trip, and to salute the bishop-sanctified Tiger ascension, I'd enjoyed a beer or two more than I should have the night before. I hoped the alcohol would slow my racing mind. It didn't. Sleeping poorly, I woke at 5 am, dehydrated and sick in the stomach. I desperately wanted to lie in, hit pause and reflect on all I'd learned. Dozing, and feeling increasingly worse for wear, I recalled that we'd agreed to attend the 8.30 am Palm Sunday mass at Immaculate Conception. Sandy and Kate were right, it was an opportunity too good to pass up: observing Vin's church in full flight on a significant holy day.

Palm Sunday provided the palms that were traditionally burned on Shrove Tuesday. I browsed Wikipedia for a refresher: 'The feast commemorates Jesus's triumphal entry into Jerusalem . . . when palm branches were placed in his path, before his arrest on Holy Thursday and his crucifixion on Good Friday.' Still in bed, I rolled over and passed the phone to Kate to read.

'That's spooky. This has got to be one of the strangest days for the son of a priest to be making an appearance—the triumphal return—to your own father's church.' Sensing my unease she added, 'You'll be fine, what could possibly go wrong?' We both laughed, me unconvincingly. It was 8.15 already. Pulling the curtain back, I saw the morning sky was cloudless. It was going to be hot.

Already late, on an empty stomach, the four of us marched down Flinders Ranges Way. Trying to lighten my mood, Kate said, 'You get the irony here: we're going to the Immaculate Conception Church, the baby boy Jesus and all that palaver—and Vin having a child—you weren't born in a manger were you?' We cackled, having no idea what was to come.

The service had already begun as we entered the front door of the modest church. Avoiding eye contact with the congregation, we self-consciously teetered up the centre aisle. By mid-church, there were many vacant pews. The worshippers had gathered in the front and back rows, leaving a gaping no-man's-land in the middle; some things never change, I thought. As we took our seats, some in front turned to glance at the tardy out-of-towners.

Mass was conducted by Father Panton, another of the heavily accented Filipino priests increasingly serving the regional dioceses. The congregation was an elderly no-nonsense-looking Anglo-Australian flock. (Panton is a fish out of water, how long is this going to last? I thought to myself.) The only occasions that drew me to a church over the past forty years were funerals and weddings. I hadn't attended a baptism or confirmation since my own. Despite that, there was nothing new to me in Panton's service; it was slow, seemed lacking in conviction and was of no relevance to me. However, my ancestral connection to this place was profound. My flesh-and-blood father served as parish priest in Quorn from early 1964 until his retirement in late 1977. He arrived here as a sixty-one-year-old and didn't take his leave until he was a cancer-riddled seventy-five-year-old. Though his retirement from Quorn was forty-two years earlier, he did relieve there in the 1980s: if there was a community who'd be able to recall him, it'd be these people.

Trying to take it all in, I looked up at Father Panton gripping the old lectern that Vin had likely preached from. Decades ago, my father would have looked out onto a larger, and far younger, gathering. His mass would have boomed with hymns and prayer. When Vin arrived here, the Australian church was in the throes of implementing a massive modernisation program as a result of Vatican II. Priests stopped delivering mass in Latin, the altar was turned to face the congregation, and women were allowed to let loose their lust-inducing hair. The swinging sixties, the contraceptive pill, and Father Vin arrived as one.

Today, approaching sixty, I'm virtually the same age as Vin when he arrived here—it's come full circle. The differences between father and son are stark. When my father arrived at Immaculate Conception, he was a priest with a three-year-old son whom he'd abandoned. My Kate was here with me, and my kids were at home following our adventures every step of the way. My family are the driving force of my life, not so his.

As if on autopilot, I stood, kneeled, sat and recited lines in unison with the congregation. Knowing I was going to introduce myself to the priest after the service, I pondered the submissive way I'd behaved with Bishop O'Kelly. What was stopping me walking to the altar right now and introducing myself as Father Vin Shiel's son? Would Kate, Sandy and Mitch be ashamed? Hardly, they were ridiculously supportive . . . or was I remaining passive to hide Maggie's identity? To protect the sensitivities of the faithful? The truth was that I was most fearful Vin was someone I didn't want to be associated with. And these benign-looking elderly worshippers were about to recognise my dread.

Immediately after mass, still inside the church—still in our pew—we found ourselves surrounded, in deep conversation with three locals and Father Panton. All were delighted to see new faces swelling their dwindling numbers and curious to know what we were doing in town, perhaps interest further piqued when none of us received communion. I recited my standard explanation: 'Father Vin Shiel is a very distant relative . . . we're just here on holiday, thought we'd look up some far-flung family history. That's all.'

And with that, they were off. Everyone had a 'Father Vin' tale to tell. Fabulous! We'd struck gold. There were animated conversations with Geraldine, Shirley and Sue. Shirley had been married by Vin and owned several of his landscape paintings, which she was anxious to show to us. They were so generous and open; the truth sat like hot coals in my pocket. We heard many stories about 'the hard-working builder-priest', 'a character—terrific with locals in need', 'stern and autocratic . . . though typical of many of the older priests'. Vin, we heard, 'always wore full-length paint-splattered overalls, but on a Sunday, back to his holy robes'. He had a 'big beard, woolly hair'—I lapped it up, but once we moved past what a decent man he was, Geraldine subtly refocused conversation to Vin's gambling. With a lowered voice she informed us, 'The gambling was of a serious concern to the parish.'

'Really, how bad was it?' I asked, with a little too much concern. 'Are you saying he may have borrowed church money?'

Frowning, she replied, 'Well, let's just say a number of us were genuinely worried that he'd gamble away the reserves.'

What? Did she just say my father was a thief?

Eager to please, Shirley chipped in, 'He often had wads of cash in his pockets, all rolled up. He just loved the races! He'd bet on anything!'

Front-row-Geraldine was a particularly eager and clued-in parishioner. As we spoke, she probed what *exactly* my relationship was to Vin. I was vague, a bit brusque, and tried to flick her off with 'a great uncle or something . . .' I was behaving exactly like my mother, being uncooperative and annoyingly evasive. Geraldine pursued me, trying to paint me into a corner; I ducked, I weaved. At that moment, she and Shirley turned to each other, and then back to me. Without blinking, holding my gaze, Geraldine said: 'You know, you talk, move and look *a lot* like Father Vin.' They both looked hard at me, nodding slowly.

Affronted, I averted my eyes. And then I felt it. The heat rose from my collar to fill my cheeks. I hadn't blushed for decades, but I did on Palm Sunday in the Immaculate Conception, Quorn.

'Do I? Really?' Christ, my mind choked, then stalled.

Afterwards, Mitch said it was one of the few times in forty years that he'd seen me lost for words. It was too much to process. I thought I looked like my mother. Adopted people don't look like anyone older than them. And now I resembled *both* my birth parents? Mercifully Kate, Mitch and Sandy deflected conversation away as the heat gradually receded from my cheeks.

'If you're interested in Father Vin, you must talk to Evie Murphy. She knows *everything* about those Shiels, and she's only an hour or so from here,' Geraldine added.

And then the bombshell. 'In 1950, Father Vin asked Evie to fly to Sydney, to accompany a newborn baby boy: the child was to be adopted by Vin's older brother. It's always been a mystery to us— who was that boy? And why had a young girl been sent alone on a plane to Sydney with an unwanted baby? Why did Father Vin want his brother to adopt the child when there were orphanages all over South Australia?'

Without saying the words, it was clear Geraldine assumed I was that baby sent to Sydney.

I wiped the sweat from my hands onto my jeans and muttered, 'What?' Was she right? Am I that baby? There'd been so many lies and half-truths in my life—at that moment, I wasn't able to distinguish up from down.

'No . . . he's not me, or I'm not him,' I mumbled. 'I was born in 1961. If that baby was sent to the Shiels in Sydney, he would be seventy—I'm just short of sixty. It's not me. I'm sure.' I was firm, serious, as if trying to convince both of us. Kate leapt in to save me and confirmed my alibi.

My mind had dashed to 'If it's not me, who was the baby? And who are the parents? Was Vin the father? Was Evie the mother? Or was it Maggie? Did Vin and Maggie have two children?' My head tingled. Was my hair standing on end? I reached up and patted it down, just in case.

Mitch leaned in close and whispered in my ear, 'That baby must be Vin's. Watto, I think you've got a half-brother.'

Head spinning, I felt a wave of panic, torn between the urge to flee and an insatiable curiosity. Seeing me incapable of coherent conversation, Kate distracted Geraldine with stories of what she'd learned about my Shiel ancestors in Sydney. Soon the two were reeling off the names of long-lost family members and the streets where my ancestors lived in Lidcombe, Balmain and Rozelle. Kate could recall everything, she could connect the dots, but for me there were far too many dots to connect: dots and priests, and orphan baby boys on planes, and dots with nuns, all circling around in my head . . . I was in shock, as if stumbling from a car wreck, concussed.

I have an older brother?

Interrupting the mile-a-minute conversations orbiting me, Father Panton interjected with an apology; he had to lock up, as he was due in the next town for mass. We hastily arranged to reconvene over coming days.

Light-headed, I lurched out of the church trailing my three friends, trying to look composed, failing. Legs like rubber. When we finally sat down back at the pub, Kate was clearly unhappy with me for agreeing, at Geraldine's insistence, to contact Evie Murphy. I'd forgotten that Evie was Maggie's best friend— they spoke every week. Kate reminded me that Evie was the young woman who'd left South Australia with Maggie after Vin encouraged my mother to live in Sydney with his family. Kate was all over it. 'We have to stay away from Evie Murphy. She'll work out who you are and Maggie's secret will be out!'

Mitch and Sandy had been silent on the way back to the pub. When the dust settled, Sandy found her voice. 'Hey, Brendan, Kate, do you realise, well . . . I think they all know Vin's your father.'

That afternoon, needing space to absorb the flood of new information, Kate stayed in our room as Father Panton showed Mitch, Sandy and I around Vin's old presbytery, church and sacristy. Panton is a thoughtful man, about forty. Born in the Philippines, he'd spent a dozen years in Rome and then requested relocation to Port Pirie. Of all the places on planet earth, why here? 'Chocolates to boiled lollies?' I said to Panton.

Frowning, he had no idea what I was talking about.

I shrugged, 'Not to worry.'

The dilapidated presbytery was all dim bulbs and cracked tiles. There hadn't been any work undertaken here since my old man's last renovation. It looked like it needed restumping . . . or a bull-dozer. Stained blinds were pulled down tight in every room. It was grotty, miserable. It would have been magnificent in its day, high ceilings and a beautiful wide verandah—great bones—but the condition of the residence was a reflection of the state of the wider Catholic Church: shot.

Vin had been diagnosed with stomach cancer in 1976. The resulting operation reduced his stomach to the size of an orange, but he didn't hang up his tool-belt. In a fraught letter in April 1976 he said he'd just finished painting the exterior of both the Quorn and Hawker churches. A parishioner had fallen during a service in Hawker so he replaced all of the floor joists and boards, an enormous undertaking for an ill man in his mid-seventies. He wrote that he'd hoped to be able to go see the Sydney-based cancer specialist who had made the initial diagnosis. In another letter home to family in Sydney, he's hoping to be told the operation was a success. He then adds that he's exhausted and has decided to retire from large-scale building projects. He'd deliberately pushed his body hard on these jobs to test his limits and in order to leave the church property in the Hawker–Quorn parish in tiptop condition. He anticipated that the buildings in his parish would not require major repair for several years and announced that, with the various projects now complete and feeling no longer able to carry on, he would retire at the conclusion of 1977. At the end of the road in Quorn, my father was signing off.

Panton hadn't met Vin, but he shared a story. My father was known to be particularly devout—he'd fast for hours before mass. Once, when the Pope visited Australia, Vin overdid his fasting and made himself extremely unwell. The pattern of self-flagellation continued. I wasn't impressed. If you starve yourself to a point where others are aware, it sounds to me like old-fashioned attention-seeking. He'd need to miss more than a few meals to absolve himself of conceiving me and this bloody mystery child we'd just discovered.

When we got back to the pub, Kate was buzzing. She'd texted one of my relatives in Sydney and learned that the mystery child's name was Terry Shiel. He'd been adopted by Vin's elder brother, William, and his wife, Elsie. My possible half-, if not full, brother had apparently always wanted to be a racing car driver and (of course!) that's what he became.

Kate and Sandy weren't sure of my theory that if Vin arranged to keep Terry in the family it meant he was much more likely to be the father. I was convinced I had a half-brother—though I didn't want him to be—another sibling meant Vin was a repeat offender. And how many other siblings were out there? Kate reminded me that my contact at Broken Rites had said, 'I'll bet that Father Vin had more than one child.'

In the bustling Austral Hotel lounge, I googled 'Terry Shiel racing' on my phone. Amid a dozen 1980s-era race cars, there were three images of a man standing in his team-coloured race overalls. Kate, Sandy and Mitch leaned in to see. One article, headed 'Shiel of Steel', showed him close up. 'My god, that's him! What do you think? I can't see a resemblance, or . . . actually, maybe? Possibly our noses? Hairline, he's certainly greyed just like me!' I was stumped, and looked to my friends passing the phone around. They ummmed and ahhhed.

'Maybe—but you're certainly not identical twins,' said Mitch.

Sandy added, 'I'm not sure, his face is rounder, you have a long oval face.' After much discussion, it was concluded that it wasn't impossible.

That night in bed, I felt that stabbing sense of abandonment return. Why was I given away when Terry was raised a Shiel?

Just after 3 am I woke, startled, sweating, muscles aching. I'd dreamed I was rock-climbing, in a blizzard. While edging along a narrow snow-covered ledge, I lost my footing. At an ever-increasing speed I slid down an icy face, never reaching the bottom . . . until . . . I saw myself from above, head bowed sitting with the unconscious Roy in palliative care. It was the morning he died. It occurred to me as I lay, stomach in knots, that I had two very different fathers: a humble, honourable man, and a priest.

Chapter 39

QUORN, 15 APRIL 2019

'I look at it every day and never tire of it! Father Vin was such a good priest and a talented artist!' Sue was all smiles at the front door as she ushered us into the lounge to see the painting by my father, which had held pride of place above her mantelpiece for over forty years. We'd all been invited for morning tea, but as Kate needed more time to contemplate these developments it was just Mitch, Sandy and I. We'd ostensibly been invited to see my father's painting, won in an Immaculate Conception raffle in the seventies . . . but it was obvious Sue was also curious.

The painting was all sunset oranges and dense mission browns. I leaned in to study it, smell it. It was proficient, well composed, but heavily stylised—kitsch even. Kate's trained artist's eye would later, seeing a photo, dismissively conclude, 'It's of an era— amateur artist.'

I was a little stunned, and certainly impressed, that the gruff priest in my mind had produced this. The work of my father's calloused hand, a landscape featuring the silhouette of a gum tree beside a river, or perhaps a lake. 'Is it the Murray River, do you think, Sue?'

'I don't know, Father never said,' she replied.

Though not to my taste, I could see why Sue adored it. 'Oh, it's fabulous, Sue. It's terrific, isn't it?' I nodded hopefully to Mitch and Sandy. 'Do you mind if I take a picture of it?'

'Go for your life,' Sue replied happily. 'You know, Father Vin, after he got his cancer diagnosis and had his *big operation,* he took up landscape painting,' Sue called out from the kitchen. 'He had an exhibition in Adelaide, he even won an art competition in New Zealand. His paintings were in demand for fundraising prizes for an order of nuns in Sydney.' There was pride in her voice.

'Really, which one?' She told me: it was Maggie's order. I glanced to Sandy who'd already made the connection.

Sue returned from the kitchen with a tray loaded with cups of tea and sponge cake. Locking eyes she asked, 'Do you paint, Brendan?'

I thought I felt another hot flush coming on. 'No, no—just the bathroom and kitchen.'

As everyone laughed, I broke her gaze to look out to the backyard. Here we go again, I thought, beyond uncomfortable. Sandy was right, Sue thought I was the 1950 mystery baby, or another of Vin's offspring.

As we settled down on the back verandah, Sue recalled the week she won the artwork. 'It was in 1977 or 1978, he was relieving at the church, and occupied himself with his art. He insisted at the end of his sermon that the entire congregation go and buy more tickets—"We're not yet sold out!"' Sue dutifully bought a second book of tickets and got lucky.

With his characteristic heart-on-sleeve openness, Mitch had won her over, as only he could. But I was more reserved, feeling duplicitous, probing for information about Vin—and taking pictures of his art—without revealing why. There was plenty of chat about Quorn, the drought and better days. Knowing of Sue's suspicions, I wondered if I was getting a sanitised version of Vin.

In the afternoon Sandy, Mitch and I drove to the outskirts of town for afternoon tea with Shirley, another of the Palm Sunday congregation. Younger than Sue, Shirley was a woman in her fifties who had been baptised, confirmed and married at Immaculate Conception. Vin's final celebration before retirement was to marry Shirley and her truck-driving hubby, Tony.

As we entered the kitchen, we were met with seven of Vin's paintings, all thoughtfully arranged on the benches or skirting the floor. As we studied the art, I was conscious of Shirley studying me. My companions attempted to distract her with conversation about the district and the church, but she was only interested in hearing from me. I was clearly absorbed in inspecting Vin's creative works when Shirley offered, 'Brendan, I'd like you to choose one—to keep.' I was thrilled (I'd hoped she'd offer).

I couldn't decide between two. The first, an accomplished (though still bland) bush landscape, the other a striking portrait of a bare-chested, dark-skinned man. The subject is standing side-on, depicted from the waist up, in some sort of ceremonial headdress. The blood-red background is framed in a highly decorative gold-painted frame. It was compelling, completely out of character with Vin's other work—I loved it. In part, I hoped it said something about my father's appreciation of the First Nations people of this area. In 1991 he'd written to Father Cresp about the Nullarbor Parish, and said he hoped the government left the land to the local people as it was a Sacred Site.

Though I am white and middle-class, I'm also the result of a forced and closed adoption. I'd been surrendered, rejected and then misled by my mother for thirty years about my paternity. Though fortunate in my experience with Bishop

O'Kelly, the fact is that I was treated abysmally by the church. A corrosive vulnerability manifests with the experience. I had been displaced, uprooted to blot out my heritage, nullified from my past to hide all trace of the sin that had created me.

As I was taking a long time to choose, Shirley said, 'Take two—that's fine.' Delighted, I offered to pay—she refused. I felt the kitchen walls shrink in toward me when she added with a knowing look in her eye, 'The paintings will have much more meaning for you than me.'

Sandy ogled me with a *told you* expression.

It was suddenly all too much. My mind was like a dog running on lino, I had to get out of there. We hastily agreed to reconvene at the Transcontinental Hotel for dinner—Shirley and Tony would be our guests.

Having never strayed far from the Australian coast, the Transcontinental struck me as the most Aussie pub I'd ever seen: double-storey, wide verandahs, a corner block in the middle of the main street, almost as if the town had grown up around it. Over dinner it was obvious (to my relief) that Tony and Shirley were huge fans of Vin. Back in the day, as a teenager, Shirley worked in the Quorn newsagency. The TAB was next door. Vin and Shirley had a standing arrangement: at the end of each week he'd stroll to the newsagency and discreetly slip a wad of cash and list of wagers for the weekend meets into her hand. 'And they weren't small bets either,' she added. Vin's 'pet' would then dutifully place the bets, and then scoot up to the presbytery to deliver the betting slips.

Most of the townsfolk appeared to know about Vin's gambling. The farcical deceit of it all, Catholics turning a blind eye—it was a slippery slope. If they allowed their spiritual leader to be a chronic punter, what was holding him back from other risky, far less acceptable behaviour?

Tony chipped in, 'And he always won! One of his brothers was in the racing game—coulda been a trainer?—and he'd give Vin the mail. He never missed a race meeting that could be reached by car. He stood away from the crowds, alone in a big overcoat and scarf, but he wasn't fooling anyone!' I whispered to Kate, 'Remember when the Meaney family told us that Vin only gambled when in Sydney? That little piece of family folklore just got blown out of the water.'

My father loved getting stuck into manual work, forever renovating and upgrading church buildings. 'He was a larrikin,' Shirley told us. 'He'd wind up the locals . . . he'd play one group off against another. He baptised, married and buried a colossal number of parishioners all through South Australia.' I was beginning to grasp the intensely intimate connection that a regional parish priest had to his community.

Unbeknown to me, during our meal Shirley was also chipping away at Kate with questions about me: date of birth, where I was born, interests, who were my adoptive parents and what I did for a living. As the night drew to a close, Shirley asked to have a photo taken of the group. Perhaps an innocent request for a memento, a record of an enjoyable evening together, it triggered my now familiar discomfort. *She just wants a picture of me. What's she going to do with it?* It would have been churlish to decline, but it only made me more uneasy.

Rather than going back to our rooms at the Austral, stuffy after the warmth of the day, the four of us wandered the town's deserted backstreets. Heat rose from the bitumen, it was eerily still, the air was thick with the scent of the towering eucalypts that lined the streets. Freed from prying eyes and suffocating secrets, it was a chance to at last talk honestly with my companions. We buzzed with the news of Vin's contradictory personality, and how the congregation accepted the gambling holy man without any sense of contradiction.

The more we debated Terry, the *other* mysterious baby, the more incensed I felt—an anger that took me by surprise. Listening to Kate and Sandy discuss the bind Maggie had found herself in completely overlooked my situation. At that moment, it felt like they too readily gave her the benefit of the doubt. I blurted out, 'Hang on! Maggie is a bloody liar. She lived with the Shiels. I bet she knows all about this Terry Shiel. I bet he's at least my half-brother. And I reckon there's half a chance he's my full-blown brother, too.' I was hurt by a new and painful disillusion-ment. My vow-breaking priest father could at least have been faithful to my mother . . . the image I wanted was slipping away. Nocturnal creatures foraging in the undergrowth, scampering over parched ground, stopped in their tracks and tuned in.

The next morning, Kate called Maggie.

'We're in Quorn, touring Vin's old churches. Brendan's got a bee in his bonnet—he's on a mission to find out everything about Vin.'

Wearily, Maggie responded, 'Oh no. Why?'

A little incredulous, Kate reminded her, 'Well you did agree— not so long ago—that he has a right to know about his family.'

'Yes, well. Driving all the way up there, that's what Vin would have done. He sounds exactly like the Father.' Her reply was curt.

Maggie's anxiety increased when Kate told her about attending the Easter service at Immaculate Conception and that the locals had told Brendan how much he looked like Father Vin. Though Kate reassured her we'd kept her identity secret, this came as a stressful new development. Despite Maggie's relentless denial, I hadn't ceased to exist.

There was no choice but to venture further into our new discoveries. Kate laid it out, as tactfully as she could: 'A parishioner told us the story of a baby who'd been flown to Sydney in 1950 under instruction of Vin. They assumed the mystery child was Brendan, though we know it couldn't have been because the dates aren't right . . . Maggie, who is that baby? Could it be Brendan's half-brother?'

Maggie, to my great surprise, was more forthcoming than I'd expected. 'Well, I don't know a lot . . . but . . . I can tell you a Whyalla doctor asked Vin to place the child, who was born on a station in Iron Knob. He wanted him placed in a good Catholic home. Vin decided that good Catholic home would be with William, his older brother, in Sydney. So the child was brought up a Shiel. He's still alive, too,' she added, 'a nice boy. He'd be nearly seventy now.'

Drawing her back to the original question, I heard Kate repeat: 'Is Terry Shiel Brendan's brother? It's important he knows.'

Maggie was adamant. 'Oh, no, no. He isn't. That boy wasn't Vin's child.'

'How do you know?'

Evidently growing impatient, Maggie reasoned, 'Because, because he doesn't look like a Shiel. Because . . . well, he's short.'

'Maggie, Brendan knows so little about his parents' relationship, his ancestry—it's not unreasonable, is it?'

With that my mother lightened up a little, and then changed the subject completely. 'In the early 1980s Vin asked if I'd move in and look after him. I considered the proposition carefully and in time agreed. Kate, he was an old man by this stage. It'd only be for a few years—I assumed—but it ended up being about a decade.' I'd never known her to put it so bluntly. It struck me as mercenary, transactional. It stank of poverty, even desperate calculation. It was confronting to hear her talk that way, their cohabitation a pragmatic decision, not my hoped-for fantasy of two soul mates finally free of the church and able to live as one.

'He was an extremely persistent individual. When we disagreed, I'd say, "Can't you just drop it? Let it go, please!" But he never would. He was impulsive . . . and it sounds like Brendan is much like his father!' Now the sudden segue made sense: Maggie was scolding me.

'If Brendan gets an idea in his head, he cannot be stopped,' Kate agreed, and she and Maggie were as one again, as they had been surprisingly often over the past twenty years.

But Maggie was at her limit, eager to end an unsettling call. 'That's all I know, Kate. This doesn't involve me. I must go.'

Kate managed to get in one final statement: 'The locals urged us to contact Evie Murphy.'

That came as a bolt from the blue for my suddenly exposed mother. 'Please, Kate, please don't let Brendan contact Evie. She'll never talk to me again.'

Kate reassured her, 'We won't, I know, he won't . . . don't worry.'

Now pacified, in a despairing voice, my mother's last words were, 'He's just like his father!'

As Kate wearily relayed the details of the call, it began to spill out of me: 'I feel like a friggin' hostage. There's always an exchange taking place—she only discloses information when presented with our new findings. She'll release a morsel of my story only if I agree to keep her secret . . . Jesus Christ. I'm going for a walk.' Like glass buried in a wound, eventually her lies always worked their way to the surface.

As I meandered up and down the deserted streets of Quorn, behind high fences dogs barked at the unexpected pedestrian. So Maggie didn't love Vin after all?

Kate was drained by her conversations with Maggie, all made at my insistence. In 2009, when I asked Kate to persuade Maggie to meet our family, an indelible bond between the two had been formed. Maggie only agreed to meet me because Kate asked her to. In convincing my reluctant mother, Kate had created an obligation to protect my mother. Oblivious to it at the time, my asking Kate to be the go-between put her in an unenviable position of competing loyalties. I'd made her the meat in the sandwich.

Kate's phone rang early the next morning. It was my mother. 'I didn't sleep a wink last night. I'm so worried Brendan is going to contact Evie.'

For decades, Kate and I have initiated almost every communication with Maggie. She has reached out just twice. Both occasions had been when my existence seemed close to becoming public knowledge.

Now, more pieces were added to my puzzle. Terry Shiel's mother was a young girl from an outback station that had fallen pregnant to a stationhand. 'Terry met his birth mother,' Maggie noted, 'but they were never close.' (The intimation was that he knew his place, being a grateful adoptee.) Without prompting, Maggie then revealed that the executor of her will was her nephew, the son of her eldest sister. Why in God's name did she want us to know that?

That night, after everyone had gone to bed, I sat at my laptop, trying to calm myself, and bring some order to it all:

1 My biology matters. What does Maggie think I'll do after she dies? In my mind I'll respect her wishes and not make contact with maternal family until she's gone; but after that, all bets are off. Should I write and let her know? Maggie's behaviour is cruel.

2 Is Terry Shiel really my half-brother? What evidence is there? How can I find out? Who will I upset?

3 Who is the most appropriate recipient of my parents' assets? Surely it's not the bloody Catholic Church? Or Pell's legal

team!?! Is it Vin and Maggie's only two grandchildren? Or
Maggie's nieces and nephews? What's right?

4   20+ years ago Maggie said when she dies her solicitor will
    contact me. With what advice?

5   Feel I've been bound and gagged!

Much of what I've read on church abuse speaks of opportunistic coercive control over children, the weak, the broken,
the vulnerable—the most pitiful. Yet, here I am, a successful,
educated, independent 58-year-old feeling like a marionette. One
moment a thread is tugged and I leap to attention; the next,
a thread is released and I fall to the floor.

I turn off the light and try to sleep.

Chapter 40

QUORN & WHYALLA, 16 APRIL 2019

The Great Northern Lodge and the Quandong Cafe vied for our ongoing breakfast custom. The Lodge led by a short half head. Over a generous helping of scrambled eggs and buttery white toast, I handed Mitch a copy of *Witness*, the SA Catholic news, from October 1977. It carried a feature story about Vin published the month before his retirement, when he was living just a few blocks down the road. The cover photo was Vin looking like a late-in-life Monet. 'Look at him, decked out in priest clobber while painting at his easel, he's pitching himself as some sort of Renaissance man.' This was just one of several mind-blowing photographs of him. 'It's his whole life story: builder, traveller, Ireland, the Trappists, the desert, Sheen, his famous Kombi, New York, uranium mine . . . The revered Holy Man chased by German U-boats as he left Europe during the war . . . I dunno, he must've cultivated the reputation . . . I still can't believe that guy there is my father. And funny . . . they left out the bit about his bastard son!' I was feeling uneasy about the angst I'd inflicted on Mitch and Sandy for a couple of days now. 'Anyway, I wish you both a highly uneventful day, it's been a bit intense, hasn't it?'

Heading back through the Flinders Ranges to Whyalla, Kate and I had an appointment with Father Liam Ryan. I was apprehensive, unsure how I'd cope with any more thunderbolts like the discovery of Terry Shiel.

I'd done a background check on Liam. He was an outstanding example of the contribution priests can make to a community. As the one-time parish priest of Woomera and Roxby Downs, he supported hundreds of asylum seekers locked in the detention centres. He was a member of the Compassion & Justice for Refugees Group, as well as contributing to the Prison Ministry, Alcoholics Anonymous, Good Sam Inn Kitchen, Men Alive, Nature Retreats, the Catholic Women's League and St Vincent de Paul.

We arranged to meet at a decommissioned presbytery Vin had stayed in when posted to Whyalla, which was situated over the road from an equally derelict convent. After handshakes, and as an icebreaker within minutes of meeting, Liam recounted 'the infamous tunnel story', a decades-old community joke about a subterranean tunnel that supposedly joined the priest and nun accommodation. Liam knew who my parents were . . . all I could offer was a grimace. He looked away hurriedly. Mine clearly wasn't the usual response.

Over a cuppa at a nearby cafe, Liam told us of the day he met my father, up in Hawker, north of Quorn. 'Father Vin was in the throes of excavating a water pipe requiring replacement. Though it was late morning and the heat intense, your seventy-plus-year-old father was out in the full sun, sweating over a crowbar and mattock. And strangest of all, he was wearing his full-length black robes. Odd . . .' My father, fixed on finishing the job, didn't even invite the young padre in for refreshments. 'We shook hands and spoke very briefly. I don't recall about what. I'd heard he was a no-nonsense sort of man. Brendan, that's all I know.'

I steered the conversation to the state of the church, Pell being the first topic. Liam was dubious about the allegations. 'It's unlikely anybody could remove the heavy robes in the short amount of time alleged. It's just not satisfactory that he could be found guilty of such a heinous crime without a witness or forensic evidence.'

To my mind, he was talking nonsense. 'But Liam, there are hundreds—thousands—of rape and abuse victims who don't have a witness or forensic evidence. They're telling the truth . . . aren't they?'

'Pell was hated by many, within and outside of the church. He's an easy target.'

Confounded, determined not to swear, I faltered, trying to find the right words. Was he seriously suggesting that the complainant—and the fellow altar boy who'd committed suicide—made up the claim? I sat quietly, exchanged a nonplussed expression with Kate, stupidly surprised that a senior cleric would seem so ignorant of contemporary research on the nature of sexual abuse. Attempting to right the ship he conceded, 'Yes, there's a lot of smoke surrounding George. I hope more charges will be laid so they can be tested and proven—if correct.'

We discussed our parish experiences. I shared the discovery that Vin had sent a South Australian baby to Sydney to be adopted by his brother in 1950.

'Yes. I know the story.'

I was dumbfounded, managing only, 'How do you know?' My mind raced. Why hadn't he shared it in previous calls? Why wasn't the story recorded in Vin's records? I'd been told the file on my father was complete—I'd assumed that was true.

Giving Liam the benefit of the doubt, I speculated that the church might be trying to protect me. But whatever was going on, I had no leverage. I stayed silent on the topic. Instead, I explained how uncomfortable it was meeting parishioners who said I reminded them of Father Vin.

'It's not the end of the world for the church if the fact that you're Vin's son gets out.' Liam's face was expressionless.

Confused, I countered, 'For the sake of the parishioners, if this sort of news got around it would only further harm the reputation of the church—it could end up in the media—and I'm worried about Maggie. The last thing the church and local parishes need is more scandal . . .'

A picture of ambivalence, Liam shrugged.

I felt like shaking him. Had he absorbed the enormity of my situation? That my flesh-and-blood father was a remote South Australian priest, just like him. He didn't get it. (Did anybody?) As we rose to leave, just as Shirley had done the night before, Liam asked if he could take a photo with Kate and me. Trophy hunting? Again, we reluctantly agreed.

In the car, Kate looked at me and said, 'I'm not comfortable with these people taking our photo.'

'Yep,' I replied. 'He'll be in the presbytery tonight saying, "Look, that man there—he's the son of a priest and a woman that was a nun. See, there really was an underground tunnel!"'

He hadn't been how I'd imagined. Perhaps stupidly, I'd half-hoped the clouds would part and a beam of enlightenment would bathe us all in a glow of clarity. At the very least, I'd hoped he was a man with some answers, conviction, some emotional intelligence. I turned to Kate. 'All these clerics are flying the flag at half-mast.'

Chapter 41

PORT AUGUSTA, 16 APRIL 2019

Deflated from our encounter with Father Liam, we hightailed it out of Whyalla. With Kate behind the wheel, we headed to Port Augusta, Maggie's home for the first eighteen years of her life. The town where my parents met. My mother was sixteen. My father forty-seven.

Scanning in my mind through the revelations of the past few days, and now this confounding Whyalla meeting, I turned to Kate and said, 'Bloody hell, mate, what a cheery day. We're gluttons for punishment—thanks for being here.' I sat in the passenger seat and read some notes set aside for the day. 'Here's a letter from Vin's bishop from 1946. He commended Vin on his excellent work in town and then goes on to say there's scope in Port Augusta for Vin's well-known "zeal". The direction from the bishop was to find the young people, to make visits to their homes. It was the welfare of the young he had to pay most attention to, it seems.' The word *zeal* jumped out. I googled it. Zeal—noun: fervour for a person, cause, or object; eager desire or endeavour; enthusiastic diligence; ardour.

'Ow, those words: "fervour", "desire", "ardour".' Given the appearance of Terry, and knowing Maggie's age when Vin arrived in Port Augusta . . . it's so uncomfortable, sinister even. Particularly after seeing the ambivalence of some of these priests.

I found an ABC article online titled 'Celibacy, order and obedience: Inside the Christian Brothers'. Though it dealt with brothers, I read out the comments on religious life: 'It stunted their psychosexual development . . . they were uneasy with adult relationships . . . the dominance over young people exerted itself in a very catastrophic way, in the way of abuse, both physical and sexual.' The article then referred to the royal commission and how religious life led to men becoming 'cognitively rigid'.

'Not that I'm suggesting Vin and Maggie were sexually active in these years—I hope not—but it highlights an explosive combination of forces, doesn't it? A bishop instructing psychosexually stunted priests to pursue with ardour young kids. Arrrgh!'

Approaching Port Augusta, I reviewed what we knew. 'Firstly, Vin started here in 1948. His forties had been tumultuous— PTSD, ill health, restlessness in the desert. In 1947 he'd hit a roo on his way back to Sydney. Though the vehicle was badly damaged, he pressed on until a front wheel broke off in Mittagong and he flew off the road. As you do. Badly banged up, he took leave in Sydney. While there, at his own initiative, he attempted to arrange a permanent exchange with a local priest. When word of his meddling made it back to SA, the bishop struck it down. Six months later, his mother died. Vin was then an orphan . . .

'Fast forward another few months and he applied to be a missionary in Japan after the *Enola Gay* dropped the A-bombs. Also knocked back. He fell ill—chest pain, lung issues and rectal bleeding. He took himself to Adelaide for X-rays, leading to lengthy medical interventions, and more leave in Sydney . . . and yet another run-in with an increasingly irritable bishop, who shunted Vin here . . . Welcome to Port Augusta! Thanks for attending my TED Talk . . .'

As we turned off the Stuart Highway, I summarised: 'He'd lost his mum, been injured in a bingle, was worried about potentially serious health issues, craved escape from the monotony of these tin-pot-town priest gigs, and was approaching fifty. He was despondent, I assume lonely, and sexually frustrated . . . and he lands here . . .' With a grand gesture, I sweep my arm across the dash toward a drab concoction of town-fringe factories, supersized roadhouses and run-down houses. 'He was a self-made builder from Sydney, he had money. He should have handed in the dog-collar and walked.'

The many boarded-up shops along Commercial Road looked like missing teeth. Some of the prominent civic buildings appeared long closed; one had been torched. If location scouts were searching for a dystopian Mad Max-styled backdrop, they'd be wise to check out Port Augusta. Few people occupy the street, most of them kids, some in groups, drinking. Since learning of my maternal roots in Port Augusta, and knowing how unhappy Maggie was there, I'd built a grim, soulless picture in my mind. And that's what we found.

As Kate parked, without thinking, I gathered up the few valuables from the car. Windows up tight, doors locked. We strolled the main drag. I pulled out a photo Maggie had given me of the Becker family home. The tin cottage in Flinders Street, more than a hundred years old, should be just around the corner. I'd hoped, irrationally, for some DNA-imprinted recognition of the house, a scent of the familiar, but was distracted by thoughts of what we'd do if the car was gone when we got back. We marched up and down Flinders Street in the heat, where the hell was it? After twenty-five minutes, sweating and frustrated, I checked the satellite map and realised the Becker home had been levelled and the land repurposed as a side-yard for a neighbour. Strike one.

We then drove to a street on the outskirts of town where maternal relatives once lived. It's populated by a mix of reasonably well-maintained homes, most with aluminium window shutters sealed tight. Elsewhere, broken windows, overgrown yards, front doors ajar, or missing entirely . . . it unsettled me. I'd rarely seen this degree of poverty firsthand. How sheltered I'd been.

As we cruised to our destination, half-a-dozen Aboriginal teenagers laughed and roughhoused along the side of the road. Decked out in a mix of worn AFL and NBA singlets, they looked like good kids with few good options. They met our eyes briefly as we passed, knowing we weren't locals.

Found at the southern edge of town, our destination boasted a panoramic vista of the Spencer Gulf, a view Melbournians or Sydneysiders would pay seven figures for. But there was nobody enjoying the view; there wasn't a soul to be seen. We pulled over onto the raised gravel riverbank. I googled house prices. 'A three-bedroom house here averages $150K and is trending steadily downward. Look,' I said, attempting to pass the phone to Kate. 'Let's buy that one!' I wasn't serious, she knew.

She shrugged, wordlessly. It had been one of those days.

We swigged from our water bottles, ate an apple, stared across the gulf. 'I don't know what any of this means, frankly . . . Terry Shiel, the Father Liam meeting, no family home, this bloody street—I don't belong here. All I want to do is leave.' With exquisite timing, a magpie then swooped low and, at speed, shat right in the middle of my windscreen.

We decided after this unedifying hometown visit to head northward and seek inspiration from a huge solar farm I spied on Google Maps. Relieved to be departing, and with me now driving, Kate pulled out the iPad. Our son has his own YouTube channel, and his biggest fan is his mum. She'd been monitoring his video view-count all trip, and now she saw Pat's channel view numbers surging. It was apparent he'd reach the magic one million target this very day. As we navigated our way along a corrugated red dirt road toward the Bungala Solar Power Project, Kate tried unsuccessfully to text and call him back in Melbourne. He'd just posted content—the numbers were exploding—we had to talk.

There we were, smack bang in the middle of nowhere, rolling down a dirt track—dodging suicidal emus—pulling over every ten minutes to screenshot a count up to 1 million. And just as we sighted an ocean of life-affirming solar panels glinting on the parched red plain, the digits clicked to 1 million. Kate successfully captured the 1 million hero shot. Could there be a more unlikely location to share this family highlight? It took a little while, but we raised the lad on the mobile, and gushed excitedly while walking the perimeter of the sun farm. He was thrilled. We happily talked over each other—our family has ridden on the successes of his social-media meanderings for years—and then the mobile signal failed.

They say you're only as happy as your least happy child, so we checked in on our daughter, Nell, too. She was out with friends, buzzing, and thrilled about Pat's achievement. It lifted Kate and me—elated, nothing else mattered, least of all the crazy-sad ancestral secrets we were stirring up in South Australia.

We had watched the first couple of seasons of *Game of Thrones* as a family over the previous year or two. I particularly enjoyed the parallel of the *GoT* lead Jon Snow (a bastard like me). As it happened, Snow had discovered his true ancestry shortly before our South Australian trip. Referencing that Kate and I hadn't quite got around to marrying, our son had begun jovially describing himself as 'the bastard son of the bastard son of a priest and a nun'.

The phone bleeped. Pat. We finished the chat, told him we loved him, then stomped the red dust from our boots and got back in the car to return to the refuge of dear friends and the mighty Flinders Ranges. With Port Augusta in the rear-view mirror, our fabulous son and daughter back in Melbourne were the only reality that counted. The unhurried, twisty road back to Mitch and Sandy in Quorn was a tonic.

I think back over the conversation with Pat, him hearing the disappointment of my Whyalla and Port Augusta visits, and repeating a Jon Snow line: 'We're not defined by our blood. We make our own choices.'

For once, the right words pop into my head at just the right time. 'Life isn't about finding yourself or finding anything, life is about creating yourself.' It's a Bob Dylan quote from an interview I had recently read, though I suspect old Bob had recycled it from George Bernard Shaw.

Those lines never felt more true than on that day.

Chapter 42

HAWKER, 17 APRIL 2019

'Father Vin liked to annoy the nuns. Though I was extremely fond of him, I would have to say he was an unusual character.

'Even though they insisted he write down mass times each week, he'd often start the service half an hour late, or earlier, and they'd miss it. Also, he'd regularly leave out the sermon to allow members of sporting teams to get to their games on time—none of the other priests did that! And my brothers, they'd complain about him to me . . . when out working in the paddocks of a Sunday morning, Father would sometimes fly past and yell from the window "Come in, we're doing mass and you're the altar boys!" By the time they got cleaned up and over to the church, it was half over—he didn't wait—he was forever testing people, winding them up.

'He'd provoke just to get a reaction. I don't know what it was, if it was fun . . . or if he was bored. I was on the Hawker church council when Father Vin first arrived. I suppose I'm from his inner sanctum—you were either in or out with Vin, and I was definitely in.'

Hawker is four hundred kilometres north of Adelaide and four hundred kilometres west of Broken Hill. Mitch, Sandy, Kate and I were with long-time church assistant Margaret O'Shea in the Saints Philip & James Church presbytery. Built in 1922, the presbytery is a proud stone-block building with detailed internal finishes, wide corridors, high ceilings, half-a-metre-wide stone interior walls and verandahs all around. Resilient design for a punishing climate.

An upright and clear-eyed woman, Margaret was hard to put an age on. I'd guess mid-eighties, possibly nineties. She spoke with a determination that suggested she'd outlive all of us. 'I remember one day, well, you need to understand it was not the done thing to overtake a priest out on the dirt roads after mass. Custom was for the priest to be the first to drive away from church—no stones and dust for God's messenger. One time after mass, Father Vin, while leading the procession of cars, deliberately drove so slowly as to provoke a reaction. Now—my son was a bit of a hothead—and fed up, he flew past the line of cars and kicked up gravel all over Father's vehicle. And, oh my, this incident brought about some grief within our family! Father *never* allowed us to forget it!' Margaret arched her back and let out an infectious belly laugh.

'He was different, yes—unconventional. For example, he didn't like the pulpit and performed mass from ground level. He wanted to be close to the congregation. It was a little confronting for some . . . oh yes, and after mass, in the winter, he'd emerge from church wearing a Geelong footy beanie. I've no idea if he was a fan of the Cats. Maybe he was given the beanie, or found it, but it was a very odd sight—a priest in full holy regalia wearing a striped beanie!' Becoming slightly lost in her reminiscences, Margaret righted herself. 'But he was also a very holy man. If you were very sick, he was there, generous and thoughtful.'

We were taken on a tour. The two front rooms were crammed full: Jesus and Mary statues, altar boy vestments, chalices, pews, candles and an enormous crucifix. In one corner sat an old twenty-litre steel drum with black handpainted words: 'HOLY WATER'. Vin may have painted those words. Waving a hand toward the unexpected collection, Margret explained, 'They're all from inside the church. It's not in use at the moment, we're renovating. We received a windfall from a group who want to build a uranium storage plant at Wallerberdina Station, just out of town. It's causing much distress for some locals . . .'

We'd seen several homemade posters around the Flinders Ranges—mostly against the dump-site construction—competing with a handful of professionally printed pro-job, pro-dump signs. It was jarring to see my father's old church being resurrected courtesy of uranium dollars. Never get between the Catholic Church and a buck.

Margaret uncovered a large timber honour board. Among the priests listed, it showed *Shiel. V 1962*—my father's first appointment in Hawker, the year after my birth—and a second notation from 1969 to 1977, the year of his retirement.

'When he preached, he liked to talk about Archbishop Sheen. He'd call him *The Archbishop*. He'd often preach about Lourdes.' Margaret was on a roll. 'Hmm . . . what else . . . ? He despised the Queen and that Labor Party. Loved old Ned Kelly. And he'd let you know it, too!' Margaret laughed out loud while shaking her head. She was easy to like.

'He didn't like other priests at his mass. He'd rarely deliver a sermon if another preacher was in attendance. He thought of himself as an Irishman, too. He'd often come out with the phrase, "You're not going to best me, woman!" His father apparently often said it to his mother.'

'How'd he occupy his spare time, Margaret?' Kate asked. 'What about his landscape painting?'

'Ah yes, he took up painting due to his health issues, and his advancing years, of course. The hard physical building work wasn't possible after the stomach cancer, the tumour on his arm, a few bouts of pneumonia. He built himself an enclosed space underneath the rear verandah of the presbytery and would spend hours out there teaching himself to paint.' She pointed out the window to the location; I snapped furiously with my camera. This was one of the most expansive descriptions of Vin we'd heard, I was delighted. As my companions engaged with Margaret, I quickly typed notes into my phone, as she went on.

'Father Vin seemed to have cancer quite a few times. The first time was under his watch, where he wore it. He said at Radium Hill there wasn't sufficient water to wash with—he couldn't get away from the radioactive dust. He was a colourful man, though he did run hot and cold. Some days were far better than others. Father had bad nerves after the closure of Radium Hill—heartbroken at the disappointment, I think—he was so proud of that church that he'd built.'

I felt an overwhelming urge to tell Margaret that his emotional state was quite possibly because of me. To say, 'The year before Vin arrived in Hawker he had a son. It was me. Vin is my father. He was in mourning because he'd gotten a young woman pregnant. They put me up for adoption . . .'

Maybe Margaret reminded me of Bet. I felt like giving her a hug, and I didn't want to conceal the truth again. But I did.

When Kate and I were in Whyalla, Father Liam told us that the Hawker church was being renovated and they'd uncovered something of Vin's that I'd like to see. Margaret duly led us across to the church. She explained that when the altar was being removed

by tradesmen, a large sheet of timber with an inscription had
been found. Now inside, treading cautiously across the bearers
and polished timber flooring, she gestured to a large sheet of
chipboard. In a thick chippies' pencil, in a beautiful elaborate
hand, was an inscription:

AD MAJOREM DEI GLORIAM [For the Greater Glory
of God]
Built by Father Shiel Parish Priest Hawker Quorn 1976

I took photos, and then placed my hand on his writing. I
looked up and saw Margaret studying me with kind eyes. What
did she know?

Later, back at the Austral, we contemplated what people would
be told if they drove around our old workplaces forty years after
we'd departed. 'I'm sure some'd say I was a cantankerous prick,
hopefully a couple would add *with a good heart*. My point being,
my work persona is harsher than the person I am at home.'

I half-jokingly added, 'We could end the tour here, today.
That was a good thread told by Margaret. I sure as hell don't need
another Terry Shiel whack—why push my luck?'

Kate, Mitch and Sandy looked back with sceptical faces. They
knew that once I'd got started on a project, it was going to be
finished, come what may.

As if to punctuate conversation, the bartender turned up the
TV news. The Notre Dame cathedral in Paris had caught fire
two days earlier. Five hundred firefighters battled the flames.
They were now dousing the smouldering embers; smoke poured
from one of the most widely recognised symbols of Catholic
pre-eminence in Europe. Drone footage showed vast destruc-
tion to the Gothic masterpiece. Officials marched through
smoke, salvaging artworks and priceless relics. Stunned onlookers

watched helplessly. An elderly couple on the footpath held hands, sobbing.

A blank-faced old man told an interviewer, 'It can never be what it once was.'

Chapter 43

QUORN, 18–19 APRIL 2019

No rain. No green.

Ribs protruded vertically along the sides of the few dirt-caked sheep. They had no value, weak, beyond redemption. The entire week in Quorn, I spotted just three domesticated animals: a gluggy-eyed tabby with barely half a tail; the publican's mangy three-legged dog; and Quorn locals Sue and Peter's white cat that could pass for a snow leopard. Just three pets in a week, and all of them could get a gig in the circus.

I've known Frank for almost as long as I can remember. Another of my flashbulb memories is reclining in the early-evening sun on the warm scalloped brick fence of Frank's family home. We were waiting for Roy to pick me up. I was around nine, about 1970. I'd bring my shoebox of stamps and we'd swap them all afternoon, in between drinking cordial and watching *F Troop* on TV. What hip kids we were.

Frank had left Melbourne at 4 am, aiming to reach Quorn by mid-arvo. He pulled in to the Austral around 3 pm, looking as fit as a butcher's dog. Travelling 1080 kilometres is a fair effort for a solo driver. With Frank here, the Fabulous Five Tour Party was now complete. After giving him a quick debrief, he retired for a kip and I returned to my laptop: it was a recording and contemplating day for me.

That night over dinner at the pub, we brought Frank up to speed. It sounded exaggerated, hyperreal, there'd been such a volume of information gathered in such a short time. Frank sat wide-eyed, listening intently.

After a couple of beers, at last feeling I didn't have to be on guard, I opened up. 'Sandy, Mitch, I gotta let you know how much I appreciate you being here. I hadn't anticipated any of the things that we've discovered . . . wow, particularly Terry Shiel! I've felt overwhelmed . . . it's not like me. I thought I'd take it in my stride, but . . . It's fabulous that you've been able to step in and distract the locals, at all the right times . . . making the atmosphere light when necessary. And that you, Mitch, can talk engines and cars stuff with the blokes—the crap I'm clueless at. It's been a godsend—nah, hang on, there's gotta be a non-religious word? A blessing?'

Kate chipped in, 'And I'm so happy to have Sandy here to exchange family theories with, and escape to the oppies and get away from you guys rabbiting on . . .' Tilting her head toward me, she added, 'He would have been a nightmare if you two weren't here.'

The next morning, shortly after dawn, Frankie drove us twenty kilometres north to Warren Gorge. Though not the most spectacular formation, it was a welcome visual relief from the parched expanse of this southern section of the ranges. Relaxed, we chatted and stretched our legs along the walking tracks. Frank still hadn't said anything about our discoveries. Getting back into the car, it was as if the surreal threads he'd heard the night before finally locked into place. 'So, hang on—your brother is a racing car driver?'

At the Quandong Cafe for breakfast, happy for a new tour member to chat with, conversation ended up with the church and the sanctity of the seal of confession, an issue that had been in the media. Without warning, I found myself agitated, finger-pointing at Mitch. 'Listen, the Catholic Church has a choice to make. It's either going to obey the law and compel priests to report abuse allegations or lose its tax-free status and government funding. It's been proven via court hearings and most comprehensively in the royal commission that the church places its bank balance and reputation above the suffering of victims!'

At the end of my rant, I registered Frank, Kate, Sandy and Mitch all silent, looking a little put-out. I glanced around the cafe and noticed that the people at the table next to us had stopped talking, too. They stole a glance at me in unison. I'd been talking louder than was reasonable, and about a subject not at all appropriate for a sleepy cafe at nine in the morning. Taken aback, I felt I should apologise to Mitch, but I didn't. He'd found a nerve close to the surface.

My unresolved questions about church silencing loomed large. I was angry at myself for lying about my identity. Why was I putting everyone else's feelings above mine? There was much investigation to do around the children of priests in Australia when we got back to Melbourne.

Yet again, we'd noticed parishioners eyeing us, knowingly. Sometimes in the pub and general store, it felt as though people stopped their conversations, craning to hear what we were saying. Was I paranoid? No, the others sensed it, too. We agreed to code future conversations: when discussing Vin's exploits, he would be referred to as 'Kev'. Any reference to the church would be referred to as 'the shed'.

Chapter 44

QUORN, WILMINGTON & PETERBOROUGH, 20 APRIL 2019

After seven nights at the Austral, it was time to head to Peterborough, where the opening of the Radium Hill Museum was to take place the following day. Vin's years at the long-abandoned uranium mine were what he was most renowned for. The museum opening was the event that instigated our tour of South Australia. We set off in convoy.

We made a fuel stop at Wilmington, one of the most defeated-looking towns we'd happened upon. As our travel mates wandered the few shops, Kate and I grabbed a quick coffee. In the cafe, a local-history brochure spoke of the heritage-listed Catholic church: 'Rev Father Shiel will be remembered for his untiring work in personally renovating the interior of the church.'

St Alexis and St John Nepomucene Roman Catholic Church was at the edge of town. We gulped our coffees and went for a wander. Inside, I got chatting to a local parishioner and Sister Lily, a Josephite nun, busily arranging Easter decorations. 'We hope we might get as many as six or seven for the mass tomorrow.'

Sister Lily was a fit and determined-looking woman, probably in her sixties, short grey hair, black eyebrows and striking watery blue eyes. Maybe because of her remarkable eyes, or because of my own wonky eye, she looked away every time I attempted eye contact. When pressed, she volunteered that she'd heard the name Father Shiel but had never met him. I found her quiet intensity fascinating. I wanted to engage, to hear her story, but was abruptly cut short. I left her to her decorations and inspected the cavernous stone building, looking for traces of Vin.

Not long after, I saw Kate and Lily sitting at the rear of the church, deep in conversation. As I approached, the just-a-moment-ago-highly-animated nun lost her words. Prompting her, Kate repeated what she'd just been told: 'We were talking about the grumpy old Irish priests; how they move in, don't ask the nuns or the locals what's required, make sweeping changes that nobody asked for and then ship out.' Though Kate encouraged Lily to elaborate, she wouldn't. Providing an opening, I said, 'We've learned Father Vin was a man who played favourites and always wanted things his own way: he had many detractors.' Lips sealed, Lily eyed me suspiciously. I read that look and headed outside.

After half an hour, Kate emerged. 'Poor thing, the priests have messed up the Catholic Church. In her mind the dislocation of the church from the community was all the fault of the priests.' As we walked along the rocky shoulder of the road back to join the others, we speculated on what it would have been like to meet Maggie when she was a nun. It was revealing that Sister Lily had no interest in talking with me, but was candid with Kate, just as Maggie is.

'Do you think she knew something about Vin that she wasn't letting on?' I asked.

Kate set me straight. 'There was no indication. We'll never know everything. Smoke and mirrors, church secrets—it was a long, long time ago—you can't jump at every shadow.'

That night we visited both of Peterborough's finest pubs, the first to dine in, the second to watch the revitalised Tigers defeat the Swans. Bishop O'Kelly's influence in high places continued to shine a light on Punt Road, Richmond. Miraculously, pimple-faced kids played like veterans, warhorses like colts. Back from an unjust, indeed immoral, suspension, Dusty Martin ran amok like a fox in the chook shed. We met a well-hydrated local looking for an ear to chew. Fishing for compliments, Tom, with a wobble of the head, boasted, 'People say I look just like that actor Gary Sweet!' Admittedly, he was bald.

Tomorrow promised unseen photos, town records and hopefully revealing conversations with old mining families who knew my inscrutable father at the peak of his powers.

I awoke early the next morning with a stiff neck, shoulders taut as though I'd swum the English Channel.

Chapter 45

PETERBOROUGH, 21 APRIL 2019

Over breakfast, we amused ourselves with an ongoing joke about the book I'd threatened to write about my ancestry, and who'd play the main characters when it was turned into a blockbuster movie. For months I'd insisted Brad Pitt was already signed to play me. It was a non-negotiable that Claudia Karvan had to play Kate. Hiring Telly Savalas for Frank would be problematic, as the lollipop man had long since sucked his last Chupa Chup. Mitch wanted Mick Molloy to play him, and we all agreed Sarah Snook was a shoo-in for Sandy. Though the tour party was lighthearted, I carried an uneasy tension. Today could easily turn sour.

Nine months earlier, after Kate had resolved my paternity, I trawled the net for information about Vin. There were several references to his years at Radium Hill. This led me to Kevin Kakoschke, President of the Radium Hill Historical Society. Kevin is a tireless media spokesperson, annual reunion host, museum administrator and author of the society's newsletter. He began his working life as a fitter and turner at the mine in 1953, and remained there until it closed in 1961. Like many in the historical society, he has relatives buried in the mine site cemetery.

From our first phone chat it was evident Kevin didn't mince words, but there was a softer side. He recounted how, many years earlier, he'd installed a large stainless-steel cross in Vin's church. (The cross is still there.) He explained how during a full moon the silver cross turns gold. He also confided that back in the fifties the local policeman saw an apparition inside Our Lady Queen of the World. Was Kevin pulling my leg?

After I explained Vin was a recently identified distant relative, Kevin became impatient, almost agitated. It was an unnecessarily het-up response. He eventually calmed himself, and over three conversations said he'd mail me a newspaper article featuring Vin, a photo of Vin, and email addresses for some of the Catholics from Radium Hill. Nothing came. In my final call, in desperation, I confessed: 'Kevin, this will sound a bit unusual, but . . . Father Shiel is actually my father. It's why I've been pestering you.'

'Well, that doesn't surprise me at all, Brendan!'

It came at me like a train.

'There were stories that'd travelled from Whyalla about Father Shiel. He wasn't popular at all with many in town—a few of the Catholic women had little nice to say about him.' Kevin spat the word 'Catholic' with disdain.

I asked Kevin if he was a member of Vin's congregation.

'No way!'

Trying to sound composed, I asked, 'What exactly were these stories from Whyalla, Kevin?'

To my relief, he wouldn't go any further. Slightly light-headed when I got off the phone, I rationalised that Vin may have flirted with some of the non-Catholic women, but I was kidding myself—I knew the truth could be far worse. Unable to put it from my mind, several weeks later l left a couple of messages on Kevin's answering machine. Nothing. Communication had been terminated.

Lounging in the Peterborough cafe with my mates, the penny dropped. 'Kate, hey, hey, remember when Kevin said—months ago—there were some stories that had travelled from Whyalla about Vin? Well, that's Terry! I reckon Kevin knew the story of the baby flown to Sydney by the priest, just as the Quorn parishioners did. The story must have spread across the district like wildfire! That's why Kevin was so agitated six months back.'

Kate could read the apprehension in my face. She smiled. 'Yeah, that could be it. Let's hope so! How many more half-brothers or sisters do we need?'

Lost in thought, I consoled myself. It's not that bad . . . my father may have only fathered—and fled from—two sons.

Though Kevin had excommunicated me, I'd read about the grand opening of the Radium Hill Museum on the historical society's website. He didn't know what I looked like, but I'd seen his photo on their website—I figured I'd just steer clear of him on the day.

Just after lunchtime, we pulled up at the Peterborough Steamtown Heritage Centre, the new home of the museum, which until recently had been located at the Tikalina Station, outside Radium Hill. There'd been some acrimony between local leaseholders and the historical society that operated the museum. Kevin and his mob had been told to pack and leave.

In one version of the story, the dispute was essentially between Kevin and Mark Francis, leaseholder of the enormous Maldorky Station, which encompasses the mine site, township and cemetery. Neither of the two bulls had a reverse gear.

For decades, the Francis family had allowed those with a family connection to the town to visit each Easter. They could celebrate their history, pay respects to relatives in the cemetery, and undertake preservation works. Many of the annual visitors had been born, married or baptised there. Issues arose when a heritage listing was granted for the site, and grey nomads began venturing down the dirt tracks, getting bogged or lost, leaving gates open, and allegedly killing stock. Kevin, I was told, continued to treat the site as his own, to Mark's frustration.

The rift escalated when Kevin appeared on *Today Tonight*. 'South Australia's Cemetery Scandal' aired in October 2018. It portrayed Kevin as a grieving, vulnerable old man barred from visiting the graves of relatives. That didn't go down well with the rough-and-tumble pastoralists up at the uranium site. All visitors were immediately banned. I'd heard an (unconfirmed) story that a couple had been turned away by the landholders brandishing a shotgun. It sounded like a scene from *The Beverly Hillbillies*. Who knows what the truth was?

After explaining my history with Kevin over breakfast, it was agreed Mitch, Frank, Sandy and Kate would engage with the Radium Hill attendees. My companions were excellent conversationalists; if there was information to be gleaned, they'd be able to collect it. I wasn't going to reveal my identity and would simply wander and enjoy the collection.

After a lifetime of bending the truth of my adoption, then discovering my mother had been a nun, and now that my father was a priest, I could deflect with the best of them. It was second nature to fudge, and at times lie, about my ancestry. Entering the museum, I realised it was another step to ask my friends to be complicit in protecting my nun and priest parents. My lying meant they had to lie, too.

In the museum foyer, a snaking queue waited to sign the Radium Hill visitor book. At the head of the queue, a greeting party of elderly ladies helped guests complete name tags. It was obvious I couldn't write *Brendan Watkins* on the tag. Kevin, and potentially others in the society, knew my name. Without a thought, I wrote *Paul Becker*. The name Maggie had given me at birth.

As I fumbled to pin the tag to my jacket, one of greeters ventured, 'I know your face. What's your name?' I didn't look up. The question was repeated. I raised my head sheepishly and saw two women beaming. They looked at each other, then back to me, eyebrows raised. Flushed, I replied, 'Hi, I'm Paul Becker,' and briskly crab-walked away. I'd endured fifty years of wise owls swearing they could see a family resemblance between Roy, Bet, Damien and me, when there was none. Now, twice in a fortnight, people who hadn't seen my father for thirty years had spotted similarities between us. I didn't know if I should laugh or cry.

The Radium Hill Museum would be of limited interest to anyone without a connection to the site or a fascination for the history of the adventurous, largely immigrant, miners who'd signed up for Australia's first uranium mine. Although by big-city standards the museum is light on for content and professionalism, it does reveal an incredible story. Avoiding eye contact with guests, I took in the rich history. During its life, the mine produced nearly a million tonnes of davidite-bearing ore. A young Sydney geologist, Douglas Mawson, later lauded for his Antarctic expeditions, confirmed that the ore contained radium and uranium. It was Mawson who put forward the name Radium Hill. Early assessment of the radium was conducted by Marie Curie.

In addition to the expected ephemera there were several intriguing, previously unseen, photographs of Vin. But I was most taken by the contents of a glass display cabinet. An exhibit card read 'This crucifix was worn by Father Shiel at all times during his time at Radium Hill. Kindly lent to the Museum by Kay Tulloch.' Underneath lay a heavy silver chain with Christ nailed to the cross, head bowed in sorrow. Discoloured by time, it was crudely produced, rough and beautiful. Did Vin make it? Next to the crucifix was his Latin Bible. Protected by a hand-stitched brown-leather cover, the Bible was opened to page 689, *Lection V*, a monastic practice relating to scriptural readings, meditation and prayer. These were his sacred tools of trade. These two items *were of him*. I craved those outback relics from his years constructing his doomed house of worship.

Kate asked around to see if Kay Tulloch was in attendance. No luck, but she learned Kay had kept in touch with Vin for years after the mine closed, and found out where she lived. *Yes!*

A theatrette ran a loop of a 1962 British Pathe newsreel, *Australia's First Atom Age Ghost Town*. In it, the recently abandoned township was shown, including the remains of Our Lady Queen of the World. Vin's forty-two thousand bricks stood, defiant to the extremes. At 2:02 minutes, the foundation stone of the church was shown: THIS CHURCH WAS BUILT BY REV FR V. B. SHIEL AND SOLEMNLY BLESSED AND OPENED BY RIGHT REV MONS M. B. CLUNE VGPA ON 2 OCTOBER 1956. It's the only foundation stone that carries my father's name.

We spent two hours at the museum. I'd avoided Kevin, and my team had managed several conversations with former residents, steering conversations to Vin. They reported attitudes that fell loosely along religious lines: the Catholics were generally positive, the non-Catholics, ambivalent—a reprieve.

Our tour was coming to an end. Easter school holidays had ended in Melbourne, and it was time for Kate to get back to work. I'd be driving her to Adelaide airport first thing the next morning. That night at dinner, as though contestants on some trash-TV reality show, we joked she'd been voted off the island. In truth, we were all emotionally spent. My partner was not disappointed to be getting on that plane.

Before heading back to the motel, I made an announcement. 'Guys, I can't get that Our Lady Queen of the World foundation stone out of my head. Look, I know the site's radioactive, and I know we're already a thousand kilometres from Melbourne— but I'm going home the long way—I'm going to Radium Hill. There's got to be a way to get out to the church without getting shot. Any takers?'

Chapter 46

ADELAIDE TO PETERBOROUGH, 23 APRIL 2019

I'd decompressed. The drive south with Kate to the airport the day before and a dreamless sleep had put me at ease, at last.

Not long after sunrise, I ambled to a cafe around the corner from my hotel. It promised to be a gorgeous, clear Adelaide day. Calm, I sat in the sun and was taken by the green of the gardens, the lushness of the lawns, flowers saturated in colour. What struck me in that golden light was the contrast to the dense ochres and browns of the northern plains. This was another reason Vin's bishops had to haul their reluctant padre back to his Far North pew after every escape.

For some unknown reason, in that Adelaide cafe I turned a corner. The spiky anxiety that I was sullied by Vin's actions had gone. So much had happened on the road, but I was still me, would always be me. Suddenly, on top of the world in the City of Churches, I tipped the waitress, and fuelled by egg, bacon and two coffees, I headed north, the drive an opportunity to phone some of the locals on my to-be-called spreadsheet.

Dorothy from Crystal Brook was thrilled to hear from me. 'I've been so looking forward to this conversation, since I heard someone from Melbourne was asking around about my Father Vinnie . . . He spent a lot of time at Mum and Dad's, regularly came for dinner on a Sunday. Mum would have the house spick 'n' span, got the good linen tablecloths and napkins out for Vinnie's arrival! It was the weekly special event!

'He was a lovely priest . . . would regularly drop in for a cup of coffee and chat during the week, too. Mum'd make a special rock cake that he was fond of. When he'd arrived unannounced, during the week, Mum'd stress that the house hadn't been sufficiently tidied . . . he'd insist all was fine, he wasn't stuck up, Brendan. Imagine that, a priest, happy to sit in the kitchen? Most unusual behaviour, that!

'Now, who *exactly* did you say you were again . . . ?'

The sky is always blue in Burra. As I'd made good time, I pulled in for lunch. After the Adelaide diversion, I was aiming to be back in Peterborough in time for dinner with my three comrades.

Regular long solo drives are cathartic for me. Blasting playlists of singalong music, sad songs, favourites from decades back. Kate and the kids can't bear my preferred volume, so out on the Barrier Highway I let it rip. With both front windows down, the sun on my bare arms, dry air blasting through, I thought of pulling up at Adelaide Airport with Kate yesterday. She told me she loved me as she turned to leave. I wished I'd said it first.

I reflected on my brilliant four-person family—life has been so kind. Though beyond middle-aged, I'd just discovered the man who made me. From the day we found him I'd been wary of my father and the sins he may have committed. But at that moment I knew that regardless of who he was, and what he'd done, my anxiety about him had to be released. My hiding had to stop.

I was exceptionally thankful to have Sandy, Mitch and Frank waiting for me up the road, knowing we were sharing a trip we'd talk about when we were old. At that moment Paul Kelly's 'I'm On Your Side' came on. It never fails to move me. Somehow, out on that open road, it seemed Kelly had crafted every line for me. I shook my head, laughed out loud as he strummed. Allowing myself to float on a wave of gratitude, I started sobbing, then crying hard. It came out of nowhere. I hadn't cried like that since the morning Roy died. I pulled over and rewound the song to the start.

> You've been crying a long long spell
> You've been drinking from the Devil's own well
> You're just hanging on to your pride
> Oh, hold on to me now
> I'm on your side
> I'm on your side when you think there's no one
> I'm on your side when darkness falls
> I'm on your side
> All you gotta do is call

Chapter 47

PETERBOROUGH, 23 APRIL 2019

Pulling into the motel in Peterborough in the fading light, I spotted Sandy, Mitch and Frank about to sit on the rickety motel chairs outside for an end-of-day catch-up. Delighted to see my companions, I parked and sprung out.

'What time are we leaving for Radium Hill in the morning?' Frank called out.

'Really?' I was grinning wide.

'Yeah, we're all coming—it'd be a privilege.'

I knew Frank was due back at work, and Mitch and Sandy, like Kate and I, had been emotionally depleted by the past couple of weeks. 'You beauty!' I said. 'Well, it's 280 Ks of bitumen from Peterborough to Broken Hill—we can stay the night there—and Radium Hill is about three-quarters of the way to Broken Hill. It's probably thirty-plus Ks of random private dirt tracks to what's left of the town and Vin's church. Dunno, best hit the road at dawn.' Although I would have done it, the last thing I *should* do was attempt to get to there on my own.

The best summary of Vin's time at Radium Hill was in an article by Kevin Kakoschke, published in the February 2017 edition of *Witness* magazine:

In 1955, Fr. Shiel was appointed parish priest of Radium Hill and considered a church to be an essential part of his new parish. He was well qualified . . . having previously qualified as an architect and gained experience in the building trades before becoming a priest. Monies for the material to build the church were raised from running fêtes, bottle drives, dances, beetle evenings, collections and even operating a 'roulette wheel' on occasion. The local 'SP' bookmaker, Tommy Ryan, would donate ten pounds every week for the cause . . . An excellent carpenter, Frank Kannerman, made many fittings . . . including the Gothic windows . . . beautiful coffins . . . As a German commando he had been awarded the 'Iron Cross First Class' for his part in rescuing Benito Mussolini from Gran Sasso, Italy in 1943 . . .

Sisters of St. Joseph Uriel and Mercedes arrived at the school on February 6, 1958, and taught sewing and music . . . They lived in the convent. Fr. Shiel had built himself a 'garage style' accommodation cum presbytery between the church and school . . . An unbelievable 114 baptisms were conducted in the church between 1956 and 1961 . . . A number of baptisms were performed on adults. This was a lot of baptisms when you consider that there were only 117 babies born at the local five-bed Australian Inland Mission Hospital between 1953 and 1961. Thirteen weddings and a number of funeral services were also conducted within the church.

Since the first day I'd read about Our Lady Queen of the World, six months earlier, I knew I had to lay eyes on it. I'd thought that somehow Vin's decades of struggle might make sense to me out there. Also, I was conceived and born while Vin was scratching about in the radioactive Radium Hill dust. Maybe I'd been made somewhere in that desert. Though Kate and Maggie were close, Kate was never going to ask an ex-nun where she'd conceived me with my priest father.

There was a certain savage romance to the land, too. Vin's 1950s East–West rail corridor (now the Barrier Highway) was one of the largest and most inhospitable territories for any priest on the planet. In the middle of the last century, Vin was a missionary in a desolate terrain of blood reds and bleached whites, where the only white inhabitants were miners and railway workers and their families, men on the run, and half-mad clerics like my father.

On October 5, 1961 the official announcement was made that the mine was to close . . . Every building . . . was ordered to be removed . . . After the entrance doors of the church were removed, a big Caterpillar D6 bulldozer nosed in to lift the big two-ton concrete lintel from above the main entrance doorway and push it inside. Well that big Cat went in too far before it lifted its blade. The result: the lintel slid back along the arms of the bulldozer, smashed the radiator and busted the head of its engine.

Was it divine intervention or what? . . . The salvage crew weren't game enough to finish the church demolition . . . would they be struck dead by a bolt of lightning?

The more I'd immersed myself in his letters and in news articles like the one above from the *Witness* magazine, the more I'd pictured him alone, chugging along the weather-beaten tracks in his chapel-camper-Kombi. My imaginings of my father were all of him in a solitary state: building, painting landscapes and driving. Travelling, never arriving. It was rare that I pictured him conducting a mass; I don't know why. The only destination I knew he was truly proud of was Radium Hill. I had to try to get there.

Chapter 48

RADIUM HILL & BROKEN HILL, 24 APRIL 2019

We stopped at the tiny fuel-stop-and-railway-station town of Olary. Google Maps directed us assertively east along the safety of the bitumen highway to Tikalina Road. But we'd decided against that path, as it'd take us past Andy Trelor's homestead. When I'd spoken to Andy a few months earlier, he'd explained, with determination, there'd be no vehicles going to Radium Hill. 'There's absolutely no way I'll allow anyone to enter my property and proceed through.' Kevin from the Historical Society had blamed Andy, along with Mark Francis, for the access problems—they both blamed Kevin. Whatever the truth, I was piggy in the middle.

I'd heard that Mark was a big man who possessed both a gun and a short temper, an unenticing combination. Fair enough, too, I figured, he was fed up with people showing up at his property expecting to be allowed to visit Radium Hill. I'd been given his mobile number months ago on the condition I never revealed how I obtained it. I called several times, but only got through once, the previous Christmas. To underline the importance of my request, I told Mark the truth of my connection to Vin, and came close to pleading to be let onto his land. A man of few words, gruff, though not unpleasant, he said, 'I'll have a think about it and let you know.' He hadn't responded to a call or text from me since.

The night before, in Peterborough, I called again. No answer. I left a message: 'Hi Mark, It's Brendan Watkins. I'm in the neighbourhood. I'd like to offer $1000 cash to be allowed onto the site tomorrow morning, just for half an hour. Please let me know.' There was no reply.

Given this history, we'd decided to leave two cars at Olary and have Frank, Mitch and Sandy jump in my city-slicker Subaru XV four-wheel drive. We'd try to navigate the tangled backtracks to Radium Hill and pray we could avoid the Tikalina and Maldorky homesteads and the attention of crinkle-eyed roustabouts squinting into the sun as they repaired fences (or whatever the hell it is men did out here).

Bob Matthews, a mine engineer, described himself as Father Vin's closest mate at Radium Hill. Through his eyes, I had a compelling picture of my father:

One time Vin talked me into taking leave of my job for a stint of roo shooting, *there's good money to be made!* he said . . . I was shooting and butchering 1.5 tons a month, we made a lot of cash, but it was brutal work. I went back to the mine. When I was out shooting, Vin'd drive out to the sheds for a visit. One time, thinking I was going to follow him back to Radium Hill, he drove through all thirteen gates back to his church—leaving every single gate open! He'd thought I'd close them—big problem—I didn't follow! Son, you leave every gate as you find it, and oh my! Vinnie's name was mud!

He used to regularly go to Adelaide to deliver roo meat to the Carmelite nuns—tucker for the convent guard dogs as undesirables invaded the grounds at night. The nuns spoke to the police who gave them some police dogs to roam the grounds—protect the brides of Christ! Father Vin used to drive all the way from Radium Hill to Adelaide, a 6-hour drive, to deliver free roo meat for the dogs. I think he really had a liking for those nuns! Now, who did you say your mother was again, Brendan . . . ?

But amid the colourful stories ('My favourite was him taking a visiting highly unimpressed fellow priest to the drive-in in his Kombi at Radium Hill to see the sultry *Cat on a Hot Tin Roof* . . . ') were more poignant observations:

Even though he was a very close mate, he had a habit of dropping in on the way home from the latest flick to yak about what he'd just seen—*he* didn't have to get up in the morning! *I did!* Sometimes he'd stay half the night, so when we'd hear the Kombi dack-dack up the street, the missus would turn off the lights so he'd keep driving . . . Father Vin came from a large Irish family, he was obviously a lonely man . . . He loved that church that he'd built out on the edge of nowhere more than just about anything.

As there'd be no phone reception off the bitumen, my always-thinking friend Frank had taken screenshots from satellite maps showing the main dirt-track junctions. He showed me the images: no houses, no roads, no green—a wasteland of orange and brown. This was not the place to get lost. Maldorky Station alone was 1700 square kilometres, which contained just one homestead.

Frank said the highway would become invisible not long after ploughing down the first red track, but he'd have a crack at directing us along the remaining thirty-odd kilometres to Our Lady Queen of the World. He'd enjoyed plenty of four-wheel driving in his time, and as a geologist, was comfortable in terrain similar to this. Sandy and Mitch probably knew where north and south were, and I had a Swiss Army pocketknife in the glove box, but it was Frank we trusted to put the bitumen back under our wheels.

We left the Barrier Highway on a wide, well-made dirt track. With plumes of dust spewing from behind, we accelerated past a large sign by the side of the track: PRIVATE PROPERTY STRICTLY NO ACCESS TO RADIUM HILL. Within two kilometres, we arrived at our first fork in the road. Our options were two single-vehicle, dreadfully uneven tracks.

'Left or right, Frankie?'

'Left . . . I think. Gee, this might be a long afternoon.'

I decelerated to a safe fifteen kilometres an hour. As we proceeded, the track occasionally blended into, and then emerged out of, the landscape. If the undulating dirt ahead didn't offer tyre tracks, it was near-impossible to know if we were on the track or not.

Though travelling at a gentler speed, we threw up huge volumes of fine red dust. It rose, drifted slowly west, then dispersed. Our presence would be evident to people kilometres away. The temperature was not hot, but bone dry. Due to the dust, the windows were wound up, and we were sweating inside. Our bravado had receded. We unconsciously took it in turns to alternate 'You still know where we are, Frankie?' with the occasional 'Let's hope we're not seen!'

'They can only point a shotty at us and send us back,' reasoned Sandy.

'Or chop us up for dog meat,' countered Mitch.

'Why anybody would choose to live out here is beyond my comprehension,' I said. All around was flat, red dirt with an occasional rocky outcrop followed by small undulations filled with super-fine bulldust. We pushed on for an hour, taking too many left and right turns for me to have any hope of remembering the way back. In that unvarying landscape, the only markers were the occasional fallen-down fence, dead tree, dead roo or old pump. None of our phones had reception.

As we approached the next turn, I wondered if we were going in circles. As if reading my mind, Frank muttered to himself, 'I really wish I'd snapped more screenshots.'

When the odometer said we'd travelled fifteen kilometres from the Barrier Highway, and after hearing an increased hesitation in Frank's voice, it seemed we were out of our depth. I should have done proper planning. Even so, knowing what this reckless diversion meant to me, I knew the other three were never going to say, 'Let's turn back.' It would have to be me. 'Hey guys, this dumb-arsed stunt is the sort of thing Vin would have attempted. We're under-prepared. There're zero landmarks out here to reference to. I think we should go back . . . ?'

As I spoke, I looked in the rear-view mirror and saw Sandy and Mitch looking wide-eyed out of the side windows. The previously trailing dust plumes had caught up with us, and had begun to engulf our vehicle. It became dark outside, with vision down to a metre or so. And then the air conditioner began to pump the cabin full of red dust—I couldn't breathe.

'Abandon ship!' I called, as we threw open the doors.

'Maybe we should've let someone know where we were going?' Sandy said.

She was right, of course. Leaving the four doors open, we wandered in different directions pondering the next step.

'Just a bit further,' said Frank, inspecting his screenshots and squinting toward the horizon. 'I think I know where I am now. There should be a dry creek bed a half-a-dozen Ks to the south. We're not that far from the mine.'

We got back in the car, and onward we rolled. The path now alternated between powdery sand and sharp rock that had our navigator concerned we could puncture a tyre. 'We should have let some of the pressure out of the tyres. It'd help with traction, and less chance of them getting sliced up. Did you check the spare tyre before leaving Melbourne?'

'Pardon? Did I drop the air pressure? Or check the spare tyre? . . . Jeez, I don't know, Francis! I'm not the car man! But yes, I have a spare, and yes, I think there's a jack, too . . . I think, yeah . . . should have.'

We made steady progress, though it did feel as though we'd been locked in that shrinking cabin for hours. My little 4WD was no Hummer, but we'd progressed more than twenty kilometres. We hadn't sighted a single person, vehicle or building, which was great news for a crew not wanting to be seen, but wicked news if the car seized.

The threat of disaster was brought front of mind when descending a sandy embankment to make a dry creek crossing. I took the ridge too quickly, and we slid without warning, tossing Mitch and Sandy left and then right in the back seats. We arrived far too quickly on the floor of the creek bed, where I hit a large unsighted rock with the passenger-side wheel, which could easily have jagged the tyre or the steering. Getting bogged in river sand was a real danger—and, of course, I didn't have a shovel.

At that point, Frank announced we were around six kilometres from Radium Hill. We sat up straight, suddenly brimming with hope.

And then the track vanished. Evaporated completely. We backtracked, pushed forward for a distance, then drove along the riverbed for a few kilometres, scouring for anything that remotely resembled a path. Frank took a walk through the scrub, climbed the rise for an improved view, all to no avail. By this stage, the sun was low in the sky, casting a warm orange glow over the landscape. The temperature would drop quickly.

My companions weren't going to give up—I had to call it. 'Guys, we'll need at least another hour to find the site, have a look around, and then hours to get back to the highway—it's not going to happen. Kangaroos will be out soon. Honestly, I have no idea of the way back to the highway, and we still have to push on to Broken Hill. Let's head back.'

This time my mates agreed. We took some final photos along the creek. I've always fancied a good rock, and I chose some ancient, floodwater-smooth souvenirs of our day, and placed them on the floor of the front passenger seat under Frank's legs.

'Great,' he said. 'I'm going to glow in the bloody dark tonight!'

The adrenaline had subsided, the drive out was long, every thud of the suspension annoying in a way unnoticed on the way in. Nobody had eaten since breakfast. We spoke of how fortunate we were not to get trapped in the sand. Walking twenty kilometres back to the highway would not be fun. Frank was the only one capable of navigating it.

'If one of us was bitten by a snake or spider . . . we've been stupid. There's about ten litres of water, but no food,' I said in apologetic tones.

We pushed on.

Shortly before arriving at the Barrier Highway, we saw an oversized sign bearing the large yellow uranium symbol. As we got closer, we could read it:

RADIUM HILL RESERVE—PERSONS ENTERING THIS AREA ARE ADVISED OF THE PRESENCE OF LOW-LEVEL RADIATION FROM NATURAL OUTCROPS AND FORMER MINE WORKINGS. DANGER—POTENTIAL SUBSIDENCE AND MINE SHAFTS IN THE AREA.

Close to Olary, sensing my disappointment, Mitch suggested we come back in a couple of months when it was cooler, pack proper provisions, and do a night trek. Frank favoured an assault with a big ugly 4WD and satellite phone. We'd smash through the rough backtracks well away from the homesteads. My preference was to hire a helicopter in Broken Hill and approach unsighted from the south.

'It's okay,' I said. 'It ain't over. One day I'll stand in that chapel and see his name in the foundation stone. I don't really under-stand why, but I've got to get there, to complete a circle. That broken-down church might have been his greatest achievement, in his eyes anyway. I need to do everything I can to learn about him—then I'll stop and get on with my life.

'The Far North Mission, Radium Hill and Our Lady Queen of the World are the perfect analogy for Vin, really. Access denied. Those tracks are as impenetrable as him. A million thanks for today, team.'

In the early-evening light, with an eye out for wildlife, we cruised cautiously in a three-car convoy along the highway out of Olary. Sweaty, dust in our nostrils and filling every pore, we trav-elled under a blanket of reassuring stars to Broken Hill. Though it was unspoken, we knew we shared a choked-up relief to be finished with the desert and about to head home. I wasn't despon-dent—I knew I'd be back.

Part Four

AFTERMATH

Chapter 49

MELBOURNE, JULY 2019

'Hello, Brendan. My name is Evie Murphy. I was given your number by friends in the Quorn parish. I hoped we could have a talk.'

'Oh,' was all my frozen brain could conjure.

Home in Melbourne, it was ten weeks since we'd returned from South Australia. I'd been off-colour for much of that time. After an emotionally gruelling journey, a weariness had enveloped me, lasting some months, and culminating with shingles. I'd hoped for a cathartic tour of enlightenment; it hadn't happened, not even close. Vin was still a perplexing riddle, and I now had to somehow resolve the paternity of Terry Shiel. Did I even want to know if he was my brother?

Evie went on. 'I've been thinking of ringing for some time but didn't want to seem like a stickybeak, it's just that . . . there's a funeral today for Beryl Shiel—in Sydney. She was one of Father Vin's nieces. I'm ninety-one, you see, and I have arthritis. It's hard to move around. Ordinarily I'd be there, family and all that, but my son is there representing the Shiels from South Australia.

Because of all of this, I've been thinking a lot about family. I was told you're somehow related . . .'

Evie was Maggie's friend and the woman we'd been urged to contact by the parishioners in Quorn. Flustered, my mind raced. What can I say? What *can't* I say? Who is this Beryl? *I've been thinking of family,* Evie had just said—and then she rings *me?*

Evie continued, 'I was married to Father Vin's nephew, Roger Shiel. He died at twenty-six from a heart attack. I was left with two young boys in Sydney, alone and without help. I had to move back to South Australia so Mum could help look after the boys while I worked.'

Not knowing what to say, I let her do the talking, but eventually it was my turn. The charade of deceit was now a well-worn groove: 'Yes, Father Vin is a distant relative of some sort— according to a DNA test. I'm not sure how we're related, but he just seemed to live a fascinating life, and we were at a loose end over Easter, so we decided to go for a drive west.'

Over coming months, Evie and I had three warm, revelatory conversations. A Vin fan, she possessed a terrific memory. 'Ohhh, yes, he was a character all right! An unusual individual, fascinating and determined. His stories about Ireland and Rome were very entertaining. Back in Australia, he spent much of his early years on the Nullarbor and around Woomera, Coober Pedy—a fabulous ballroom dancer, too! He and his fiancée won many trophies. Yes, Father Vin was once engaged to be married!'

Evie also volunteered that Vin had been a Bondi lifesaver, something I had read in a 1956 *Sydney Morning Herald* article. I suspected he may have made it up or somehow inflated his involvement. The paper claimed he 'had a hand in rescuing more than 100 people'. More new, important tales rolled out with little prompting. 'After Vin retired, he was the chaplain at a hospital operated by an order of nuns. You see, one of the nuns from that order was his . . . his . . .' She struggled to find the precise term. 'She was his *housekeeper*. Her name is Maggie Becker. We're still great friends. We talk regularly. Maggie left the convent and moved in with Father. If I'd gone to today's funeral, I would have also made a trip out to see her, too.'

It was too close for comfort. I changed the subject, asking about Terry Shiel, knowing Vin had sent Evie to Sydney in 1950 to deliver baby Terry to his brother.

'Yes, Vin spent a lot of time in the mining communities, including at Iron Knob. A doctor from Whyalla whom he was friendly with asked him to adopt out a child that a sixteen-year-old lass from one of the stations had. Illegitimate. I was eighteen. It was my first time on a plane! First time in Adelaide, too. You know, I'm still amazed my parents let me deliver that baby to Sydney. And while I was there, I met my future husband, Roger.'

I probed gently: did she know why Terry wasn't given to a local orphanage? Why did he end up with Vin's ill and retired brother and his wife?

'No. Now that you ask, it is puzzling, isn't it?'

Our first conversation flowed amiably for an hour. Anxious that she'd probe me about my maternal ancestry—and needing to confer with Kate—I ended the call and promised to call back the following week.

Two weeks later, we resumed our conversation. After pleasantries, I fessed up: 'Evie, Father Vincent Shiel is actually my biological father. It's a complicated story, but you've been so kind . . .' I didn't want to mislead her. 'There have been too many lies. I hope the news doesn't upset you, given you thought so highly of Father Vin.'

Evie wasn't shocked. In fact, she told me she'd suspected as much. 'You see, Father Rob, a priest from up at the Coober Pedy–Uluru district told me last Christmas that Vin had had a son.'

I remain humbled by what followed.

'Brendan, these things happened . . . We are family now—we should meet.'

I told her I'd love that, but warned her that my mother was still alive and very private. 'She insists on remaining anonymous. She's Catholic, she'd be devastated—so I can't talk about her.'

'Understood,' Evie replied.

'Secrets and lies haven't done anybody any good. I'm sorry, Evie, it's a bit of a mess. I won't ask you to lie, but at least you understand the reason for my behaviour.'

She happily agreed, and then surprised me by saying: 'In fact, the last person who should ever hear this news is my girlfriend in Sydney, the one I told you about in the last call—Maggie Becker. She'd not take this news at all well.'

I was struggling to process that a priest—this Father Rob—had breached the agreement I'd had with the church about not making my parents' identities public. And that Evie had resolved to withhold from Maggie what she probably suspected, that Vin fathered her child. Flushed, all I could do was stammer back, 'Thank you, thank you, Evie.'

It seemed my mother's oldest friend and I now had a pact . . . secrets within secrets. What was shocking about my parentage was the absence of shock, most particularly from the Catholics.

When I asked Evie if there was any chance Terry was Vin's son, she replied without hesitation: 'No!' But that was followed by: 'Weeelll, I really don't know . . . Who knows if the mother really was a sixteen-year-old from Iron Knob, too? It could all be invented, I suppose.' And then the penny dropped: 'If Vin is the father, Terry is your brother . . .'

Afterwards, Kate and I speculated that if Father Rob had told Evie that Vin had a son, he probably revealed the truth to other parishioners, too. He may have also revealed that Maggie was my mother. It was possible they *all* knew I was Vin's long-lost son. I grew livid.

I woke the next morning well before dawn. When Kate roused, I blurted out, 'They knew! I'm certain those church-people in South Australia knew I'm Vin's son! Remember when Father Liam inexplicably said it wasn't the end of the world if I revealed Vin as my father?

'That's why the locals were offloading his paintings to me! It's why they said *they'll mean much more to you than me!* That's why they were taking my photo! They all knew!

'It's why they said I sounded, stood and moved like him. That prick of a priest, Father Rob, has made a fool of me. He let me wander South Australia lying to everyone.'

On 29 October, Father Rob called, and got straight to business. His voice was measured, tight. 'Brendan, I've made a significant mistake. I revealed to one or two of the parishioners in South Australia the identity of your father . . . and mother . . . I'm afraid Evie, in particular, was quite distressed.' He was contrite, solemn. With a mixture of pain and fear in his voice, he apologised repeatedly. 'I don't know what happened, or how . . . I may have been tired or had a mental blank. I just can't explain it.'

'For fuck's sake! How could you?' I was thinking of all those elderly parishioners we met in South Australia, who'd known who I was well before we arrived. It wasn't just an embarrassment for me, but an astonishing breach of confidentiality for Maggie.

He said nothing.

Knowing this would be our first and last conversation, I didn't do what I wanted, which was to slam the phone down. Instead, I extracted more detail about where and when he told Evie, astonished that he didn't seem to grasp the magnitude of this failure. An apology and a few rounds of the rosary weren't going to cut it. 'Father Rob, more than anyone on this planet, Maggie was the one who needed my existence to be kept secret. You telling Evie reveals sixty years of Maggie's deceit of her best mate—it's annihilation for Maggie. She'd been a nun, for Christ's sake. How could you be so stupid? Gossiping bloody priests!'

I heard a shudder of panic in his voice, as he stuttered out further apologies.

'I'm incredibly disappointed in you,' I said. 'I've had enough of this. Goodbye.'

My immediate inclination was to kick out hard, to lawyer up. I spoke to several high-profile church-abuse specialists, including Viv Waller's office, which was representing Pell's abuse complainant. They were all fabulously empathetic and helpful.

My research into the children of priests gained new ferocity.

I resolved to go public, but first I had to get my facts straight.

Chapter 50

MELBOURNE, WINTER 2019

Nobody knows the precise number of children of priests, but surveys have shown that around half of all Catholic priests have had sexual relationships, mostly with adults, and there are currently around 400,000 Catholic priests globally. The most extensive empirical research into priestly celibacy is a longitudinal study of 1500 Catholic priests conducted over twenty-five years by ex-priest Richard Sipe. His startling conclusion was that less than half of the Catholic priests in the United States attempt celibacy. He was quoted in the US *National Catholic Reporter* in July 2019, 'Only 50% of the [Catholic] clergy are celibate', noting that, while most of them were having sex with other adults, 'this creates a culture of secrecy that tolerates and even protects paedophiles'.

Given these statistics, and the Catholic view on clerical celibacy, contraception and abortion, it's reasonable to conclude that many thousands of children have been born—and mostly abandoned—by their priest fathers.

I found a scathing 2014 report by the United Nations examining the Vatican's compliance with the UN's Convention on the Rights of the Child. Most of its sixty-seven recommendations relate to church sex abuse of minors, but the report's authors also expressed concern about children of priests, who 'in many cases, are not aware of the identity of their fathers'.

The report noted that 'the mothers may obtain a plan for regular payment from the Church until the child is financially independent only if they sign a confidentiality agreement not to disclose any information about the child's father or the plan'. The United Nations Rights of the Child committee recommended that the church identify these children and 'take all necessary measures to ensure that the rights of those children to know and to be cared for by their fathers is respected, as appropriate' and that it 'no longer impose confidentiality agreements as a condition to providing mothers with financial plans to support their children'. The United Nations gave the Vatican until September 2017 to formally reply to the recommendations.

There are 1.3 billion Catholics globally. It's estimated the Catholic Church is worth US$200 billion, so it's not as though it doesn't have the capacity to do what's right.

Michael Rezendes, the Pulitzer Prize–winning journalist from *The Boston Globe*'s Spotlight team (renowned for exposing systemic child sex abuse by Catholic priests), calls the children of priests 'an invisible legion of secrecy and neglect'. A *National Catholic Reporter* article on 21 August 2017 stated that 'Depression, suicidal thoughts, excessive drinking and ritual cutting habits have all been a part of the residue of being the child of a priest', and that many of these children struggle with lifelong familial secrecy, suffer a crisis of identity and faith, and have often been brought up in financially deprived situations.

If there is a wounded legion of tens of thousands of children of priests, why have only a handful come out publicly in the English-speaking world? Surely the church hasn't gagged everyone?

I'd set up a Google alert with the term 'children of priests' back when I first discovered Father Vin was my father. In my weekly email compendium, I'd kept waiting to read about priests being defrocked for breaking their vows. Where were the consequences? Where were the court cases? Reports of compensation and apologies to separated mothers and their offspring?

My research made for awful reading. I already knew that the Catholic Church's standard response to reports of priest child abuse had been to move the priest to a new parish; it seemed its response to a priest fathering a child was the same. What followed was permanent estrangement of child and father.

The fate of the mother often seemed to be considered not worth reporting. She was left holding both the infant and the secret of paternity. While some women had abortions (sometimes at the priest's behest), most appeared to have surrendered their child for adoption or placement in a foster home. The paternity of children who did remain with their mothers was always shrouded in lies and half-truths. Some mothers were compelled to leave their so-called Christian communities due to rumour or innuendo. A number became destitute or resorted to prostitution. In several instances, the church provided shelter and limited financial support—but there was a proviso, a written (or implied) confidentiality agreement. Overwhelmingly, the mothers blamed themselves.

Religion, sexual taboo and the authority of the priest insidiously shifted the guilt onto the woman.

The plight of the children, regardless of who raised them, was to be surrounded, always, by a litany of lies.

What was painfully obvious from these weekly email updates was that most children of priests had battled a diverse range of silencing behaviours from the church, their birth mothers, Catholic adoption agencies and often, by association, their wider communities.

David Weber, the founder of the Frankfurt-based organisation Human Rights for Children of Priests, explained in an article in *L'uomo Vogue,* 'Orphans of God', how the church views priests' children 'as a threat to its authority, and therefore nothing less than an enemy'. Hence, he says, 'the need to conceal the father's true identity at all costs, severing, when possible, his ties with the child and parents—a crime'.

Weber adds:

> Highly problematic, also, is having to deal with a mother who lies about your father's identity or, even worse, asks you not to reveal it to anyone—an inhuman pressure that shapes a whole life. Not surprisingly, many of the priests' children I know have developed chronic diseases, often of psychosomatic origin. Even as adults, the sense of fear is so ingrained in them that they often hide being a child of a priest even to their closest friends.

My research included joining a number of social-media–based communities that deal with adoption, DNA discoveries, church abuse and children of the ordained. Facebook groups provide direct connection with like-affected members—they have a pulse, they're dynamic. The best I found include DNA NPE (Not Parent Expected) Friends, SNAP (Survivors Network of those Abused by Priests), Adopted in Australia, DNA Friends, and Mothers of the Children of Priests. I also stumbled regularly across a website called Coping International. It offered free psychological counselling to the children of priests, but because the landing page included endorsements from a range of gawky-looking clerics, I assumed it was operated by the church itself. I repeatedly flicked it off.

Eventually, despite reservations, I joined Coping, where I had discussions with as many members as possible. At the same time,

I was also led to other children of priests who were not members of Coping. In one-on-one conversations, I was honoured to be told many painful secrets by complete strangers, sometimes secrets never shared with their own families. In turn, I shared my own intimate secrets—talking lightened the load. I was surprised to learn only a few had been adopted, like me. Some had been raised in orphanages or foster care. A number had been raised by their birth mother, usually without a father-figure. For those, often it was a DNA test that revealed that their priest uncle, guardian, or godfather (who sometimes visited) was, in fact, their father. Some had been raised by grandparents and told that they were the parents of the child. In one instance, the child had lived their whole life believing that their mother was their elder sister. More than one had been baptised by their priest father, usually only discovering the truth after his death. Some had ended up in the Catholic foster system, or orphanages, where they were raped by clergy.

One person, after discovering the truth of his priest father late in life, enjoyed a reasonable relationship with the man. He respected his father, though he was later perturbed that the priest insisted on secrecy until after his death.

Most, like me, had never met their father. Often, also like me, the priest had been dead for several years at the time of discovery. One had been offered cash to keep the paternity of the child secret.

The common denominator was deception. Virtually everyone had lived much, or most, of their lives in the shadow of lies told by parents, family, church and community. These lies in some instances were also told by legal practitioners, hospital staff and adoption agencies. I discovered that the knee-jerk inclination of the children of priests on learning the truth was to hide it. When you discover your ancestry has been a complete fabrication, the first response is to continue with the model of secrecy, to bury every last dire detail. Virtually all group members I spoke with had directly or indirectly experienced the coercive power of the priest, resulting in mental and family breakdowns, and sometimes disputes within families about financial matters. The vast majority felt great sympathy for their abandoned mother. Only one or two spoke of their priest father as having a positive impact on their lives. Without prompting, several volunteered they had been seeing a psychologist for much of their adult life. Virtually all had paid for this from their own pockets. Not that I asked each one directly, but it appeared all bore an overwhelming weight of trauma without any meaningful support or acknowledgement from the church.

Shame is sticky. Shame is contagious, and if you are the embodiment of your mother's greatest shame you must be hidden. If you are the result of rape, incest or a relationship with a priest, *you are the secret.* This is ancestral trauma.

I was told of an Australian paedophile priest who had fathered a child. Of a priest who made a mother swear at the altar of the parish church never to reveal the identity of the priest father. Of a priest who had fathered a child, overseen its adoption and later resigned from his order, only to be told by the Catholic Family Welfare Bureau, when trying to locate his child, that the child was dead, while refusing to reveal the location of the grave.

Often their paternity had been kept from the child of a priest not only by their mother but also by their extended family: 'Everybody knew, or suspected, he was my father—except me!' Most didn't learn the truth of their paternity until adulthood, and usually long after the priest was dead.

Home DNA kits are increasingly revealing clerical parentage shocks, often after one or both parents were dead, leaving many with never-to-be-answered questions. This is where the lasting, often intergenerational, psychological damage begins. If you can't trust your own birth mother and father, who can you trust?

Maggie's scenario was typical. When I was conceived, she was twenty-seven and my father fifty-seven. She was poor, uneducated and a member of Vin's congregation. In her eyes, my father was literally the hands of God. I began an ongoing dialogue with Queensland academic Dr Stephen de Weger, a specialist in clergy sexual misconduct against adults. His research confirmed much of what I was piecing together from the anecdotal, that priests took advantage of both vulnerable adult women and men. He found that those who became involved with a priest were often dealing with a marital or wider family crisis, or were seeking spiritual or emotional guidance. Some were disabled, others bereaved, isolated, unwell or poor. This insidious nexus of the spiritual and sexual, whereby a priest uses his religious authority as a grooming strategy, goes to the heart of the issue. Power imbalances and vulnerability of the woman are disturbingly common within these scenarios.

The complexity of the situation and the anger many of these women feel is captured in this extract by Theresa Engelhardt on the Mothers of the Children of Priests Facebook page:

> The immature men, lacking in moral integrity, who are priests. They are Roman Catholic clergy or seminarians who do what they please, when they please, living a parallel lifestyle of piety vs one of sexual activity that they choose to not be accountable for or bear the responsibility of their actions. Hundreds of thousands of children have been victims of . . . the broken promise of celibacy and coercive, manipulative behaviors by the Roman Catholic Church to keep it secret . . . Now adults, after enduring years of trauma, PTSD and mental health issues, clerical abuse victims, their families, along with mothers of the children of priests . . . are seeking the justice that they have been long denied.

Chapter 51

MELBOURNE, SPRING 2019

Globally, the issue of children of priests has only entered the mainstream media since around 2014, largely due to a brave handful of previously hidden sons and daughters going public with their stories. If the church has records, it hasn't made them public.

I searched high and low for reliable research about others like me. The most articulate spokesperson appearing in the media was a Londoner, Sarah Thomas. As a child, Sarah was told by her mother that she was the daughter of a university lecturer. At the age of twelve, she discovered the truth: her father was a priest. Sarah's parents met when the two were studying theology, and her father was a seminarian at the time of her conception. Though he implied he was considering ending his clerical studies, when he discovered Sarah's mother was pregnant (as Sarah told ABC's *Foreign Correspondent*), 'He went, in her [Sarah's mother's] words, berserk, and dumped her on the spot, basically, and hid behind a more senior priest, who in the end masterminded a plan of secrecy to stop her ever telling me anything about him.' Since that day, Sarah's birth father has never spoken to her mother without a representative of the church present. When the pregnancy was first announced, a senior cleric urged Sarah's mother to move away from home, have the child and give it up for adoption. She refused.

Sarah's father went on to be ordained, and her mother raised Sarah on her own. Though happy, Sarah's upbringing—common to children of priests—was far from easy. Sarah was raised in a UK housing association flat and money was tight. She first met her father when she was fourteen, but sadly he had no intention of forming a relationship. He made occasional financial support payments, but they were often accompanied by a note warning that contributions would cease if he was ever identified. Due to the vexed nature of her paternity, and struggling with low self-esteem, Sarah began indulging in risky behaviours. In 1998, at the age of twenty, she had a catastrophic accident. When her father was told Sarah was on life support and might die during the night, he was asked if he would like to see her. He said no.

Sarah's post-accident convalescence was life-changing and in time led her to commence a PhD on the phenomenon of Catholic priests' children. She 'interviewed many priest children from around the globe—and some of their mothers, and some former priests who've also fathered children'. In total, she made contact with around a hundred children of priests and has formally surveyed a number of them. In an article published by the BBC on 3 January 2018, she shared some early findings: 'Secrecy always comes up—lots of people talk about being encouraged to lie to keep their fathers a secret. Lack of identity is common, too, and the confidentiality agreements—whether official or verbal—are quite common . . .' She shared her struggle to understand why it's acceptable for a man who preaches about the importance of family and loving your neighbour to act this way in private. She also described how lack of recognition by the church creates low self-worth and guilt, and cited similarities between the experiences of children who had been sexually abused and those of the children of priests: fifty-six per cent of the survey participants had either attempted suicide or experienced suicidal ideation.

Fifty-six percent; it appalled me.

I saw exciting possibilities in Sarah's work. She was conducting her research completely independently of the church, in accordance with rigorous academic standards and overseen by highly qualified scholars. Her completed thesis would undoubtably be a powerful, authoritative document with the potential to create real change for the children of priests, and for their mothers, too.

I wrote to Sarah offering support and enquiring about her progress; we had a brief exchange. Late in 2019, she began to step back from the media and curtailed contact with some of her Coping associates. I was concerned, wondering what she might be going through, and hoped she was all right. Her university has since confirmed that Sarah has withdrawn from her studies. The evidence Sarah's research would have produced could be used as substantiation of the psychological damage caused—it would have supported legal challenges against the church by the children of priests and our mothers. The church will no doubt breathe a sigh of relief.

Catholic Church law is a complex web of evolving conventions and non-negotiable canon law. Clerical celibacy, for example, is considered a tradition that could be struck down immediately by the Pope. The application and interpretation of the church's rules varies from country to country, and within each country there are multiple orders, some progressive, others not. Local bishops have a degree of autonomy in applying these rules, which is why, thanks to Bishop O'Kelly, I'm the only person ever to have received the church's official file on an Australian priest. Importantly, though, the implementation of church doctrine must comply with the relevant laws in each country.

I spoke with several Australian lawyers who specialise in religious institutional matters, many still overrun with the repercussions of the royal commission. I wanted to understand how the issue of children of priests was seen by the law. The church has been dragged through the Australian judicial system numerous times as it sought to defend cases involving the abuse of minors, but cases brought by children of priests have not yet appeared before Australian courts. This came as a surprise to some of the lawyers. Some wondered if the children and mothers had been silenced. When I explained about the 2014 UN recommendations, it suddenly made sense.

Based on advice from those lawyers and legal academics, it can be argued that priests are the most visible representatives of Christ on earth, and that children who are fathered by priests are therefore the children of the church. And, as it is the duty of every parent to support and maintain their children, the church has a duty to financially and emotionally support its children.

A couple of the lawyers I spoke with made reference to the 'Melbourne Response' when discussing the law and the responsibility of the priest and the church in relation to sexual abuse. I thought maybe I could find links, protocols or precedents that would assist the most impacted children of priests that I had met.

In 1996, in response to a growing spate of child sexual abuse allegations against representatives of the church, George Pell, who was then archbishop of Melbourne, announced the introduction of the 'Melbourne Response', a new protocol for dealing with allegations within his archdiocese. I sought further legal guidance in understanding the outcomes achieved, and the implication for others like me. It was explained that as well as the Melbourne Response, the church operated the Towards Healing protocol, the

National Response Protocol, Pathways Victoria, the Truth Justice & Healing Council, the National Committee for Professional Standards, a National Centre for Pastoral Research, various church committees and numerous parallel legal precedents (involving the Catholic Church) that were relevant in some way to my situation. Initial scanning of these websites and reports made my head spin—I wondered if that was the intention.

In essence, the church view—and to a degree, the legal position—was that when a woman had a child to a priest it was considered to be sexual abuse—regardless of whether the sexual act was consensual or not. A vow had been breached: the extreme power imbalance had been recognised. Maggie was officially a victim of sexual abuse. The view of the abuse specialist lawyer was that I was likely to be considered a 'secondary victim' as no direct abuse had occurred. However, he cautioned that a long court battle would take place and copious evidence had to be produced to prove psychological damage and life trauma. 'Is that what anyone would want to sign up for?' he asked.

It was later suggested that compensation may be available for children of priests under cases of 'wrongful birth', another grim rabbit hole for me to plunge down. I didn't see myself as a victim. Was I? Was Maggie?

In December 2019, I wrote to Archbishop Mark Coleridge, president of the Australian Catholic Bishops Conference, who at the time could be considered the most senior Catholic in the country. I gave an overview of my story, the legal opinion I'd received, and detailed recommendations setting out the steps I believed the church should immediately undertake to support children of priests. I offered to share my experiences directly with the next Australian Catholic Bishops Conference to progress the issue.

Initial acknowledgement came from Father Hackett, Coleridge's general secretary for the bishops conference. He advised that the issues concerning children of priests were dealt with by the local bishop. He intimated that the Australian Catholic Bishops Conference was considering a national policy. I was informed that he'd pass my letter on, and he added that the bishops conference had been 'in liaison' with Coping International. I was already sceptical about Coping and its influence on and connections with the church. Disappointed, I wrote to Coleridge again, repeating what I'd already said and stressing that Coping in no way represented my opinion. When Coleridge did finally reply personally, in June 2020, his advice was that ongoing discussions about children of priests had been deferred until the November 2020 conference, due to Covid. Though polite, he said nothing to advance the issue.

Importantly, Coleridge advised that there was no central authority responsible for dealing with children of priests in Australia. Each bishop had discretion to resolve matters on a case–by–case basis. He added, 'In dioceses where children of priests have come forward to the local bishop, a policy or protocol is probably in place already.'

No consistent policy, and decentralised management, meant data was not collated. This allowed the church to deny the scale of the problem and mitigated the risk of scandalous statistics ending up in the hands of media. This approach mirrored the system exposed in the Catholic Church's sexual abuse scandal.

Chapter 52

MELBOURNE, OCTOBER 2019

'Yeah . . . to be honest, I had wondered if Father Vin was my father. And I suppose a DNA test is the only way to find out once and for all—but, but I don't know . . .' Though steady and calm, there was wariness in Terry Shiel's voice. Listening to forty-five minutes of my life's trials and traumas probably hadn't encouraged him to open this Pandora's box.

After Evie Murphy had told me of Beryl Shiel's recent death, and learning that just a few of my father's nieces and nephews remained, now in their eighties, it was clear I had a rapidly closing window to make contact with paternal relatives. Given several South Australian parishioners and at least one priest (who had broken confidentiality) knew the identity of my birth parents, there seemed little point in continuing to hide from the Shiel family, although I would continue to honour Maggie's request to not reveal her identity or contact maternal relatives until after her death.

My great paternal ally, Peter Meaney, sent me names and numbers for several relatives who could put me in touch with

Terry Shiel. As I reached out to them, I was struck by how apparently untroubled the Shiels were that Vin had had a child. A number of stories were shared, some of which I'd already heard. One new one stood out: my father had my grandparents' gold wedding bands melted and included in the manufacture of a chalice. Nobody knew what had become of it, but the family was keen to retrieve it.

My expanding paternal family was generally welcoming, but only two could be described as fond of Vin. Their general impressions were of someone 'crusty', 'stern' and 'demanding'. In stark relief were descriptions of the 'charm' and 'vibrancy' of his 'carer' and 'great mate' Maggie Becker. Unprompted, and unaware she was my mother, few relatives failed to bring her into the conversation. I was told Maggie had broken contact with the Shiels after Vin's death.

One story, repeated third hand, was disturbing. Seventy years ago, Vin had unsuccessfully attempted to climb into bed with the eighteen-year-old older sister of Terry's birth mother. 'He'd drink with Terry's stepfather at the Iron Knob station. He'd stay over-night as he was incapable of driving back to Whyalla . . .' It was a gut-punch, but confirmed in my mind that Terry was a half-brother. And there were probably more kids. I tried to push that thought out of my mind.

Although people remarked that my speech patterns—thoughtful, controlled—were just like my father's, we laboured to find common ground. Irish culture and all things Celtic (a Shiel obsession) had little meaning to me. My casual embrace of them came to feel inauthentic, concocted. I didn't want to fake connections that just weren't there, a disorientating scenario all too common between reuniting adoptees.

And then a relative just came out with it: 'The moment I was told you'd be calling, and that Father Vin had a child, I knew

Maggie Becker was the only woman who could be your mother. Don't answer if you want, but—is Maggie your mum?'

'Ahhh, I'm not going to deny it, and I'm not going to lie. Please—don't go there. I'd just like Terry Shiel's number, please.'

In the call where I had been given Terry's mobile number, I also received an unanticipated rebuff. In a matey of-course-you'll-understand voice I was told that given possible issues with the clan back in Ireland, and the risk of upsetting elderly kin who *thought highly of Father Vincent*, my name would not be added to the official Shiel Family Tree.

My family would cast shame on theirs. Okay, well screw you, buddy.

I was about to ask a complete stranger to take a DNA test to see if we were half-brothers, and I'd done my homework. Terry was married with kids and had led a full life. Racing against the superstar drivers of the day, he'd spent time on the Dick Johnson Racing team, came outright third in the Hardie-Ferodo 1000, and enjoyed high finishes through the seventies, eighties and nineties. He wasn't Peter Brock, but he was known, successful and respected.

Like me, Terry had had his identity withheld from him for much of his life. 'I didn't know I'd been adopted, that my mum and dad weren't my real parents, until I was about to get married at thirty-two. I'd gotten a copy of my birth certificate—and it didn't say Shiel. What made it all the more upsetting was some in the family knew and they kept it from me . . . I was an angry man for a time.'

Like me, Terry treasured his adoptive parents, more so after learning he was so prized and yet not blood-related. 'Elsie, my dear mum, died when I was little nipper, four years old. Dad and I were extremely close. To this day I still carry their photos in my wallet.

'The day Dad died—I was sixteen—he'd had a heart attack the week before and was recovering at my sister's. We were reading the Sunday papers, and he just looked up and said . . .' Terry paused and cleared his throat for composure. '"Just remember Terry, you are my son and always will be." I thought he was losing it, what'd that mean?

'Shortly after, we'd just finished lunch, Dad said he felt light-headed. My brother-in-law and I carried him to bed. He closed his eyes and passed away. I later learned that Vin had made my family swear to never tell me I was adopted. But I reckon on the day he died, Dad was going to reveal the truth.'

Terry and I connected on many levels, the common deceits most galvanising. 'I tracked down my birth mother before she died,' Terry told me. 'She refused to reveal who my dad was— I've always wondered.'

'Terry, there's something else you should know,' I said. 'My birth mother was thirty years younger than Father Vin. He has been with younger . . . people . . . though my mother was twenty-seven, not sixteen.'

'Oh,' was all Terry said.

Terry was particularly unimpressed with the Vin he knew as an uncle, someone who demanded to be chauffeured to the races with annoying frequency when in Sydney, who embarrassed Terry in public and who meddled unhelpfully in the upbringing of his 'nephew'. 'When I turned eighteen, I set him straight. I told him my dad would have been a much better priest than him, Brendan . . . there was one occasion I could have thumped him— I was bloody close.'

I was desperate for him to take the test, to help clear things up, but all the more aware of just how much I was asking of him. 'Terry, please don't feel pressured. It's asking for trouble, I know . . . I can't adequately explain it—even to myself really—why I've spent decades hunting the truth . . . I just don't want them—him and the church—getting away with it. Your mother was just sixteen. If he is your father, I think I'll be able to let go of him, to sever ties . . . but none of that helps *you*, of course.' I was digging a hole for myself, bumbling through my appeal. This wasn't the conversation I'd prepared for so carefully. 'The more I think of it, why would you want the truth? It's funny, my adoptive brother hasn't gone down any of the rabbit holes I have—he's the smart one. It's a big ask, Terry—too big, in fact—I'll understand if you say no . . .'

He listened calmly.

'I'll leave it with you, mate,' I wound up, before hanging up.

Terry had shown himself to be a compassionate and thoughtful man. I felt certain he was my sibling. Replaying the conversation over in my mind as I swam lap after lap in the pool the next day, it occurred to me that Terry had successfully pushed Vin out of his mind for forty years, until this discarded bastard son came knocking. Why would he overturn the story the Shiel family had been wedded to, an innocent sixteen-year-old and a young roustabout letting passion get the better of them? Terry should graciously decline my self-obsessed request—he had everything to lose, zero to gain.

A few days later the phone rang. It was Terry. 'I'll take the test.'

Chapter 53

MELBOURNE, LATE OCTOBER 2019

'The sheep will spend its entire life fearing the wolf,
only to be eaten by the shepherd.'
—AFRICAN PROVERB

One figure has emerged in recent years as the global spokesperson for the children of the ordained: Vincent Doyle, the compelling Irish founder of Coping International. He featured in the groundbreaking 'Secrets and Lies' episode of ABC TV's *Foreign Correspondent*, broadcast on 24 September 2019, and has been quoted in *The New York Times*, *The Boston Globe*, *BBC UK*, *The Irish Times*, *The Washington Post*, *Le Monde* and *The Guardian*.

Most of Doyle's media appearances have included a retelling of his personal story. Sixteen years after his adored priest godfather died, Doyle discovered that the man was, in fact, his birth father. Wanting to follow in paternal footsteps, he studied theology at the same university as his father, but the life of a priest was not to be. In 2014 he founded Coping International, and in 2016 he completed a diploma in psychotherapy.

Vincent Doyle is a brave man. Back in 2014, he was one of the first to go public with his paternity. He exposed himself to ridicule in front of the world's media. He presents as a man of confidence and conviction.

In 2017, Doyle confirmed to international media, after being granted access by the Vatican and reading the previously secret guidelines dealing with the children of priests, that the church, in effect (though exceptions exist), compelled priests who fathered children to resign. These priests are generally forced to leave their order with little or no financial support from the church. Many have limited skills to gain employment and would obviously be challenged to support both themselves and a new family. This dire prospect, together with family and community scorn, is believed to exacerbate the trend of priests leaving the mother of their child high and dry.

Gaining access to these guidelines, and later being permitted to post them on the Coping website, was a major coup for Doyle— he should be rightly lauded. He was quoted in *The New York Times* that February as saying, 'I don't believe unemployment is a response to paternity.'

Doyle claimed that a minimum of ten thousand children of priests had engaged with his organisation. He explained that number as an extrapolation of unique site visitors, assuming that a modest percentage must be children of priests. If that sounds vague, it was never questioned by the media, and given anecdotal accounts elsewhere, there was clearly something significant at play.

In 2018, when I learned my father's identity, I was thankful the ubiquitous Google could link me with my tribe, including those at Coping International. After I established my credentials, I was admitted to a closed Coping Facebook group, expecting a dynamic community of thousands of children of priests from all corners of the globe, I was dismayed to find just 134 members. Where were the rest of Doyle's ten thousand?

And who was behind Coping? Doyle and Coping seemed to be interchangeable. He managed everything and carefully curated the majority of the Facebook content. As the CEO and in-house psychotherapist, Doyle immersed himself in the lives of thousands of deeply traumatised individuals beyond the Coping Facebook group. He was often the first port of call for those who had recently received the most soul-rattling news. Some would be furious, others spiritually shattered, seeking a means to somehow retain a crushed faith. I assume a number would be suicidal. He carried a great weight. And responsibility.

Coping's media advocacy seemed to me to be based on assumptions, anecdotes and information gleaned from Doyle's one-on-one interviews with those who found him online; there appeared to be no basis for his advocacy in formal, scholarly research. Although Coping was opaque and informal, that's not uncommon for small charities where an individual (or small group) with limited professional expertise takes on the workload of many.

While compensation, the rights of women, litigation and inheritance were themes discussed by many Coping members when we spoke to each other, they did not get significant attention in the organisation's public advocacy—this concerned me. Nor were these concerns often mentioned within the Coping Facebook group or on the website.

I also saw no wide-reaching call for criminal charges to be brought against priests. What about the church confidentiality agreements? These agreements muzzle the abused and ensure bad behaviour continues. They're an insidious tool weaponised by the likes of Harvey Weinstein and Jeffrey Epstein. Why was there no prime advocacy on this from Coping? And why wasn't it agitating for women to become priests or to at least be recognised as equal to men? Coping's advocacy seemed to have just one goal: amending church law to allow priests to have sexual lives within their clerical role.

Doyle often signed off his communications with 'God Bless' and used the hands-together-in-prayer emoji. It was not what I'd expected. Was I the only one angry at the church? Nobody advocated burning down the church for the traumas inflicted on their mothers, or for the deceptions they'd endured. Several weeks into observing the group, it became apparent that most of the closed Coping Facebook members appeared to retain a spiritual faith.

After decades working in the not-for-profit sector, and being a stickybeak by nature, I'd noted the disclaimers on the Coping Facebook page that 'Coping is not a lobby group' and 'is not a charity'. The website contradicted, with 'Coping advocates for the rights of children of priests' and is 'a registered charity'. Things didn't completely add up, but I was still anxious to connect and learn from fellow members, and anyway, Doyle was obviously busy with his work—initially, I let it go.

Yet increasingly I became convinced that despite much brave and beneficial work, the influence of Vincent Doyle and Coping International required further scrutiny. The misery of the children of priests must be fully recognised and addressed; however, that will not happen unless openness and independence are central to any advocacy made on our behalf. By the time Doyle self-published a book called *Our Fathers* in 2020, I realised that his influence was only likely to grow—unless others like me speak up.

After the groundbreaking 'Secrets and Lies' program aired, I contacted Doyle in late October 2019. He told me there had been 'dozens' of new Australian contacts. I was full of questions; he was reticent. He wouldn't reveal the number of Australian members of Coping. He wouldn't give me the names of those on the Coping board but did confirm that Coping members did not elect the board and could not be nominated. He wouldn't say if the board were all children of priests, or the mothers. Doyle's belief that priests who had fathered children should be permitted to remain within the clergy did not reflect a position formally agreed by the members of the association. He did acknowledge that the organisation's travel, administration and online presence, as well as his hours spent on Coping affairs, had the 'assistance' of the Irish church, and this was later partly corroborated in a paper written by Doyle in the Irish journal *The Furrow*, in which he stated that Coping was launched 'amid little fanfare, in December 2014, funded by Archbishop Diarmuid Martin of Dublin'.

My many enquiries were clearly becoming tiresome. Outwardly Doyle was charming, but I could feel him bristling down the phone lines when I reached him in Ireland. I backed off.

It was perplexing that he'd been quoted throughout the international press criticising the Vatican's lack of transparency, and yet Coping was little better in this regard. The only discussion Doyle wanted with me involved the minute detail of my parentage, which I shared in full.

In December he offered me one-on-one psychological counselling. He'd said he was a psychotherapist; I could only assume this was backed by years of training and a formal accreditation. Though the website stated 'Coping International facilitates free psychological and pastoral support for children of priests', and its Facebook page said it 'neither endorses nor distributes, nor does it request, raise or seek, money or any financial assistance from members'— it appeared I was encouraged to make a financial contribution: 'Donation only as per affordability via PayPal'.

The counselling offer was put to me verbally and then again via Facebook Messenger. It was an immensely vulnerable time for me; I felt uncomfortable. Given Doyle's unambiguous faith and ongoing connections to the church, his proposition to become my emotional and spiritual guide felt inappropriate. I wondered how many others, who felt the same way as me, participated.

In May 2020, Doyle emailed Coping members, including me, asking us to complete a questionnaire about alexithymia, or poor emotional availability, and urging us to respond, noting the questionnaire was 'for Coping, not me'. It was signed off with Doyle's customary 'God Bless' and a link for donations to Coping.

I wrote back: 'I would like to assist all other children of priests in every way possible, but I have real concerns about who exactly wants this information about me.' As a member, I asked him to clarify Coping's status. Who is on the board? What is their mission statement?

He replied, but it didn't allay my unease. I was told the survey results were for the Coping board, of which he was a member. He added that as I had reservations, there was no need to concern myself with the test.

It's my belief that most children of priests receive more valuable support within secular abuse-centred communities than within Coping International. Coping appears to me to be at odds with most of the online adoption, church abuse and DNA advocacy and support groups that I engage with, as it is run by a single administrative voice (Doyle). Additionally, Doyle fails to engage in debate on policy and advocacy objectives. He is accountable only to himself, or so it appears.

Among the handful of active Coping online participants, all appeared content, although there must have been the occasional dissenter, as Doyle posted in September 2020 that he'd 'removed' a member. There was no detail or explanation of the breach. Such a lack of transparency only deepened my scepticism about the organisation. This lack of process mattered to me, because

Coping was presented by the world's media as the leading advocacy group for the children of priests.

As a member of Coping's closed Facebook group over several months, I watched as it appeared to me to morph into a quasi-Catholic 'ministry' (as one member literally referred to it). 'God Bless' from the spiritual leader was sprinkled about in his online comments like holy water. The following year he was congratulated for his comments in the media and responded that it was the work of God, that he was merely 'a poor pen, He is the ink'. The celibacy of priests remained the core issue for Coping's media advocacy. It appeared to me that Coping had drawn attention away from important issues that were damaging to the church.

I'd undertaken successful lobbying and advocacy campaigns in my professional life. It appeared to me that Doyle made every effort to funnel media attention toward the church—focusing on amending their rules—where I instinctively saw the correct avenue as engaging with the state: the law makers, police and lawyers.

Media discussion around children of priests boils down to two questions: how does the church stop priests impregnating women? And what should be done about the existing children of priests and our mothers? Coping only responds to the first of these, and only obliquely: Coping's view is that church rules should be amended to allow priests to have children and continue their pastoral work—that they be allowed to impregnate women. Doyle advocates overturning the requirement that priests be unmarried (in the context of the church, celibacy means unmarried) and therefore relieved of the requirement to refrain from sexual activity. In focusing on this approach, to me, Coping avoids addressing issues that are more immediate.

After two years' membership, I began to withdraw from the Coping Facebook group. I hadn't found my tribe after all.

Chapter 54

MELBOURNE, EARLY DECEMBER 2019

At close to sixty years of age, I still didn't know what time I was born, my weight or length at birth, or anything about the day I entered the world. I believed I had a right to know how many days I was left alone in that hospital nursery after my birth. I'd approached the church a couple of times about my records and had (ever so politely) been fobbed off.

I'm not one to let things slide.

A quarter of a million Australian babies were adopted in the era of closed, and often forced, adoption between 1950 and 1980. Surrendered newborns in the fifties and sixties were not held, talked to or nursed as they are now. I was picked up only to be fed and changed. Immediately after being removed from Maggie, I was taken to the nursery of a hospital, traumatised by the sudden absence of her ever-present heartbeat. We can't remember the first years of our life, as our cognitive ability develops slowly. The limbic system, however, is believed to be well functioning in utero: it regulates emotion; the fight, flight, freeze or fawn response; motivation; and the hormones that drive the nervous system. When you've been forcibly and permanently removed from your mother, your brain (and hers) is reset. A lifetime of motivations and inclinations are tangled and tainted. The longer I lay alone in that hospital nursery, the more my brain was recast. The personality I was born to inhabit had been inexorably altered.

This emotional short-circuiting explains why many of us adopted within this era process stress in an abnormal way. The experience can lead to catastrophic thinking, controlling behaviour and separation anxiety—my adoption gifted me an elevated risk of depression and self-harm. Cortisol pumped at unhealthy levels through my veins for days after birth. I was born on red alert.

I have lived a charmed existence, but there have been times of debilitating sorrow; my path would have been completely different had my adoption, and the all-permeating influence of the Catholic Church, not shadowed every step I have taken.

On a perfect Melbourne summer morning, interrupted only by the occasional unsettling whiff of smoke, I was on my way to an orphanage. Australia was in the throes of what would prove to be our worst-ever bushfire event. The east coast had been alight for weeks. The smell of burnt eucalyptus put everyone on edge and made it hard to settle to sleep. The federal government was in denial about climate change and responded with unnerving aggression to those who questioned their apparent lack of concern.

It was an interesting parallel to the aggressive responses of the church-engaged lawyers defending cases actioned after the royal commission. Doubtlessly the court cases retraumatised the already damaged. When the church lost, it immediately appealed. It dragged victims back through their anguish time and again.

The coins and notes collected from elderly parishioners were handed to barristers who stopped at nothing to discredit men and women raped by priests when children.

Thoughts of power and corruption circled through my mind as I nursed an elegant, though chipped, half-filled cup of tea in the boardroom of the children's orphanage at MacKillop Family Services, South Melbourne.

I'd made a formal request for my complete church, birth, adoption and counselling records several weeks earlier. When I first requested the file, I didn't explain to Joan, the counsellor assigned to my case, that my birth parents had been a priest and nun. I'd assumed it might make her less helpful. After we shook hands and sat, I let her in on my secret.

She didn't miss a beat. 'Quite a number of the children of nuns and priests have come forward in recent years. You're exceptional only as you have one of each.'

With no time to waste, she held an index finger aloft and nodded, instruction for me to pause. Head down, Joan rifled through disorganised notes, faxes and photocopies. My file was a dog's breakfast. Although she appeared as a kindly aunt, like most others I'd met over the journey in welfare, psychology and the adoption world, Joan was unflappable. After a few minutes of squinting at notes, she looked me in the eye. 'Your birth and adoption records show a highly unusual set of circumstances— nothing normal is happening here, I re-read the file the other day. The only conclusion to be drawn is that you are some sort of special case. I believe there's some sort of cover-up in play.'

I asked to read the file, but that wasn't allowed.

Joan leaned over the documents to be sure, as if shielding them from prying eyes. 'The first inconsistency was that you were born in the Vaucluse Private Hospital, East Brunswick. That's an odd location; almost all surrendering Catholic mothers went to either a Catholic or a public hospital—generally speaking, the mothers never had money.'

So I was born in a fee-paying hospital. 'Do your notes say who paid for it? Was it my father?'

'. . . and more importantly,' Joan continued, undeterred by my questions, 'why were you adopted to a Catholic family if you weren't born in a Catholic hospital? It's unusual.'

The listing of anomalies continued: 'There's also the question of your baptism, there's no record of it occurring. Catholic babies intended for adoption were baptised before being handed to their new family. There was a priest assigned to every Catholic hospital. As you were born in a private hospital, I don't know what's happened.'

I showed her a letter from the Sisters of St Joseph I'd found at Roy's when cleaning out his house after his passing. Dated 30 April 1962, almost fifteen months after my birth, they thanked Roy and Bet, 'praying that God will reward you a hundredfold for your kindness to the little one'. It noted an 'enclosed amended baptism certificate'—but the certificate, if it had been there, was now gone.

'It's irregular. You must have been baptised to enrol in a Catholic school . . . or at least had a certificate. There's many holes in this file, but that's not uncommon for offspring of the clergy, I am afraid.'

I'd read of several children of priests who discovered late in life that their birth father had actually baptised them. Could that have happened to me?

Joan sounded surprised. 'Anything's possible, Brendan . . . Look, there are several key documents missing. I'll have to go higher within the Catholic hierarchy to see where they've got to.'

I spoke of the firm dissuading I'd encountered from Jenny Abbott back in 1990 when I wanted to contact Maggie.

'That's no surprise. Jenny had a reputation—she didn't want a scandal to get out.'

I decided to ask point-blank how many children of the clergy had come forward. Dozens? Hundreds? Tight-lipped, Joan stood; the meeting was over.

'Before you push me out the door, there's a lot of pages there in that file—what else can you tell me? Is there *anything* about Maggie or Father Vin?'

Joan mentioned some references to conversations with Maggie in the 1990s, but again asserted she couldn't show them to me—'consent from higher authority is required'. The best she could offer was to refer my request to the CEO of CatholicCare, and ask for a meeting. An invitation from the CEO never came.

Exasperated, I stayed firmly in my seat and blurted out, 'Hang on, I've waited months for this meeting and haven't learned a thing. Not the most fundamental details: my birth weight, length, time of birth, information about my parents, my medical information, how Roy and Bet were selected—nothing about my birth parents. Joan, did the church know my father was a priest?'

'I'm sorry, Brendan. We'll probably never know.' She'd already opened the door and was awaiting my exit.

Now on my feet, I had one final question, one I'd wanted to know the answer to for decades. 'How long did it take—how many days—before I was collected by my adoptive parents?' I'd always hated the thought of me, nervous system in overdrive, waiting for days, alone in a hospital nursery.

To my surprise, she stopped. 'Yes, that information is in the court records—here, I think you've always had that material . . . ?' She held it up, and it did look vaguely familiar, something I may have seen in Roy's files . . . The typed documents said I was born on 10 February 1961 at Vaucluse and was immediately removed from Maggie and sent to the nursery. I stayed there until 17 February, when Roy and Bet collected me. Seven days alone. Shit. Another answer I didn't want.

Outside, the wind had turned, and it brought a blanket of ominous, low-hanging, copper-coloured clouds. I smelled fire; there was fine ash in the air. I'd left my car in a two-hour parking spot; I'd been with Joan for two and a bit. A parking ticket lay under the wiper.

I'd cultivated relationships with some church insiders and learned that, around the time of my adoption, the Australian Catholic Church processed the children of priests in an efficient and systematic way. My adoption in 1961 was managed by a long-term social worker from the Catholic Family Welfare Bureau (CFWB), Ellen O'Collins, the sister of two prominent priests. I'd been led to believe that priests who were responsible for a pregnancy could contact either Ellen or one of her clergy siblings. They would locate a good Catholic home for the child and ensure nobody discovered the truth about the priestly paternity.

Ellen may have collaborated with Sister Fabian of the Australian Sisters of Charity, who is best known as the founder of Melbourne's St Vincent's Private Hospital. In her 1998 obituary, *Herald Sun* journalist and future Melbourne Lord Mayor Peter Costigan wrote, 'As a young nun she was approached by the legendary Archbishop Daniel Mannix to expand the maternity hospital then being run by the Charity nuns for impoverished mothers, to look after the single women and children whose "situation" had been created by priests.'

The obituary goes on to explain that she did so despite almost total opposition from church officials, but Sister Fabian prevailed. Until her final months, she 'kept in touch with scores of the children of those liaisons'. Costigan noted: 'Her loyalty meant the views she formed over the years in which she administered the secret side of her maternity hospital stayed within her order and the Church.'

The Victorian Parliament is currently conducting a Responses to Historical Forced Adoptions in Victoria Inquiry. A submission made by Origins Victoria Inc, a not-for-profit organisation with a mission to support people separated by adoption, makes mention of Sister Fabian:

> Fraudulent information regarding birth entries . . . Origins have proof that some infants were registered in the names of their adoptive parents but we do not know how many . . . Origins Vic has been informed that when Sr. Fabian passed away a list of names of babies placed with people who registered them in their own names went with her.

When transplanting a sapling, to give it the best chance to flourish, it's essential to retain as much of the roots and surrounding soil as possible. How could Sister Fabian not see that denying ancestry was diminishing the chance of the child's success?

My birth was unusual, being in a fee-paying private hospital, well away from inquisitive Catholic nuns and staff. It appears my well-heeled priest father paid for this privilege. Even though he and my mother had little connection to Melbourne, in the weeks leading up to my birth, my mother was sent by my father to stay with a poor Catholic family (not the type to ask questions) until I arrived. It's highly unlikely my Sydney-raised, South Australian resident father would have known where to send my mother in Melbourne; it's more probable that the CFWB social worker, or her brother, made these arrangements on his behalf. My adoptive parents also appear to have been especially chosen by the church to raise me. They hadn't made application to adopt. Roy and Bet's names weren't on a waiting list.

My father renovated church properties in Ireland for six years in the 1930s to help pay for his education. His seminary was close to the Waterford Magdalene Laundry; it's feasible he worked there. The depraved abuse of children and mothers there—a number pregnant to priests—should have appalled him. Several years later, in Australia, he would have witnessed the 'stolen generation' removals, and babies placed in Catholic orphanages where treatment was often cruel. Yet he sent his own flesh-and-blood son into the 1960s Catholic system of fostering, adoption and orphanages.

Almost twenty years after his ordination, while touring Europe in 1958 and 1959, Vin had an audience with the Pope at the Vatican. Fewer than twelve months after this, he conceived me with a woman thirty years his junior. Then this prince of God abandoned me. The point being that my father, like so many priests who conceived, believed God was on his side. As so often throughout history, abject cruelty was justified by God, money, whiteness and lies.

After my meeting with Joan, I kicked up a stink with the Victorian Department of Justice. Several weeks later, some of the previously unavailable pages from my CFWB file arrived in my letterbox. A note had also been recovered from my brother Damien's adoption records. It read: 'February '61. Mr & Mrs. Watkins took a baby boy of very intelligent background direct from hospital . . . Paul Becker became Brendan Francis Watkins.' A subsequent phone conference with a representative from the Department of Justice and another from the Catholic Church confirmed that it was 'extraordinary' such critical information had been recorded in a different file, and 'highly irregular' that I was collected direct from hospital rather than from the Sisters of St Joseph Receiving Home in Carlton, and that the term 'a baby boy of very intelligent background' was very likely Catholic shorthand for 'child of a priest'. A senior nun had told me previously that when nuns left the convent to give birth, the absence was recorded as 'cared for an ill relative interstate'. Each order apparently had their own shorthand for activities they wanted hidden.

It was also depressing to learn from the just-received CFWB notes that Maggie was deeply disturbed by my adoption, and that our first adult contact had also caused her enormous distress. It didn't fit the character of the woman described to me at the time. I was incensed. The anguish disclosed to me was the opposite of what Jenny Abbott had conveyed, when she called Maggie a *very intelligent, determined and devout woman*, which I heard as *cold and uncaring*. As a result, my communications with my mother— for decades—were forthright and devoid of empathy: fighting fire with fire. If only I'd been told the truth, my approach, and the outcome with Maggie, might have been slightly better. The church-sanctioned deceptions, the gaslighting, the pitting of children of priests against our mothers—how could they? I was reminded of the words of American writer H.L. Mencken: 'Morality is doing right, no matter what you are told. Religion is doing what you are told, no matter what is right.'

I now saw my adoption, and Maggie's response, in a new light. My conception was the worst thing that ever happened to my mother. There would be no salvation for her after I arrived. Her trajectory—and mine—had been deliberately thrown into opposing orbits. In a purely objective sense, my birth ruined her.

Chapter 55

MELBOURNE, DECEMBER 2019

I've kept a journal for decades. I can't fully scale the consequence of tumultuous life events until they've been tamed by my short, sharp sentences. Each annual journal used to run to around forty thousand words. Since submitting my DNA to Ancestry, they average seventy thousand.

In December 2019, I had significant news to mull over:

Terry Shiel called, received his DNA results. We're not related—we're not half-brothers. T reasoned 'the Shiels were always my family'. He only did the test to see if he and I were brothers—because I asked—to satisfy me. In my self-absorption, I didn't comprehend how monumentally compassionate this act was. I'll always be indebted to this kind man. In a single conversation, my father has been transformed from a monster rapist of a 16 yo to a charitable priest who appears to have saved a friend's underage daughter's unwanted child from a remote SA orphanage. I got it wrong. (Maybe someone will fund a movie now? Brad Pitt's back on the casting couch!)

I have to now adjust to a better Vin. Was he good or bad? Does it matter? . . . T's long past mulling over the what-fors and what-could-have-beens. He's moved on . . . as my wheels spin. T closed the conversation with, 'If you ever want to talk, call me anytime.' Ironically, we ended feeling somehow like siblings (or at least I did). We shared a life-altering experience— trust. I didn't need his blood to feel an unbreakable bond. Eight months has elapsed from first learning of T's existence at the Immaculate Conception. Eight months of dreading we were united by an appalling paternity. Never again will I submit my DNA to another agency, bugger that.

It took months to recast Vin in my mind.

Terry's result still didn't explain why he'd been sent to the Shiels when I wasn't. Kate had an answer, and sat me down with my paternal family tree: Vin was the youngest of fourteen; Roger (who adopted Terry) was the next youngest. At the time of my birth, in 1961, Roger's wife had died, and he had his hands full with eleven-year-old Terry. Now, of Vin's surviving siblings, Mary had died four years before. Vin's remaining brothers and sisters were elderly and all passed away not long after I arrived: Anastasia in 1962, Francis in 1965 and Margaret in 1973.

'The pragmatic reality is, there was nobody to take you! Had Vin been the firstborn, and not last, you could have been raised as a Shiel, if that's what they wanted. And how fortunate were you? Because no Shiel could have prized you more than Roy and Bet.'

After my surprise appearance a year ago, the Shiels had gradually begun to share information. The yarns, flattering and otherwise, flowed freely. The veracity of each was something Kate and I had been conditioned to question. One claim, so ridiculous it sounded like an invention, was that my late-life artist father had painted his name over an original artist's signature on more than one painting and passed it off as his own. I asked, 'Who has these paintings now? Where are they?'

The informant had no idea. 'Oh . . . it's just what I was told.' The claim put this person at odds with others who said my father had an exhibition of his works in Adelaide and that he once won a painting competition in New Zealand.

The Catholic press stated several times that Vin was a 'fully qualified architect'. Although his architectural education would have been in the 1920s (making any record of it less accessible), we can't find evidence he was qualified. Should we shut up and accept what the press had said? Was I obsessing about the unimportant?

Another anecdote, which I hope is true, comes from a visit to Archbishop Sheen in New York. Vin volunteered to assist with the restoration of Our Lady of Victory Church in downtown Manhattan. The tale goes that the heavy-handed Antipodean priest was in the basement with a sledgehammer, steadily punching through a wall. His ultimate blow, with an excess of force, saw the basement wall give way to expose a gaping black void. My curious father poked his head through the opening to see the tracks of the New York subway. An invention? You tell me.

Another family legend, from the early 1950s, was that he returned from a US trip with a gift: a colour television. The fundamental flaws in this act of generosity were not only that the curious-looking box wouldn't plug into local power sockets, but also that Australia didn't begin broadcasting a television signal until 1956.

He'd owned a chocolate shop for a few years on Victoria Road, Rozelle, before he became a priest, and decades later (post-retirement—when he and Maggie lived in the Blue Mountains), he bought into the heritage-listed Paragon cafe in Katoomba, which specialised in handmade chocolates. I'd also been told by multiple family members that he won the lottery twice and gave the proceeds to Maggie's convent. A cousin, with great pride, told me he had built an ornamental structure ('possibly a timber archway') in the grounds of the Vatican.

Could it all be true? Was Vin having a lend?

The week before Christmas, an email arrived from Sister Callisita, a nun who manages the Mother Teresa Center in India. Maggie had told Kate that in 1970 Vin travelled to Melbourne to ask Mother Teresa, who was opening a community house in Gore Street, Fitzroy, to let him go back with her to India. He wanted to become a missionary in Bombay. During their meeting, Vin gave Mother Teresa his prized outback chalice—the one given to him by Archbishop Sheen. Maggie said Mother Teresa laughed at the 68-year-old and said words to the effect of 'Look at yourself, you're old and sick. You'd be dead in weeks. Go home, Father Shiel!'

I'd written to two nuns who managed the Mother Teresa Center in India, as well as Mother Teresa archivists in the United States and Italy. Their interest in pursuing the fabled chalice was acute, given Sheen was again in the Catholic press—his case for canonisation had recently been put to the Vatican. Sister Callisita wrote back saying I could be very proud of my zealous uncle (there was that word again). She was certain his endurance through trials had saved many people and that Vin would be enjoying his reward in heaven. There was no news on the missing chalice, however; their search had drawn a blank. Mother Teresa apparently gave away the gifts provided to her as quickly as they were received, so maybe the chalice remained in Australia?

I'd also contacted various Archbishop Sheen historians and archivists. All were taken with the romance of Father Vin's Holy Grail, if suspicious of my motivations. An American archivist forwarded two letters sent to Vin by Sheen in 1966 from New York City to the far-flung *Catholic Presbytery Box 43, P.P. Quorn,*

South Australia. The first speaks to the closeness of their relationship, with Sheen sharing news of a forthcoming TV series and making mention of the trials Vin had endured, before signing off with expressions of fondness and highest regard.

The second letter, sent six weeks later, is surprisingly affectionate, and it includes updates on mutual friends and notes the mutual admiration he and Monsignor Schultheiss shared for Father Vin. He reminds my father that as a busy carpenter he was doing the same noble work as 'Our Blessed Lord' and encouraged Vin to continue his construction on behalf of their Lord and ministry.

Vin basked in the reflected glory of the American. Presenting the chalice to Mother Teresa only propagated the legend further. He also used the Sheen friendship as a way of persuading his bishop to agree to various extracurricular favours.

Sheen, in turn, benefitted from association with the fervent missionary in exotic Australia. In his published memoir, he further magnified Vin's travails to present him as a kind of masochistic Reverend Father Crocodile Dundee. The inflation of Vin's suffering, and reverence, would have also played well for my father as he travelled the world. It can't be denied that Vin toiled harder—in the physical sense—than many of his peers, but he was far from the pure-hearted soul created by Sheen.

●

The Shiel relative I most closely resemble is Bill Shiel. He's a thinker, softly spoken—I like him a lot. He believes some anti-Vin sentiment in the family stemmed from money disputes, usually relating to his houses, rent or money he'd lent. 'Brendan, I thought he was great, impressive—a bit of a larrikin, too. During uni breaks, I'd labour for him on the Hawker, Crystal Brook and Quorn churches. Particularly when out doing building works, he'd swear like a trooper. To pass the time, Vin'd tell stories about his travels. When he was on a trip to the United States, he was filmed giving mass; apparently that recording was replayed frequently on American television.'

I pushed him: 'Some stories I've heard just don't fit with the character of the man I have in my head. There's so much contradictory information, bizarre stories—I don't know what to believe . . . I've heard from a few relatives that he'd been engaged and was a trophy-winning ballroom dancer in his twenties. It sounds odd for a man who was to go on to become a dour priest— is it true?'

Bill paused. 'Hmmm—I'll email you something in the next few days.'

The following week my inbox pinged. I clicked the attachment and saw a striking, professionally shot photograph of Vin wearing black tie with one eyebrow dramatically raised. (I raise mine exactly like that.) My father has an arm around a beautiful woman with a flower in her hair who wears a glamorous satiny dress. Their bodies face each other, heads theatrically turned to the camera, both oozing self-assurance. They each have a raised knee and are obviously dancers, at any moment about to glide across the polished floorboards. The young woman is thought to be my father's fiancée.

Sitting on a decorative plinth in the background are trophies.

Chapter 56

MELBOURNE, MARCH 2020

After Terry's DNA confirmed that I was possibly Vin's only child, I wanted a break from untangling my parents' lives, but I'd launched so many balls into the air that I was receiving near-daily calls and emails from people offering assistance, as well as ongoing contact from numerous children of priests.

Though Vin had died twenty-five years before we identified him, I knew a great deal about him. My mother was still alive, but I knew hardly anything about her life, except that she'd had to grow up quickly. Maggie's early years were focused on withstanding childhood neglect. All I can do is speculate.

I was conceived through a liaison in which she was not an equal in any sense. As a direct result of my birth, she sacrificed twenty-five years of her life to a convent. The thirty years following were essentially spent working as a domestic helper and then housekeeping for my father, all while anxiously trying to evade me. Her single indulgence was mortgaging Vin's flat, mysteriously assigned to her after his death, and treating herself to two overseas holidays. Good for her!

The adult Maggie was dogged by her difficult childhood; I wondered what she could have become if provided with opportunity. So many of my paternal relatives were drawn to this sunny, handsome and diligent woman. What a loss. Vin, by contrast, had learned a trade, been engaged to marry, accumulated wealth, swapped a career for a vocation, travelled the world, been creatively stimulated, and, though a priest frustrated by his mundane desert responsibilities, had a certain freedom by being away from his bishop. He could decide how to spend most of his days and would frequently sneak away to build, gamble, return to Sydney or enjoy socialising with favoured parishioners.

Maggie had no celebrated life story. I've heard no suggestion of her exploring interests or grand passions. Her potential had been constrained by the sexism of the era, and particularly the patriarchal nature of the church hierarchy, as well as the reparations she believed she owed after falling pregnant with me. She became a nun, the embodiment of subservience, a safe way to retain a semblance of dignity.

An ex-priest led me to Sister Jude, who has a PhD and is a qualified counsellor. She supports nuns, some after they've endured abortions, been raped, surrendered newborns or raised babies of their own. After listening to my unspooling story over the phone, Jude began to talk. Her candid assessment was that my birth mother had been subjected to coercive control: 'Maggie's order was notorious. They're backward. Doubtlessly, after your birth, your mother chose that order as the most pitiless atonement possible. She deserves a medal for lasting twenty-five years.

'And once she was in, you should understand, leaving the convent was a frightful option—if you abandoned your post, you were left high and dry. "No one who puts a hand to the plough and looks back is fit for service in the kingdom of God"—it's from Luke . . . I'm not surprised she told not a soul she had given birth. What a trauma . . .

'You won't find many well-educated women—no daughters of the wealthy—in our convents, Brendan. Novice nuns are often seeking a safe harbour. Maggie's story is far from unique.'

Jude knew of a few children of nuns or priests, but no others with a nun mother and priest father.

She attributed Maggie's disinterest in me and her grandchildren to a dissociative disorder, common in these circumstances. 'The spiritual and earthly lives of nuns are placed in compartments, silos. Understand this—it's a survival mechanism.' She explained how victims are often unaware that they are victims. 'Nuns talk to me of sexual abuse as if they are witnesses, not as though it physically happened to them. They're completely powerless,' she said, adding, 'It sounds as though your mother is still atoning for her time with your father. And for surrendering you.'

I wrote to Maggie and explained we'd be in Queensland the following month, and asked if Kate and I could see her. 'You and I have been greatly impacted by the past—I only wish you well. If there is anything I can do to help, now or in the future, please just ask.'

Not long after, she called Kate: 'Thrilled to bits with Brendan's letter.'

It was the first and only time I had made my mother happy. But, she declined my request to meet.

I decided that if I never heard from my mother again, that was the best possible last exchange.

Though my own faith had long lapsed, I realised that I still behaved like a member of the church that formed me. Taught by experts, I'd evaded making public the truth about who I really was. My adoption, rejection by Maggie, and discovering the truth of my parents' lives caused episodes of unsettling grief, years of my life interrupted as I searched for answers. The burden of colossal secrets can present as hypervigilance—the impulse to hold back, and to control. That is me. And that is Maggie.

Trauma is a thief of time. There is also the often unacknowledged 'opportunity cost' of life prospects not pursued. That is a price Maggie and I have both paid, my mother by far the most dearly.

All children of priests pay this price, to varying degrees, sinking their energy and attention into the past, not able to live in the moment or focus on the future. When I finally solved my paternal riddle and began engaging with the quixotic Doyle, a couple of my peers—at the peak of their earning arc—were buying beach houses; I'd just walked away from my well-rewarded career and spent three years floundering about trying to make sense of who I was. The church must be made to take full responsibility for the losses suffered by all the sons and daughters it has tried to erase.

In the final reckoning, my story is one of love. I was saved by the kindness of strangers. While the largest religious institution in the world, professing compassion and charity to all, callously annulled my heritage, it was Roy and Bet, people with whom I shared not a drop of blood, who rescued me.

Exactly how does a cabal of old men, accountable only to another unseen old man in the clouds, live beyond the law? I hurt for the mothers who wanted to keep their babies, and the women who needed the right to abort, both denied choice by these 'Christians' and their laws.

The asymmetrical power dynamic between priests and nuns is the bedrock of the Catholic Church, and this dysfunction is what allows abuse to flourish. There are thousands of children of priests. Our stories reveal a systemic pattern of institutional lies, secrecy, corrosive trauma and weaponised intergenerational poverty. Every day, somewhere in the world, somebody will open an email from a DNA lab with news that the unthinkable has happened: their father is a Catholic priest.

Priests will continue taking advantage of vulnerable women unless stories like mine become known. I decided to come forward and encourage other children of the ordained—and our mothers, too, if they are inclined—to find their voice. Breaking stigma means talking.

Chapter 57

MELBOURNE, MAY 2020

Sitting at the kitchen table, low autumn sun streaming through the window, I hold a timeworn leather-bound edition of *Breviarium Romanum*, a liturgical book of Latin rites and canonical prayers. As I open it, the dry scent of age and the desert fills me.

Inside the cover, in heavy black letters, is the owner's name: *Rev Fr. Shiel RADIUM HILL, SA*. The leather of the inexpertly constructed cover, which I hope my father hand-stitched, contains 274 fine gilt-edged pages. (Is it kangaroo leather? From one that he shot?) Five satin page-markers record the liturgical readings he revisits most often. The year 1935 is stamped at the bottom of the first page, the year he arrived at Mount Melleray Abbey, Ireland. My father may have carried this book for more than fifty years. I grip it tightly.

Alongside the book, wrapped in tissue, is his weathered crucifix. A sturdy, once gold-plated chain bears a cross made of steel. Instantly, I treasure these gifts, sent by Kay Tulloch, Vin's ally from the Radium Hill years. Kay and Vin maintained a friendship from the sixties through to his death in 1993.

And there are photos: Vin and Maggie posing with friends in the driveway of their Blue Mountains house in 1991—the year I sent my first letter to Maggie. At first glance, they appear carefree. My mother is fifty-seven, a couple of years younger than me now, fit and capable. She offers the still-waters smile of somebody who carries a secret. Vin is obviously much older, his hair snow white. Surrounded by three women, he manages to extend his arms around the trio; he pulls them close, feeling the warmth of their bodies on his. Back in Melbourne, on that day in 1991, Kate and I were contemplating starting a family. And Maggie—or Maggie and Vin—had already decided they wanted no contact with me.

Vin is eighty-eight in the photo. He has fewer than two years to live. He will pass away without a sound as Maggie dutifully drives him home from another day at the races.

Though his crucifix and liturgical book have no material value, they represent the most fundamental spiritual commitment of Vin's life. His sacrifice to his God. Although I'd cobbled together his letters, photos, news articles and paintings, what I'd hankered for was a possession that held profound meaning for him.

Some weeks earlier, thinking of Vin's possessions marked 'Kindly lent to the Museum by Kay Tulloch' at the Radium Hill Museum, I'd called her. Over three conversations, we spoke for seven hours. An increasingly common chain of events unfolded. In the first chat I said I was a distant relative; in the second, Vin's son; and by the third, Vin and Maggie's son. Kay had guessed all along, of course, declaring 'How wonderful!' after hearing the truth. Wildly impressed by Vin, she'd once told the bishop, 'Father Vincent should have been made a bishop . . . he was the only holy man I've ever known!'

In our final conversation, Kay said, 'Your story is a beautiful one. Your father was a good and decent man—which is why you turned out so well.' Though I accepted the compliment, the reality is that Vin and Maggie had no bearing on me becoming good and decent. Although I look very much like them, they didn't raise me. Roy and Bet are the heroes of my life. And not because they adopted me, but because they provided a lifetime of love. They showed up. I'm good and decent because they were. Kate has helped to shape me, too, by example, showing me extraordinary compassion, far beyond reasonable expectation: more goodness and decency than I will ever have the opportunity to repay.

If only I had a dollar for every time I've had people gush 'Your story is just like *The Thorn Birds*', which is described by its publisher as 'a sweeping family saga of dreams, titanic struggles, dark passions, and forbidden love in the Australian Outback'. I have to admit I've never read the novel, but I have seen the 1983 TV adaption. As Kate and I nestled on the couch and watched the opening credits roll, we wondered if Vincent and Maggie had done the same thirty years earlier. Did they hold hands as we did? What did my mother and father think of this beloved drama about another Father who had fathered a child, in the sun-baked Outback, with a much younger woman?

It is the story of Father Ralph, a handsome Irish Catholic priest who had been banished to the Australian desert for slighting a bishop. Highly principled, noble, he denies female temptresses who tempt him to break his vow of celibacy. The central relationship is between Ralph and Meggie, a woman eighteen years younger than him, whom he has known since she was eight. As the years pass, Meggie makes several grave errors of judgement, and Ralph frequently comes to her aid, his priestly compassion and nobility coming to the fore.

After a great many years of resisting Meggie's womanly wiles, in time temptation gets the better of poor Father Ralph and a child is conceived. Meggie, duplicitous, then sleeps with her estranged husband to trick him into believing he is the father of the unborn child. Many years later, Ralph has risen through the clerical ranks and is based in Rome. On a return visit to the Outback, he meets Meggie's child, Dane, and feels a magnetic connection, though unaware he is the boy's father. Dane then becomes a priest and is mentored by Ralph, both men still ignorant of Dane's paternity, though the similarities between father and son are obvious. Dane eventually dies attempting to rescue some drowning women. Before Dane's funeral, Meggie reveals to Ralph that he is Dane's father. Ralph then dies in Meggie's arms.

I thought the ending was a cop-out. In having Father Ralph die after learning he was Dane's father, the author, Colleen McCullough, dodged the grisly truth—priests desert their children. Had Ralph not died, he would have been on the next 747 to Rome. In Meggie concealing the truth of Dane's paternity from childhood, McCulloch also sidesteps the conundrum Ralph would have faced: does he resign as a priest and raise his son with Meggie? Or does he cut and run? The person McCullough cites as making the majority of unethical decisions is the woman, Meggie.

The Thorn Birds is a work of fiction, of course, but it's what Catholics desperately want to believe: that clerical sex is an expression of love, respect and mutual passion. Published in 1977, with sales in the millions, it's no surprise that the sprawling drama is one of Australia's highest-selling novels. McCullough isn't responsible for the trope of the naive, noble priest, or the dangerous and deceptive woman; she was merely reinforcing hundreds of years of religious and societal misogyny. From the day the Bible placed an apple in Eve's hand to tempt Adam, Maggie was always going to be blamed for Father Vin's behaviour.

As for him, he'd been buried twenty-five years before I knew his name. A priest, decades older than my mother—I felt immediate weariness. My expectations of him were low, though he did sacrifice increased wealth and a family. A personality comprised of madly contradictory traits, he was vainglorious, hypocritical and a misogynist. Seemingly driven by the adoration of his Mammy, he was emotionally immature and unavailable. My father would have told himself he saved Maggie, and maybe he did, but he also used her. I have been prodded by older friends not to view my father, born in 1902, through the lens of modern conventions. I'll admit his controlling and sexist ways were not exceptional, and many relationships of the day were entirely pragmatic, but I'll never know the true nature of my parents' relationship. Others remarked 'they were great mates', and maybe there was love at one time. But when Kate finally asked Maggie, at my urging, if she loved Vin, my mother demurred, 'No, not really.'

I reveal my story in honour of the thousands of mothers of priests' children around the world who cannot be loved by their own flesh and blood because of the lies of priests, bishops, archbishops and cardinals, and the institution they serve.

I cannot love Maggie, but I can forgive. My absolution is complicated though; there's a begrudging element to it. My mother's lies over the past three decades were concocted to shield her shame—there was not enough consideration of her only child. And if I'm completely honest, I have inherited her ruthless pragmatism. If I'm ever going to stop living life distracted by what I see in the rear-view mirror, I must pardon the betrayals.

Aspects of my life's story are tragic, but I didn't break. I owe that to the boundless love and sense of belonging that two strangers, Roy and Bet, gave me—a 'special child' whose past had been deliberately erased—when they carried me into their home sixty years ago. If you'll excuse the old-fashioned terms, my adoptive parents were charitable, honourable and dignified. They literally would have given their lives for me. How lucky am I? Kate, my children, Damien and Maire, my wider family and friends are everything. Nothing else matters.

POSTSCRIPT

'The child who is not embraced by the village
will burn it down to feel its warmth.'
—AFRICAN PROVERB

Vincent Doyle's debut book, *Our Fathers: A Phenomenon of Children of Catholic Priests and Religious*, was released in December 2020. When I saw the news posted on the Coping Facebook page, my hackles rose. It was a misrepresentation. *Our* Fathers?—how dare he purport to speak on behalf of the thousands of children of priests! As a cohort, we are the physical embodiment of a silenced mass, muteness personified—how dare he presume?

Our Fathers was first made available from a self-publishing website with a Vatican acknowledgement, by Father Ardura, president of the Pontifical Committee for Historical Sciences, who wrote: 'To my knowledge, this is the first time that a book has been specifically and exclusively devoted to this subject.' Following its publication, Doyle received several glowing comments from members of the Coping Facebook group. I didn't concur with their praise, but I remained silent, as I'd already witnessed Doyle's summary expulsion of another member.

Our Fathers recounts Doyle's paternal story and presents a detailed philosophical, psychological and theological debate concerning canon law and the attitude of the church to celibacy. It focuses on what Doyle believes the church should do when one of the ordained becomes a parent. As his media appearances attest, he advocates for priests to be allowed to marry and/or for the church to make celibacy optional, while still allowing a priest to remain in that role if he fathers a child.

This position foregrounds the sexual appetite of priests. Where are the women? And what about the welfare of the woman impregnated by the priest? It's the mothers who bear the greatest burden of stigma and shame. Like the church itself, *Our Fathers* proceeds from a patriarchal perspective, at the expense of the most vulnerable and disempowered.

Doyle's perspective contrasts with that of Dr Jane Anderson, an anthropologist at the University of Western Australia, who interviewed fifty Australian priests about their sexual lives for her PhD thesis, published in 2005 as *Priests in Love: Roman Catholic Clergy and Their Intimate Relationships*. Anderson wrote:

These men sacrifice their psycho-sexual development in order to fit within the clerical culture, which demands intellectual conformity and asserts a male-dominated theology of God as Father, Son and masculine Spirit. In this culture, emotional affirmation is given to men who are revered and powerful (pope, bishop, and priests), and boys are treasured as the future of the church. Women, on the other hand, are shunned, except for those female tokens that are venerated as mothers and/or virgins. These are forbidden objects of sexual fantasy.

In my interviews, many children of priests expressed outrage at the neglect and unacknowledged pain suffered by their mothers. Doyle misses the opportunity to meaningfully address inequality within the church. Women remain as handmaidens to men.

The church must do its Christian duty, making amends for the past by means of compensation, public apology and a commitment to reform. *Our Fathers* fails to prosecute this case with sufficient force. It doesn't prioritise bringing criminal charges against clerical perpetrators. It doesn't encourage victims to engage lawyers, litigate and seek compensation. It doesn't call for royal commissions or other independent investigations into the negligence of the church. It doesn't demand an end to the church use of confidentiality agreements. It doesn't instigate the collection or publication of data or research into the experience of children of priests.

Why not?

In *Our Fathers*, Doyle expresses little of the visceral outrage that so many children of priests have communicated to me. This is partly because he hasn't suffered the trauma that so many of us have experienced, the pain of being disowned by a priest father. I don't believe it's possible for Doyle to appreciate the sense of loss that the rest of us suffer. Hearing the devastation of others, as he does in his counselling sessions, is not the same as feeling it. As a devout Catholic, it's perfectly understandable that Doyle seeks to remodel the church to accommodate the sexual needs of his much-admired birth father. He is in the envious minority of those who spent quality time with their fathers.

Coping's advocacy is simplistic. Allowing priests to have children and remain in the clergy will not fix the myriad problems that the group's members face. Each child and mother has a unique experience; there is no single solution—aiming for one is futile.

Our Fathers is forward-looking in that it talks of solutions to stop priests abandoning their children. But it fails to meaningfully address the damaged and destroyed lives that wayward clergy have left in their wake. *Our Fathers* cautiously skates around some of the most tragic outcomes: how many sons, daughters and mothers have taken their own lives?

Equally disturbing, and just plain wrong, is Doyle's advice to children of priests to not enlist legal representation: 'Talk to the Catholic Church provincial and bishop . . . You do not need a lawyer, representative, attorney or mediator'; 'On earth, you are your lawyer, judge and jury.' After three hundred pages illustrating the outcomes of celibacy—psychologically depleted victims, where 'Harm and emotional abuse permeate the duration of their lives; harm is normalised for these people'—for Doyle to advise a survivor to front up to the church, the perpetrators, without legal representation and attempt to negotiate justice is ludicrous.

Doyle does proffer a suggestion to involve a journalist. To locate, and to then intimately brief a local journalist, to ask them to act as a support person when meeting with the church and insist that this be done off the record (and to forever keep the secret). My mind boggled with the proposition. None of the damaged, highly vulnerable mothers or children of priests that I've encountered were in a position to establish such a complex relationship, particularly not with a story-hungry journalist. I could only think that Coping's within-church resolution advice exposed the survivor to possible spiritual manipulation, ongoing control and further trauma.

A review of *Our Fathers* published on a Vatican website on 18 February 2021 is laudatory. It endorses his advice: 'The last chapter provides helpful tips and advice for anyone wishing to navigate canonical issues related to children of priests, or wishing to right the injustices children of priests often face.'

The same article quotes Irish archbishop Diarmuid Martin, the master of ceremonies at the ordination of Father Doyle (Vincent Doyle's father), as having provided financial backing for the Coping website on the condition that it be 'done right'. What *exactly* does that mean? It poses the question, who is Coping working for?

Also, it must be said: I am no longer a child. 'Children of priests' is a manipulative term propagated by the church and its agents. Yes, we were once children, but every 'child' I've spoken with is now over forty years of age; our truth is usually hidden until late in life. 'Children of priests' justifies others speaking on our behalf, as though we are forever infants, incapable. It is coercive, condescending and paternalistic. As a marginalised and voiceless legion, we have allowed others to do the talking for us for far too long.

•

Some of the stories I became aware of regarding clerical sexual behaviour leading to the birth of a child are shocking. Aside from the church, Coping is the only English-speaking institution that seems to have any concept of the scale of criminal activity. How many times has Coping reported sexual abuse by priests to the police? Its Board must have a sense of the numbers of suicides, rapes and underage pregnancies, as well as the enormity of the ongoing emotional scars of survivors. I decided to write to Doyle.

> As you would have seen in our Coping Facebook group, I'm interviewing as many children and mothers of priests as possible. It's been both fascinating and desperately sad. In *Our Fathers*, you said you presented the Vatican with (non-identifying) data on the experiences of the members of Coping, in which my story would have been included. As a member of the association, I would appreciate it if you would send me a copy of that material.

He declined, saying the material was for a new project. He did acknowledge the highly sensitive nature of the material, and advised that the Board of Directors of Coping was in agreement with the decision to deny my access.

No plausible reason was given. It seemed to me it could only be to not offend the church.

What troubled me most was the thought that the church might have already muzzled hundreds—possibly thousands—of children of priests worldwide with meagre payments, or worse, ignored their pleas for compassion.

Is the church still compelling children of priests, and our mothers, to sign confidentiality agreements? What had become of the 2014 UN recommendations?

Investigative journalist Michael Rezendes noted in his 2022 essay 'Father's Child' that 'The [UN] committee gave the Vatican until 1 September 2017 to respond. It has yet to reply.'

•

What children of priests need is a centralised response from the church in the form of a global protocol of support, rather than the current case-by-case approach.

I am offering a framework for a church response to fund support by way of:

1 unlimited psychological counselling by a practitioner selected by the survivor
2 assistance to trace next of kin and research identity and ancestry
3 legal advice about amending birth and death certificates, rights and other similar questions
4 funding to help establish credentials by procuring DNA evidence (for example, the payment of exhumation fees)
5 provision of access to church records containing information about birth parents

6   where appropriate, compensation for pain and suffering

7   cancellation of all confidentiality agreements that restrain chil-
    dren of priests and our mothers.

Recently, I wrote to Archbishop Coleridge and again provided
the above suggestions. I reminded him of my circumstances and
shared what I had learned from interviewing other children of
priests—that the majority feel abandoned, silenced and unsup-
ported by the church.

I requested an assurance that the Australian Catholic Church
has banned the use of confidentiality agreements with regard to the
children of priests and our mothers, and asked for information about
the Australian church's response to the 2014 UN Convention on
the Rights of the Child report. I reiterated my concern that as
long as each Australian bishop could establish their own protocols,
the silencing of victims would likely continue. 'The treatment of
the children of priests worldwide betrays every principle of love
and inclusion taught by Jesus. You have a rare opportunity to be
a compassionate agent for change.'

I urged him to consider the words of Pope Francis:

How can we issue solemn declarations on human rights and the
rights of children, if we then punish children for the errors of
adults? If a child comes into this world in unwanted circumstances, the parents and other members of the family must do
everything possible to accept that child as a gift from God and
assume the responsibility of accepting him or her with openness and affection.

This time it didn't take six months for the archbishop to reply.
I had his response in three days.

Coleridge had been given a clear opportunity to explicitly state
that the Australian Catholic Church does not use confidentiality

agreements against the children of priests and our mothers—he didn't take it up. Though there was talk of meetings, committees, restructures and processes, I was advised there is no Australian policy concerning children of priests, or any commitment to implement my seven support suggestions.

And there was a new twist in the tale. The archbishop advised that Doyle had contacted the Australian Catholic Bishops Conference in 2018 and had intermittent contact with him through his General Secretary. He advised that the Conference obtained a copy of the Coping publication *Alma Sanctus*, and that the data it contained had been reviewed by the National Centre for Pastoral Research. During all of the research I'd done, I'd never seen a reference to *Alma Sanctus*. I googled, no trace. What was it?

•

I managed to locate a copy of a December 2018 letter from Coping International Ltd headed 'Alma Sanctus'. It declared that their research on the children of priests globally was now available to the Catholic Church. It appeared to be a form letter, one I presume that was sent to leaders of the church worldwide. It went on to describe the 87-page *Alma Sanctus* contents, which included: critical web search results and key search phrases, non-identifying testimonies from the children of priests, psychiatric reports and a statement from a leading theologian.

Signed by Vincent Doyle, the closing lines of the letter floored me. It said that Alma Sanctus would not be made available again, and that the public would never be granted access to the material.

Coping appeared to be covertly lobbying the church with data that the children of priests, and the wider Catholic community, were denied. If Doyle had said to me, 'tell me your most intimate secrets and I'll include them (anonymised) in a clandestine report for the church and will also exclude you from ever seeing the results', I would have refused. I'd assume many other children of priests would do the same.

•

Though Coping has gone to pains to only allow senior clerics access to *Alma Sanctus*, I have recently been able to read a copy.

In truth, much of the material has already been cited or alluded to by Coping in the media or on its website. It includes copious explanations of internal church processes, the psychological trauma of children of priests, and much theological discussion; from my perspective, some of the more striking data were the website visitation numbers. The Coping website was launched in December 2014. Between 2014 and 2017—prior to the site receiving promotion or public announcements—it organically recorded 6628 unique visitors originating from Australia and a further 3948 from New Zealand (Ireland 80,000 and United States of America 105,000).

These visits were generated by a range of search terms, the most arresting: 'I am pregnant, and the dad is a Catholic priest.'

Perhaps only a small minority of the 10,000 Australia/New Zealand unique visits were from the child of a Catholic priest, their mother or another relative. However, it does suggest the existence of hundreds, if not thousands, of very much alive and curious children of priests in Australia.[1]

Alma Sanctus states that Doyle also consults with the Commission, which I took to be the Pontifical Commission for Protection of Minors, where he would provide non-identifying

---

1   By March 2021, Doyle had been quoted in the *Roscommon Herald* as saying he now believes there 'is anything between 10,000 and 20,000 children of the ordained around the world' and 'The Coping website has had close to 200,000 interactions.'

information about the children of priests. It was a disconcerting statement given it appeared to me that he was doing so without the collaboration or consultation of the discarded sons and daughters of the church.

•

The children of priests issue is a matter for the state, not the church. Just as the police don't investigate matters of police integrity, and politicians shouldn't investigate improper acts of other politicians, Coping and the Catholic Church should not be permitted to engage with or attempt to resolve the coercive, spiritually improper, sinful and/or criminal acts of priests.

How can the leader of Coping say 'children like me, if not aborted, are harmed almost beyond psychological recognition in the alleged name of holiness' (13 May 2021, *The Tablet*) and 'many of the mothers in question were raped as girls or teens by priests . . . more often than not, there's rape and pedophilia involved' (23 October 2017, Getreligion.org) and 'Prolonged depression, prolonged anxiety. These children are crushed the moment they are conceived until the moment they die' (17 December 2020, *The Tablet*), yet not make the first goal of his organisation reparations, transparent enquiries and retrospective criminal justice?

At worst, Coping engages with and almost leverages from the misery of the survivors of the church in order to bring about an end to celibacy.

In 2022, Doyle began a monthly article in the British religious journal *The Tablet*. Buried in his long online biography was the line, 'Doyle is also the founder of Coping International, an organisation and apostolate dedicated to the wellbeing of children of the ordained and religious globally.' Apostolate? I had to look it up. The dictionary confirmed that Coping practises a form of 'evangelistic activity'. Its goal is to herd the bewildered, spiritually jolted sheep back to the flock. Though the Coping website does not repeat the 'apostolate' term, it appeared that my suspicions had at last been formally confirmed in print.

Finalising my research, I did a Google Maps search for Coping International Ltd. The result highlights an obvious conflict of interest: the global epicentre of the children of priests is head-quartered in what appears to be the presbytery of the Christ the King Church, in Roscommon, Ireland.

I believe a new secular organisation is required to support the children of the church, and our mothers. It must be independent, transparent, survivor led and governed, and collaborative. It must strive to support survivors, protect children and vulnerable adults at risk, as well as raise community awareness (I am drawing here on the mission statement from the Survivors Network of those Abused by Priests).

In the Western world, sexual coercion is increasingly being recognised as a criminal offence. Church silencing is an immoral and abusive act of violence. While the attention of the inter-national media, restorative justice processes, courts and royal commissions has rightly focused on the abuse by clergy directly upon children, there has been insufficient in-depth investigation into children of priests and the role that the church and its agents play in controlling us.

For hundreds of years the stifled primal howl of our mothers, abandoned by their spiritual guide, has echoed across oceans. Make no mistake, the children of priests issue is yet another form of Catholic Church abuse of minors—the yet-to-be-born offspring of the ordained.

Aside from the obvious preservation of personal privacy, and church-imposed confidentiality agreements, there are many compel-ling reasons why the children of priests don't appear in the media:

not wanting to bring shame upon extended family, or their faith, or if their priest father had several children—to multiple women— or if they are the result of rape. It is not easy to speak out publicly.

Maggie, a devout twenty-seven-year-old woman, with limited education and non-existent financial resources, could not consent to a sexual relationship with her worldly fifty-seven-year-old priest. Catholic priests see themselves as above the law because the church tells them that they are. So many priests who have had children, my father among them, sincerely believe God is on their side.

I have uncovered a staggering amount of material on my celebrated father. In the late 1950s, almost twenty years after his ordination, he toured Europe. He had an audience with the Pope at the Vatican, and less than a year later Maggie was pregnant with me. This noble servant of God then abandoned me and maintained a complex hidden relationship with my mother for another thirty years. Bishops celebrated my venerated Rector Emeritus Reverend father's funeral.

And he almost got away with it.

The children of priests are the sleeping giant that the Catholic Church prays will never fully awaken.

ACKNOWLEDGEMENTS

This book may never have been written had I not met Linda Kelly-Lawless. Linda is the South Australian who appeared on ABC TVs 2019 *Foreign Correspondent* episode about the children of priests (now at 1.5 million YouTube views). Angry at an unresponsive church, Linda revealed the depths of her grief on national television. She bravely showed her face when few anywhere in the world had the guts to do so. She is the groundbreaker. Empathy from others is all good and well, but there's nothing like talking to those who have felt the concussion of hidden clerical paternity. Thank you also to Cait, Theresa and the many others like me, and our mothers, who have shared the weight of this burden.

I've received enormous compassion and generosity from those with professional writing expertise. Nobody has been as immersed in the process and provided as much EQ, as well as peerless nuts-and-bolts editing and structural guidance, as Stephanie Holt. Thanks for making me slow down, thanks for making me think and thanks for deleting a thousand exclamation marks! Stephanie is a very wise woman; I am indebted.

Lou Sweeney has a rare gift of stringing sparkling, evocative words together. Always envious of what looked like an effortless sleight of hand, I apprehensively asked Lou for help two years ago. Though we were mates, we weren't big-ask mates, she had every right to politely back away. However, with unwavering goodwill she contributed hours, patiently nudging me toward a method of smoothing my lumpy sentences, delving deeper into my still-evolving thoughts and keeping the bloody thing simple.

When I first approached Sian Prior, author of *Shy: A Memoir* and *Childless: a story of freedom and longing*, I could barely compose a shopping list. Sian bravely agreed to become my writing mentor and began the unenviable task of trawling through the tens of thousands of words in my most raw copy. A frown on the wrong day could have sent the whole book project into the bin—thanks for your patience and good grace, Sian.

On several occasions, my niece Leah Watkins ditched the scalpel for an editor's red pen and slashed through a couple of drafts, providing copious well-considered suggestions and edits—thanks, darl.

Bill Hampel, author of *Mallee Roots* and *Against The Grain: Fourteen Farmers Adapt to Climate Change*; Monica Raszewski, author of *The Archaeology of a Dream City*, and her hubby, Dieter; Jill Brady; and Pat Watkins all read drafts and made much appreciated observations and corrections. My sincere thanks to you all.

Though there were a few publishers who expressed interest in the manuscript in the early days, I was gone, hook, line and sinker, after the great Jane Palfreyman from Allen & Unwin sent me an email saying she'd read the book in one sitting. She added so many comments somebody who is just bursting to tell their story craves to hear—she got it. I'd heard about Jane long before, about her championing of authors and ideas; she was the only publisher I wanted and somehow it came to pass. And though we've only been working together for a reasonably short amount of time, I'm thrilled to have Courtney Lick and the meticulous (with a big heart) Elizabeth Cowell as well as Samantha Kent in editorial, who have improved my work immeasurably, and also Isabelle O'Brien in publicity to help guide this project toward success.

Big thanks also to my agent, Clare Forster from Curtis Brown, who has been a wonderful source of industry information and support.

Suzie Smith, author of the must-read *The Altar Boys*, opened important doors for me from the first day I came knocking on hers. She is a fierce champion of church survivors; I'm so pleased she has taken up this cause. Also, from the ABC, I thank Amanda Collinge and Belinda Hawkins. And to the uber-supportive Sarah Macdonald from the BBC London, and the fabulous June Christie and Emily Webb from the BBC's *Outlook* program, my sincere thanks for your commitment above and beyond. Likewise, to Phillipa Hutchison from Artemis Media and doco maker Yana Bille-Chung.

And there are so many others: Catherine Lynch, Kate Stowell, Rachael Brown, Damien Cave, the team at Vanish, Broken Rites and SNAP (Survivors Network of those Abused by Priests). To several survivors of church abuse, to a gaggle of church-specialist lawyers, academics and a number of ex-priests and nuns, you know who you are—and though I cannot list your names, I can say that I am very thankful to you and you will receive my thanks privately.

It is also important to state that although I am critical of the institution of the Catholic Church, I am indebted to Bishop Greg O'Kelly, who acknowledged the lacerating harm of secrecy. Tanja Stojadinovic from Professional Standards has also provided friendship, plus copious empathetic and practical supports, and is one of the good eggs. There are several others within the church establishment who have been supportive, but for obvious reasons I cannot acknowledge them by name here. Thank you, each one of you.

To Brian and Marg Howard, for thirty years of stability and acceptance, my deepest gratitude to you both. Sincere thanks to Peter Meaney, Terry and Sue Shiel, Bill and Craig Shiel and Kay Tulloch for your unquestioning acceptance and contributions in clearing the roadblocks to my paternity. And, of course, to the wives and partners of the Shiel–Meaney men who (most likely) gently steered the boys toward making the right decisions for the wonky-eyed priest-kid blow-in.

Blood doesn't mean family: to Mitch, Frank and Sandy, for the desert drive and the travels to come; who knew the 2019 road trip would lead us here? To Jai, Gem, Mick, TB, Gee-Oh, Cath and Dave, Heti and Ludger, Rit, Fiona, MDS, Mr. D'Arcy and Killer, Timby and Holly and the Richmond Football Club.

I'll forever be staggered by the fact that the people who raised me, loved me and made me the man I am were not genetically related to me. Dumbstruck by my good fortune, for over two years this book was to be called *Gratitude*, and later *Kindness of Strangers* (the marketing team had their way with *Tell No One!*). The only faith I have is in people.

To my brother, Damien, a rock—thanks mate. To Maire, Joe, Jane, John, Leah, Katherine and extended families, and our much-loved Aunty Marl.

To Roy and Bet, Kate, Pat and Nell—this is for you.

For more information: www.brendanwatkins.com.au

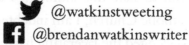 @watkinstweeting

@brendanwatkinswriter

RESOURCES

Works Cited and Further Reading

Anderson, Jane: *Priests in Love: Roman Catholic clergy and their intimate relationships*

Bok, Sissela: *Lying: Moral choice in public and private life*

Bryant, M. J.: *Treasured Lives Sacred Lands at Crystal Brook*

Bull, Mimi: *Celibacy, A Love Story: Memoir of a Catholic priest's daughter*

Byrne, Kathryn R: *Understanding the Abuse of Adults by Catholic Clergy and Religious*

Chick, Suzanne: *Searching for Charmian: The daughter Charmian Clift gave away discovers the mother she never knew*

Daly, Peter J and Myslinski, John F: *Strange Gods: A novel about faith, murder, sin, and redemption*

Dessaix, Robert: *A Mother's Disgrace*

Down, Jennifer: *Bodies of Light*

Doyle, Vincent: *Our Fathers: A Phenomenon of Children of Catholic Priests and Religious*

Forbes, Heather T: *Beyond Consequences, Logic, and Control: A love-based approach to helping attachment-challenged children with severe behaviors*

Foster, Chrissie and Kennedy, Paul: *Hell On the Way to Heaven*

Fox, Peter: *Walking Towards Thunder: The true story of a whistleblowing cop who took on corruption and the Church*

Francis, Susan: *The Love That Remains*

Fronczak, Paul Joseph and Tresniowski, Alex: *The Foundling: The true story of a kidnapping, a family secret, and my search for the real me*

Harkness, Libby: *Looking For Lisa*
Harlow, Harry F.: *The Nature of Love*
Heffron, Anne: You Don't Look Adopted
Johns, Catherine: *Maggie*
Johnston, George: *The Meredith Trilogy: My Brother Jack, Clean Straw for Nothing* and *Cartload of Clay*
Keneally, Tom: *Crimes of the Father*
Lockwood, Patricia: *Priestdaddy: A memoir*
Lucy, Judith: *The Lucy Family Alphabet*
Maddison, Abraham: *Crazy Bastard: A memoir of forced adoption*
Manseau, Peter: Vows: *The story of a priest, a nun, and their son*
Marr, David: *The Prince: Faith, Abuse and George Pell*
Martel, Frederic: *In the Closet of the Vatican: Power, homosexuality, hypocrisy*
Maugham, W. Somerset: *The Razor's Edge*
McCullough, Colleen: *The Thorn Birds*
Milligan, Louise: *Cardinal: The rise and fall of George Pell*
Morton, Rick: *One Hundred Years of Dirt*
Ormerod, Neil: *When Ministers Sin: Sexual abuse in the churches*
Osborne-Crowley, Lucia: *I Choose Elena*
Piketty, Thomas: *Capital and Ideology*
Scally, Derek: *The Best Catholics in the World: The Irish, the Church and the end of a special relationship*
Sheen, Fulton J.: *Treasure in Clay: The autobiography of Fulton J. Sheen*
Sipe, Richard: A Secret World: Sexuality and the search for celibacy
Smith, Suzanne: *The Altar Boys*
Sumner, Barbara: *Tree of Strangers*
Verrier, Nancy: *The Primal Wound: Understanding the adopted child*
Wheatley, Nadia: *The Life and Myth of Charmian Clift*
Winterson, Jeanette: *Why Be Happy When You Could Be Normal?*

Select Academic Research and Reports

Anderson, Jane: 'The Contest of Moralities: Negotiating compulsory celibacy and sexual intimacy in the Roman Catholic priesthood', 2010

Ball, Robyn: 'Open Adoption in Victoria, Australia: Adoptive parents' reports of children's experience of birth family contact in relation to child wellbeing', 2005

Brock, Megan P: 'Force of Habit: The construction and negotiation of subjectivity in Catholic nuns', 2007

de Weger, Stephen: 'Clerical Sexual Misconduct involving adults within the Roman Catholic Church', 2016

de Weger, Stephen: 'Unchaste Celibates: Clergy sexual misconduct against adults—expressions, definitions, and harms', 2022

Doyle, Vincent: 'Children of Priests', The Furrow, Ireland, 2019

Kennedy, Margaret: 'The Well From Which We Drink is Poisoned: Clergy sexual exploitation of adult women', 2009

Moran, Frances M. Magnum: 'Silencium: From legislation to foreclosure within the Catholic Church', Australasian Journal of Psychotherapy, 2019

'National Apology for Forced Adoptions' (Australia), 2013

Reisinger, Doris: 'Reproductive Abuse in the Context of Clergy Sexual Abuse in the Catholic Church', 2022

Royal Commission into Institutional Responses to Child Sexual Abuse (Australia) 2013

Shepard, Ashley; Diamond, David; Willard, Laura; et al: 'Discovering Misattributed Paternity After DNA Testing and its Impact on Psychological Well-Being and Identity Formation', 2022

Taglia, Kathryn Ann: 'On Account of Scandal: Priests, their children and the ecclesiastical demand for celibacy', 1995–96

United Nations Convention on the Rights of the Child, 2014: https://docstore.ohchr.org/

INDEX